THE GENIUS OF EUROPE

SOME WORKS OF HAVELOCK ELLIS

Author of "Studies in the Psychology of Sex"

1890: The New Spirit

1890: The Criminal

1892: The Nationalization of Health

1894: Man and Woman

1898: Affirmations

1900: The Nineteenth Century

1904: A Study of British Genius

1908: The Soul of Spain

1911: The World of Dreams

1912: The Task of Social Hygiene

1914: Impressions and Comments, I

1916: Essays in War-Time

1919: The Philosophy of Conflict

1921: Impressions and Comments, II

1922: Kanga Creek

1922: Little Essays of Love and Virtue

1923: The Dance of Life

1924: Impressions and Comments, III

1925: Sonnets, with Folk-Songs from the Spanish

1931: The Colour-Sense in Literature

1931: The Revaluation of Obscenity

1931: More Essays of Love and Virtue

1932: The Song of Songs (Translation of Ernest Renan's drama)

1932: Views and Reviews

1933: The Psychology of Sex (Manual for Students)

1934: My Confessional

1936: From Rousseau to Proust

1936: Questions of Our Day

1937: Poems

1940: My Life

1950: The Genius of Europe

THE GENIUS OF EUROPE

by

HAVELOCK ELLIS

WILLIAMS AND NORGATE LTD
36 GREAT RUSSELL STREET
LONDON, W.C.1

First published 1950

MADE AND PRINTED IN GREAT BRITAIN BY PURNELL AND SONS, LTD.
PAULTON (SOMERSET) AND LONDON

AUTHOR'S NOTE

T HIS VOLUME, as will be seen at a glance, represents interests of the writer spread over forty years.

Nearly all the essays here brought together *have* appeared at the time in magazines or reviews, but none of them has ever been included in any of my published volumes. The shavings of a literary workshop, the reader may hastily conclude. Not at all! They were left aside not because I thought they were not good enough to preserve but because I intended them for a future volume I had planned but now find I can no longer hope to complete.

I had *The Genius of Europe* in mind during many years. It seemed to me that one should put on record one's personal impressions of the world in which one had lived, and that world was for me mainly the European world in many parts of which I had been a fairly observant wanderer. Round about the time of the Great War (1914–18) I was specially engaged with this subject. That event itself, however, eventually diminished my activities in this direction. It seemed probable that my readers would feel that European conditions had been so changed as to render my observations valueless. That supposition would not, however, be justified. I was not concerned with temporary and merely political conditions. It was the psychological and anthropological characterization of the European peoples which interested me. I hasten to add that this interest was entirely outside the disputes concerning supposed "racial" superiorities and inferiorities which have lately become so fierce. The word "race", though it is sometimes convenient to use it, has no meaning for us in any primitive sense. We are all more or less mixed and we cannot set up any hierarchy of European races. *We Europeans*, by A. C. Haddon and Julian Huxley, authorities of high rank, is a survey of "racial" problems which may be profitably read in this connection. But though we cannot expect to find any primitive or exclusive "racial" characters, we have to remember that the characters of stocks, however mixed, differ, as do the hereditary traditions amid which they grow up, and are only slowly to be modified, so that a nation still has its own specific traits, even

5

though we cannot in any precise scientific sense term them "racial". It was with such national traits constituting what we may term the "genius" of a nation that I was concerned. It is a subject that remains interesting and significant when we have put aside those absurdities of "race" which to-day have become so tragic.

I have also felt that there would be advantage in not attempting to bring these essays up to date at those points where political changes have taken place. I was not dealing with temporary conditions but seeking to reach traits which remain comparatively permanent during many centuries, and it is curious to note when they remain unchanged under widely changed political conditions.

HAVELOCK ELLIS

Spring, 1939

PUBLISHERS' NOTE

The Publishers would like to acknowledge their indebtedness to Mme. Françoise Delisle for the assistance which she has given in the preparation of this volume.

Spring, 1950

CONTENTS

Left with this volume unpublished at the time of Ellis' death, I had to arrange the order of these essays. I have framed those on Europe between two philosophical ones representing the author's latest outlook. These—Foreword and Afterword—date from 1939. The European essays proper are given in chronological order.

FRANÇOISE DELISLE

	PAGE
AUTHOR'S NOTE (1939)	5
FOREWORD: MY CREDO (1939)	9
FRANCE AND GREAT BRITAIN: TWO CIVILIZATIONS (1901)	18
THE GENIUS OF ENGLAND (1916)	36
THE GENIUS OF RUSSIA Practically all rewritten in the summer of 1917, after the Kerensky Revolution, and never published before.	73
THE GENIUS OF FRANCE (1918)	179
THE GENIUS OF SPAIN This version reshaped in 1918, and never published before.	186
THE GENIUS OF GERMANY Reshaped by Ellis in 1925, but only published after his death, 1940	218
AFTERWORD: NATIONALISM AND PEACE (1939)	234
INDEX	241

FOREWORD

LIKE MANY others of my generation I was brought up
in a religious family, and was the eldest child and only son.
My mother was not merely conventionally but genuinely
religious, belonging to the Evangelical section of the
Anglican Church. As a girl she had been considered "volatile", but
at the age of seventeen she was "converted," and that event influenced
the whole of her subsequent life. Nothing disturbed her firm
character, which was, however, never harsh and with increasing
years became increasingly tolerant, so that she accepted without
protest the varying religious tendencies of her children. My father,
a sailor away from home nine months of the year, accepted my
mother's religion and decorously went to church with his family
every Sunday when at home, but really had no religion of his own.
Familiar with many lands and at home with people of all creeds,
he was indulgent to all. His own temperament, moreover, was so
equable, so free from any tendency to vice or excess, that, liked by
everyone, he might be said to have been scarcely in need of any
religion. I mention these facts because I regard them as of essential
importance. A man's philosophy can never be properly apprehended
unless we know the foundations for it which he inherited from his
parents.

I was mainly my mother's child, whatever tendencies I also
inherited from my father. I spontaneously carried a little Testament
in my pocket; I read Bunyan's *Pilgrim's Progress* all through. And in
due course I underwent the church rite of "confirmation" without
any sense of incongruity. But meanwhile my insatiable intellectual
appetite was leading me to devour books, especially serious ones, of
all kinds. In this way I was somehow induced to buy a cheap edition
of Renan's *Life of Jesus*. It was new to me to see Jesus treated so
sympathetically and yet apart from all supernatural elements. I read
the book with interest, yet critically, and I made critical comments
on the margins. But Renan's attitude was more congenial to my

own temperament than I at first realized. It was not long before books of more or less similar tendency became convincing, or before I definitely rejected as intellectually out of court the whole supernatural foundation of Christianity and miraculous theology in general. This did not lead to active hostility or to any sense of liberation from restraints. My life remained the same. But I was conscious of loss. The supernatural universe had melted away and I was without a spiritual home. There were moods of desolation in spite of constant and varied mental activities. This continued from my seventeenth to my nineteenth year.

Later, as a solitary teacher in the Australian bush, I was somehow stimulated to procure James Hinton's *Life in Nature*. I read it, and it made no pronounced impression. But it may have touched something in my unconscious mind, for a few months later I read it again. This time it produced nothing less than a mental revolution. I still recall the details of that revolution and the day when I walked across the hills, a new being, feeling as light as air, with a new vision, as yet unformulated, of the universe. That moment has influenced the whole of my life.

What had happened to me was what is commonly called "conversion". But that process is usually misunderstood. It is not the sudden acceptance of a new religion, or a change of life, or anything to do with creeds. It is simply, as the word itself may be said to indicate, a complete psychic change, however produced; the method of production will vary according to the intellectual and emotional calibre of the person experiencing it. "Conversion" in a John Stuart Mill has little in common with conversion in a costermonger. In my own case, as I later realized, what had happened was that the two psychic spheres, intellectual and emotional, which had been divorced and in constant active or passive friction, were suddenly united in harmony. Hinton's vision of the universe, even though I could not at every point accept it and would never at any time have considered myself his disciple, presented a universal unity of life which was new to me. The world was no longer dead and repellent; there is the same life everywhere; man and "nature" are fundamentally one. Henceforth I was at home in the universe. With that realization there came a peace which passes all understanding. I never had any more moods of religious depression.

The revolution remained entirely private. I had no impulse to confide it even to intimate friends and still less to preach it to the world. Perhaps I obscurely felt that such experiences are necessarily personal, under the direction of hereditary and constitutional factors which cannot be transmitted. I regarded the experience as religious and not as philosophic, and so I still regard it.

In the years of my mentally formative period I was, however, much concerned over philosophy. It seemed to me that one ought to have a philosophic system, and I had none. I bought philosophic books, notably Spinoza's complete works in Latin, as well as the standard history of philosophies of that time. I was a constant reader of the chief English philosophical journal, *Mind*, and I even wrote a rather lengthy article—a study of Hinton's later thought—and sent it to the editor, Professor Croom Robertson, who welcomed it in a friendly spirit, though it was from a complete stranger, and published it at once. That was in 1884, when I was twenty-five years of age. Almost immediately afterwards I chanced to become personally acquainted with a genuine philosopher, one of the most remarkable men I have ever known. This was Thomas Davidson. The books he left behind are not of the first importance, nor was he, indeed, so impressive a writer as speaker. He was above all an original personality, of almost passionate philosophic temperament and that eloquence which sometimes marks the Scotch intellect in its more exalted shapes. He was an outsider in philosophy, and without academic associations, though attracted to various lines of thought, ancient and modern.

Davidson was at this time collecting around him a small band of young men whom he desired to indoctrinate with his opinions and personally lead in the formation of a sort of quasi-communistic establishment in which to carry them out. My friend Percival Chubb, afterwards known as an ethical leader in the United States, was prominent among them, and by him I was introduced to Davidson and induced to join the little group who listened to his eloquent speech. Davidson told me later he had been especially drawn to me, and it was therefore a grievous disappointment for him, after he had expounded his doctrines during a long evening, to find next day that though I had seemed to drink in his eloquence, I had really remained unmoved. Davidson was so disgusted at my failure to respond as he desired that a little later in a letter from Rome he broke off relations with me. At a later period, however, when there was no longer any question of my becoming a disciple, occasional friendly relations were resumed.

The outcome of this episode doubtless seemed to Davidson entirely negative. But it was far from being negative for me, or I should not have felt called upon to introduce it here. It had a very positive result, though one that would have been by no means pleasing to Davidson. It convinced me that philosophy is a purely personal matter. A genuine philosopher's credo is the outcome of a single complex personality; it cannot be transferred. No two persons, if sincere, can have the same philosophy.

I made this discovery for myself, but a few years later, when I began to study Nietzsche, I found that he had vaguely suggested a similar viewpoint. In my essay on Nietzsche in 1896 I clearly set forth my attitude:

> It is as undignified to think another man's philosophy as to wear another man's cast-off clothes. . . . Let Brown be a Brownite and Robinson a Robinsonian. It is not good that they should exchange their philosophies, as that either should insist on thrusting his threadbare misfits on Jones, who prefers to be metaphysically naked. When men have generally begun to realize this, the world will be a richer and an honester world and a pleasanter one as well.

Though I made the discovery for myself, nowadays of course it is quite taken for granted. It has, for instance, been recently stated clearly by Bertrand Russell: "The logical quality of the cosmos as it appears in each of the great systems is due to the fact that it is one man's cosmos." But even for Bertrand Russell this attitude seems to be recent.

It must have been shortly after the Davidson episode that I read Lange's *History of Materialism* and was thereby fortified in my attitude toward philosophy. Not only was Lange's book a notable history, fascinating and sympathetic, of the development of the materialist doctrine, but it culminated in the conclusion, for which I was now fully prepared, that metaphysics is a form of poetry. I might not, indeed, myself put it quite that way. I would draw a distinction between metaphysics and poetry. But I was willing to see the justification of a metaphysical system no longer placed on an abstract, pseudo-scientific foundation but on a personal, aesthetic foundation. I was thus prepared to view later with sympathy and admiration the metaphysical view of the world as a beautiful spectacle put forward by Jules de Gaultier, one of the most notable thinkers of our time though outside academic circles.

While I thus reached the conviction that every man who thinks should have his own philosophy, I do not seem to have shown any anxiety to acquire a philosophy for myself. As I now, long afterward, look back at this period of my life I am disposed to put this indifference down to a sound instinct. It has come to seem to me that one's philosophical attitude can only be reached by an unconscious process, that it is a spiritual growth as much beyond our control, and often beyond our consciousness, as physical growth.

Not only in philosophy are the soundest results thus reached. We are probably here faced by a general law. I am interested to see that in the recently published volume of collected essays by the late A. R. Powys, an architect with a sound and penetrating insight into the art of architecture, precisely the same principle is enunciated that I find to hold true in philosophy. Discussing the "Origin of Bad Architecture", he regards dependence on the reasoned theories of others as the source of feeble architecture. We need, he declares, first of all a digested experience. "By 'digested experience' is meant the subconscious result of experience, or in other words the certain feeling and assured knowledge which are in a man without resort to conscious feeling or thought." This does not mean that the art product comes solely from within. Powys insisted, on the contrary, that the experience would come from without and include distinctive elements of the age in which the artist lives. But they are unconsciously absorbed and transformed; that is the significance of the term "digested experience". So far as I acquired any philosophy, it was the outcome of varied contacts with the world during long years, unconsciously assimilated and transformed into an unrealized personal credo.

It was not until later life, when I was contemplating the publication of my book *The Dance of Life*—largely made up of essays written during the immediately preceding years—that I realized that I had, without directly aiming at it, attained a philosophic attitude and even what may fairly be described as a philosophic credo. I was now sixty years of age, but as I view this matter—though I know that few professional philosophers would agree—that is quite early enough in life for a definitely conscious philosophic creed to be established. Much earlier than this, of course, it must have been slowly constituted and actively operative, but the less consciously the more genuinely. Otherwise it runs the risk of being merely artificial, adopted on grounds that were not the real outcome of personality.

In the determination of my own philosophic outlook it seems evident that there was from the very outset the instinctive impulse to embrace the elements of life harmoniously. When I discovered that there was a discordant break between the emotional religious life as I had been experiencing it and my strong intellectual aptitudes, I was profoundly unhappy. Some of my friends, when they discovered a similar break in their psychic lives, had cheerfully selected the side of intellect and poured only contempt on emotional religious demands, while in the mass of mankind, needless to say, neither intellectual nor emotional demands are strong enough to involve any conflict, and the result is an attitude of indifference rather than of serenity. It has been my experience that people of sensitive intelligence have often remarked on my "serenity". This is not the outcome of any conscious intention on my part, and I have often enough been far from conscious of any inner serenity. But I can well believe that the conquest of opposing psychic elements into a single harmonious whole naturally results in an attitude of serenity.

During the Great War I came to realize that the harmony I had attained between the two opposing elements was really only a particular application of a deep-lying tendency of my nature. This came about through my contemplation of the disputes between militarists, whether German or English, over the term "conflict", which they confused with "war". I realized that while war was undoubtedly a form of conflict, we must regard conflict as a much wider term, including forms of opposition which were not war and might be of totally different tendency. That brought the disputes between nations into line with that general tendency to opposition which is essential to life and opened out the possibility of super-seding war, not in a merely negative manner, but by the fruitful necessity of the presence of opposites. Conflict is in nature, but it is a fruitful conflict in which each opposing element may have its essential value. I might have recalled the saying of Heraclitus that "conflict is the father of all things", since conflict that was violent could hardly be fatherly. I set forth the result I had reached, together with some of its wider implications, in an essay, "The Philosophy of Conflict" (ultimately embodied in a volume with the same title), which I regard as of significance in the presentation of my philoso-phic outlook. Those pacifists who supposed that the supersession of war by more civilized methods of adjusting national differences meant the abolition of conflict fell into an error which was fatal, it seemed to me, to a sound conception of life and the world.

Our planetary system, we are taught, must be viewed as carried on harmoniously by the action of opposing forces, centripetal and centrifugal, pulling in opposite ways. The same conflict is even clearer in the vegetable world. We see it in every seed in its vital pressure against the inclosing capsule, and every unfolding frond of fern bears witness to a similar opposition of forces. Opposition is not a hindrance to life, it is the necessary condition for the be-coming of life. No doubt this realization of opposing forces in the vegetable world came to me as an early suggestion from Hinton's *Life in Nature*. Now I am ever increasingly impressed by the resem-blances of vegetable life to animal life. I see how closely akin are the laws that rule in both spheres. I find that the behaviour of plants is what my own would be under the same conditions and with the same limitations. That the same law of conflicting forces as the necessary condition of life prevails in the animal world needs no proof, nor that it is most marked in the highest forms of life, and notably in the mammal with its expanding ovum, which only develops under the pressure of the firmly constricting womb. I reach out toward a conception of the unity of what we call the universe. What we call life really prevails throughout.

It was not until later that I realized that the vision of harmonious conflict I had attained in an entirely different direction might be seen perfectly in that sphere of sex the study of which had been my chief life work, and I made no clear statement of it until 1931. At that time, in the *Forum Philosophicum*, Professor Del-Negro put forth his view of the problem of sex as one of "antinomies" only to be resolved by compromise. Dr. Schmidt, the editor, invited me to write a reply—which was reprinted in the Second Series of my "Views and Reviews". I was unable to accept Del-Negro's doctrine of compromise between essential elements of life. Here as elsewhere I saw the harmonious conflict of opposite tendencies, each necessary to the other and supporting it, while compromise would merely mean weakness. All the phenomena of sex seemed to illustrate this conflict, from the physical opposites of tumescence and detumescence to the erotic conflict of courtship and the social balance between sex indulgence and sex abstinence. Sex and culture are perfectly balanced. To desire freedom from this balance is to desire annihilation.

Man in his conscious arts illustrates this same conflict. Nowhere is it better revealed than in the primary art of architecture by the device of the arch. Here we see how in the conflict of two opposing forces each supports the other, and stability is insured. If the opposition ceased, the arch would collapse in ruin. In the other primordial art, more ancient even than architecture, that of dancing, we see the same harmonious conflict beautifully illustrated. Every pose of the dancer is the achievement of movement in which the maximum tension of opposing muscular actions is held in the most fluid harmonious balance.

In other arts, even if this principle is less convincingly illustrated, it is still present. In poetry there is the conflict between the centrifugal impulse of expression and the centripetal restraint of form. From an early period men drawn to poetry seem instinctively to have felt that the impulse to emotionalized expression should be held in check by an impulse to rigid form, and that only when these two opposites were combined could the result be accepted as satisfactory. When, as sometimes happens, a poet rebels against this need for the harmonious opposition and seeks to concentrate either on form or on expression, there are but few of his readers who enjoy his results

One could, I believe, detect a similar law in other arts. The demand for the harmonious conflict of opposites rules in nature's operations, and since man is a part of nature it also rules in his operations. He disregards it at his peril and at the sacrifice of that serenity which comes of an even unconscious sense of oneness with our universe.

So much, it seems to me, may serve to indicate all that I have been able to achieve in the general attainment of a philosophic credo. Since, even to myself, it has only been a slow, gradual, and largely unconscious achievement, I have naturally made little attempt to preach it to others. But it has been clear to any sympathetic reader of my books, and to some it has been helpful in aiding them to reach their own outlook in the world.

The reward of being simple and sincere with what seem the facts of one's universe is that one sheds abroad an influence that may be incalculable. It is worth while.

FRANCE AND GREAT BRITAIN: TWO
CIVILIZATIONS

THE QUIET observer of politics, more especially as made in haste by journalists who are politicians and politicians who should have been journalists, is seldom so often compelled to smile as when France and the question of Anglo-French relations are discussed in England. When the new journalistic diplomat sets forth to deal with this matter he makes a clean sweep of the facts of geography, history, anthropology and economics, while he betrays equal ignorance of the conditions which are the outcome of these facts. Thus he is enabled to give free scope to his own prejudices, and to play upon the passions of his hearers. Nor is this new superior person without the support of precedent furnished by an elder, and perhaps greater, age. Even Tennyson referred complacently to the "red fool fury of the Seine", and Matthew Arnold once discoursed concerning "French lubricity". Such utterances, with the grain of truth they contain, are as sagacious as the proverbial sayings about the French which we find scattered among the bulk of our unintelligent population. "Do what you will," said Thackeray, faithfully mirroring the feelings of his most ignorant fellow-countrymen, "you can't respect Frenchmen." The traditional British attitude towards the French during the last century is no doubt largely the outcome of British terror at the end of the eighteenth century in the presence of the Revolution and the subsequent military activities of Napoleon. At that time, it is clear, men of all classes, from statesmen and poets to the dregs of the population, were wrought into a condition of horror, fear, disgust, and, after the defeat of Napoleon, contempt as regards France. The notable part of this change was that it largely affected our thinking and educated classes. Up to that period there had existed a mutual and respectful admiration which wars had not been able to destroy: Sir Philip Sidney sang of that "sweet enemy, France", while a little later England became the educated Frenchman's ideal of a free country. Throughout the greater part of the eighteenth century French and English social and literary relations were intimate, with the best results on both sides; the admirable chapter of history written by the late Professor Texte around the great spiritual revolution centring in Rousseau shows how close and cordial were the relations between French and English. Not only Diderot and Rousseau but Voltaire—the most truly French of writers and thinkers, as we commonly believe—were largely moulded by English influences, while one of the most fruitful elements of English life and thought was brought to us by Huguenots. How far down among the English people the sympathies of the educated classes extended we may, no doubt, question. A seventeenth-century traveller noted that while Englishmen were received with courtesy at Calais, the Frenchman arriving at Dover was liable to less pleasant experiences, and the way in which the more or less Shakespearian play of *Henry VI* finally turns Joan of Arc into a caricature shows how long and how deeply the expulsion from France prejudiced the English mind. We need not, however, attempt to unravel the complex causes of the sympathies and antipathies which have brought together and pushed apart the two countries. Here we need only concern ourselves with the situation as we find it, more especially with certain fundamental facts of French life and civiliza-tion, and with certain fallacies in common British judgments concerning those facts.

There is, for instance, the common assumption concerning the "Latin races". The Latin race, we say, is decadent; France, we assume, is Latin; therefore, France is decadent, in striking contrast to the superiority of the "Anglo-Saxons". The fallaciousness of these flourishing beliefs has often been pointed out; but since the anthropological evidence which has accumulated enables us to expose them with complete precision, it is worth while to call attention to the matter once more.

It is now widely accepted by anthropologists that the numerous human varieties in Europe may be grouped into three races, which may ultimately, it is probable, be resolved into two: the long heads and the broad heads. If, however, we take the minor criterion of pigmentation (i.e. colour of skin, hair and eyes) into consideration there are three: dark long-heads, fair long-heads, and broad-heads. Roughly speaking, these races are arranged in three layers running east and west, dark long-heads to the south, fair long-heads to the north and broad-heads across the centre. Now Rome lies at the upper border of the lowest level, whence a faint and thin layer of long-heads is continued up along the Italian and French coast of the Mediterranean. This so-called Ligurian layer of southern long-heads on the French Mediterranean coast is not, it must be noted, the outcome of any historical migration from Rome to France; it is merely an aboriginal extension of the southern long-heads, older than Rome itself. Nor is there any evidence to show that Latin blood was powerfully infused into the French population at any period. On the contrary, it appears that no western country was so free from Roman blood as Gaul, only a few thousand colonists having settled on the Rhône and elsewhere. Moreover, the Roman legions, as we know, were made up of any but men of "Latin race", being recruited from all parts of the empire, wherever fighting men were to be found. That the soldiers and functionaries of the empire left offspring in the conquered countries we may have no difficulty in believing. But such an infusion of foreign blood always tends to be rapidly lost, and to leave little or no perceptible trace. Moreover, in both these respects the arguments for the "Latin" blood of France would apply to Great Britain also. Not only was England occupied by the Romans for several hundred years, but those anthropologists who have most carefully studied the British Isles will probably agree that a very large proportion of the inhabitants of Great Britain, and still more Ireland, which the Romans never occupied, belong precisely to that southern dark long-headed race of the area in which Rome was situated, a race which still occupies almost all Spain, and in a prehistoric but not entirely unknown and incalculable period crept up along the coast to reach England, leaving its dead in the Long Barrows of neolithic times, and its recognizable descendants over a great part of the country. Whatever arguments, therefore, may be brought forward to show that the French are of Latin race apply with even greater force to our own country. In so far as France is a country of "Latin" race, Great

Britain is still more genuinely Latin, and when Professor Sergi of Rome, one of the most brilliant of Italian anthropologists, tells us that England is the modern Rome, his contention may or may not be just in other respects, but is not wholly without basis in fundamental affinities of race.

When, however, the British publicist refers to the French as a people of Latin race he is not always much concerned about the anthropological accuracy of his statement. He is chiefly concerned to make a contemptuous and damaging charge of inferiority of race, and to indicate the decadence of France as against the superiority of England. It is therefore worth while to compare France and Great Britain from the racial point of view, in order to discover the real differences that may exist. The most fundamental indication of deep difference of race in Europe, i.e. that furnished by the head form, is most conveniently measured by the length-breadth or cephalic index. Dr. Deniker, of the Paris Museum of Natural History, has lately prepared an elaborate map of the cephalic index in Europe, for the first time gathering into a connected whole and reproducing in a simple and graphic manner the known facts concerning the distribution of the long-headed and broad-headed population of Europe, the degree of long-headedness being represented in the map by relative depth of blue tinting, and of broad-headedness by relative depth of red tinting. When we look at this map we see at once that there is no country in Europe (except, on a very small scale, Greece) where the long-headed and the broad-headed elements which make up the European population are so fairly and fully represented in their well-marked forms, and so finely mixed and tempered, as they are in France. It is, moreover, the only country in Europe in which all the three great constituent elements of the European population—northern, central, and southern—are thus fairly and equally represented. The deep-red of the broad-heads from Asia, short and usually dark, covers the mountainous backbone of the country with a prolongation into Brittany, the tall fairish Teuton northerner occupying the pale blue and mixed country to the north of this, while the Eurafrican dark long-heads occupy the pale blue and mixed country to the south.

France thus represents Europe in miniature, in a sense that no other country, great or small, can claim to do, and if we had to choose one country as representing the quintessential racial elements of Europe we should be compelled to select France. Russia is predominantly red and broad-headed on the map, with blue patches owing to the occasional presence of fair northerners; Germany, strange as it may seem, is in much the same case; far from being long-headed it only shows blue tinting in its western and extreme northern portions, the really "Teutonic" country being Sweden. Turning to the remaining great European country, that which most closely concerns us, we find that Great Britain is blue throughout; it is almost the most uniformly tinted country in Europe; one minute reddish patch in the north-west of Ireland alone remains to show any possible trace of that broad-headed race who are known to have invaded England in prehistoric times. It is true that the uniform blueness of Great Britain is to some extent deceptive. If we turn from Dr. Deniker's map of head-form to the map of hair and eye-colour which Dr. Beddoes, the first of English anthropologists, has prepared on the basis of a vast number of personal observations spread over many years, we find a somewhat different set of phenomena; we see that along the east coasts of our islands the people are fair; and along the west coasts dark, being thus admirably disposed for the maximum amount of mixture. The two elements correspond respectively to the northern and southern long-heads of Europe, but these are those two of the three constituent elements of the European population which may, it is probable, be ultimately regarded as one, and they are so similar in head-shape that Deniker's carefully-graded map fails in the slightest degree to make them distinguishable. Thus the racial representation of Europe in Great Britain is seriously defective and one-sided. Our country unites indeed the two more energetic and restless of the three European races, but lacks the harmony, balance, and many-sidedness of a more complete representation, and misses the special qualities of the central European race. France, on the other hand, is the racial epitome of Europe.

The stereotyped phrase regarding the "Latin race" of the French is thus wholly incorrect and meaningless. There remains, however, a sense in which France is truly Latin, and it is so significant a sense that we cannot too vividly realize it if we wish to understand the genius of the nation or the secret of French civilization. The French cannot be called Latins, but French civilization may be called Latin. The Gallic tribes with which the Romans came most closely in contact were those of the south; they were that section of the population which, though not Latin, really belonged to the same great stock as the Romans. The qualities attributed to the Gauls by the Romans, their fierceness, oratory, versatility, and sociability, seem to indicate the presence of the Ligurian race, though modified by other elements, while the obstinate and tenacious people whom the Romans found in Iberia were of their own race unmixed. This fact may be taken into consideration when we note the different relations of Spain and France to Rome. Spain, when finally subdued and placated, sent her best men to Rome to gain immortality among the greatest Romans, but left no permanent and independent Roman civilization on her own soil; France also sent an important contingent to Rome, but devoted her chief energies to the establishment of her own civilization. The alien Visigoths practically swept Latin civilization out of Spain; all the invasions that have passed over France, and are still pouring in, have left her civilization unaffected, because almost from the first it grew up independently among a mixed population; every invading element could be assimilated by that civilization because every possible invader had, from the first, his racial representatives in the country.

When we understand these facts we learn to understand how it is that France gained, and still retains, so definitely marked a civilization which is yet primarily of classic origin. The real racial affinity of the population of the thin and exquisitely situated slip of southern Gaul which was the early focus of Gallic civilization began the process, and the gradual incorporation of the various other elements in the country continued it. Italy was too near the towering influence of Rome for such a development; Spain was too far. France was situated at the point where the various elements could most easily absorb and develop a finely tempered civilization, which was largely exotic and not the outcome of the races that have chiefly occupied and ruled France.

Yet it is in this fact that French civilization is, in a sense, an exotic or artificial growth that its strength really lies. At the first glance, indeed, one might say that here was a disadvantage. But even if any civilization can be called precisely natural, it would not be easy to see how the same civilization could be "natural" to all the elements of so complex an organic whole as France. How would a Breton civilization suit Provence? What is there in common between the Norman and the Gascon? How could a Picard enter into the manners and customs of the Basque? Yet all the various component peoples who make up France are loyal to the traditions of their common language and civilization in a manner that we certainly cannot say that Ireland, or even Scotland, is loyal to the traditions of English civilization.

France has reaped the advantage of these somewhat foreign origins, not only in the early maturity which makes hers the oldest of European civilizations, but in a certain abstract, formal, impersonal quality, associated with those elements of clearness and reasonableness which render the finest manifestations of the French genius truly classic, not only by lineal descent, but in a sense in which no other civilization evolved in Europe during the last two thousand years can be called classic. France interprets for us, at a distance, it is true, the genius of Greece and Rome, while France also furnishes a modern civilization which is truly classic in type.

In all other countries—and this is true to some extent of Italy and Spain—civilization, whether expressed in literature or in life, is a more or less crude attempt to obtain personal expression by a compromise with such chaotic elements of tradition as chance to be nearest. French civilization is fundamentally a discipline into which the novice can only obtain entrance by arduous effort, and the consequent sacrifice of his personal idiosyncrasy, however completely in the end he may reconquer his personality. Language, the most intimate manifestation of a civilization, is at once the best example and the most conclusive proof of these qualities in French tradition. It is a truism to say that every educated Frenchman can write; in science, for instance, it is often a relief to turn from the

bald, painfully laconic manner of the English writer, or the barbarous
verbosity and circumlocution of the German—neither of whom has
been taught to write—to the sanity, clarity, and equipoise of the
Frenchman. It is doubtless largely, though not altogether, because
his speech is not an obscure growth from the instincts of his remote
ancestors, but a creation within historic times that, for a Frenchman,
language is not a merely bungling and instinctive attempt at self-
expression but a great and precious possession, to be treated with
reverence and an artist's care for fine human creations.[1] Thus it
is that French has become the most perfect of all living prose instruments, equally adapted for the most solemn and the most trivial
ends. There has never been any prose literature which attains such
precision and so high a degree of perfection in so many various
fields. Certainly the conditions under which French civilization
developed aided in bringing the language more quickly to maturity,
and so gave its literature a longer history. But the qualities of the
language and the literature lay in the people who created them.
It was not an accident that *Petit Jehan de Saintré* was written in the
fifteenth century, three hundred years before the days of Swift and
Sterne; its fine perfection is the outcome of personal qualities, of
psychological insight and ironic vision of life, subordinated to the
impersonal ends of art; it was by no means altogether or chiefly
because of the difficulties of our own magnificent language that
Pascal was a master in controversy while Milton was struggling
hopelessly in the magnificent chaos of his own eloquence. It was not
until the end of the seventeenth century that in England we began
to learn, with Dryden, what prose is. Until then, and too often since,
the masters of English prose had been writing poetry all their lives
without knowing it, while the French were consciously cultivating
the possibilities of their own exquisite prose medium; they never
wrote prose without knowing it, and that is the real point of the
simple-minded Jourdain's discovery.

[1] I may refer to the work of a French man of letters, M. Remy de Gourmont's
Esthétique de la Langue Française. It is difficult to imagine such a book written about
our own beautiful language; our men of letters lack the erudition, perhaps even the
interest, to write it, while the philologist cannot put himself at the aesthetic point of
view.

This power of looking at things from the outside, the remarkable fact that we see here people of the most widely different races yet loyally attached to the same tradition and helping to build it up, explain not only the development and special qualities of the French language, but the essential facts of French civilization generally and the whole temper of the people. The philosophic tendency, the willingness shown even by a people so tenacious of their traditions to overturn those traditions, as at the great Revolution, in obedience to what seemed the higher claims of reason and a wider order; this, together with that gaiety which can condense the most poignant experiences of life into a smile or an epigram, this reasonableness and this gaiety are not only two aspects of the same attitude towards life, but they are both the outcome of a special civilization demanding the subordination of the personal claims of the individual. French gaiety has often been the object of foreign contempt, and no doubt in its lower manifestations it can be as plebean as the gaiety of any other nation; but in its finer manifestations it is, when rightly understood, of the very essence of French civilization, the expression of that sense of detachment, of universal and impersonal reason, which is never very far from any Frenchman. It is the expression of the man who heroically rises above his own misfortunes to a vision of them "under the species of eternity"; thus it is—as has been said by the wisest of young French philosophers, himself meeting courageously an early death—a less theatrical rendering of the ancient *non dolet*. It is not less heroic because it manifests itself, as all fine civilization must, in the pettiest details of daily life. I have noticed a Frenchman hastening to an omnibus, to find every place occupied, and lifting his hat, turn away with a good-humoured "Bon voyage!" Not so our own countryman. The Englishman is so convinced that he is himself the end to which the whole creation moves that any sudden shock to this conviction deprives him momentarily of any impulse of courtesy or humanity; the Frenchman instinctively conquers his own disappointment, to realize the impersonal fact that if he has lost others have won.

It is obvious that the traditions of such a civilization as that of France inevitably make for sociality and urbanity. The sociality of the French is a somewhat complex fact, curiously and intimately related to every characteristic feature of French civilization. The fact that the literary genius of the people shows itself in prose and not in poetry is closely connected with this sociality, for prose always implies an external and social standard, while the poet is swept away by the current of his own personal emotion, and indifferent to the standards of reason inspired by social claims. Even if we compare so genuinely humanitarian a poet as Wordsworth with so personal and egoistic a prose writer as Montaigne, it requires little insight to see which is more truly social in temper. The genius of prose always involves an appeal to reason which is necessarily impersonal, and it always infers a community of ground with the reader. But the essence of poetry is personal emotion, and the poet's wings would be paralysed if he had to insist on his fellow-creatures all soaring with him. Again, the democratic quality of French civilization is inseparable from this sociality, and both alike are only possible with a tradition and a language which are independent of race and of class. I have elsewhere pointed out how significant in relation to the anti-democratic or oligarchic structure and tradition of English life is the fact that our language savours at once of race and of class; its different elements have been furnished by different elements of the population, so that long ago, as regards, for instance, domestic animals, while the Saxon serf was only familiar with the ox and the calf and the sheep and the pig, his Norman lord knew only of beef and veal and mutton and pork, a difference which bears witness not only to a distinction of language and race but also of class, for while the man of the people furnished the names for the animals as they were bred, it was the man of the classes who gave names to these same animals in the only form in which he knew them well, on the table. In England we have two main sources for the enrichment of our language, one from Latin, reaching the language mainly through the scholar, the other from the popular Anglo-Saxon and allied dialects, reaching the language mainly through the people. Hence a perpetual conflict between two dissimilar elements, one of which has a pseudo-superiority over the other, due to its class character. The heterogeneous character of our language has its advantages, for it has given us some of the most magnificent effects in our poetic literature, from Shakespeare to Rossetti; it is a dubious advantage in prose, and in social intercourse it is the reverse of an advantage. It accentuates the distinction between the upper class man and the lower class man; it introduces an unfortunate difference between familiar language and ceremonious language, vulgarizing the one and stultifying the other, and probably it serves to increase the awkwardness and unreadiness of the Englishman in speech. The French language, on the contrary, is homogeneous and built up from a single source; with whatever finer shades of distinction there is no such fundamental difference between the language of upper and lower classes, or the same embarrassing choice of synonyms; it is perfectly adapted for the expression of social equality.[1] Moreover, this sociality is connected with French courtesy. That indeed was a fundamental condition for the constitution of any civilization on a basis of such widely unlike racial elements. Friction could only be avoided under such conditions by the institution of a ritual courtesy, so guaranteeing the social rights of the individual in his own person. Courtesy thus is of primary value for the community, even apart from its inevitable development in a community in which social intercourse is so highly prized. French politeness is sometimes treated as a sham by English people. But to suppose that politeness must only be exercised when it is the expression of deep personal feeling is to betray absolute ignorance of its elements. French politeness, to me at least, seems of less fine quality than Russian politeness, the watchful yet unobtrusive anxiety to help others which is the outcome of a singularly humane temperament developed under inclement conditions involving constant mutual aid. In French politeness there is sometimes a little too much of ostentation, as it were a conscious homage to a great ritual tradition; so expressed, its superficiality is emphasized. But it has always to be remembered that nine-tenths of our relations with our fellows are only superficial,

---

[1] It is no doubt true that this quality of the French language has tended to the great development of slang in France, so that, it has been said, to the very lowest classes in Paris French has become almost a dead language. To some extent, however, we witness the same phenomena in London, and without the compensating advantage referred to above.

and how great a relief it would be if we could ensure that those
superficial nine-tenths of life were fittingly lived in an atmosphere
of equally superficial politeness! Our English minds, grasping
greedily at the things which alone seem to us real, are only too apt
to forget that politeness, superficial as it may be to our deep personal
life, is after all one of the most real and essential features of life in
common, the prime quality of city life, of politics in the true classic
sense of the word.

It is because France has thus brought into the modern world
traditions which spring largely from the civilization of the world's
supreme city that her civilization is peculiarly adapted to an age
which is primarily an urban age, and in which therefore the virtues
of urbanity must inevitably come to the front. In our insular
arrogance we speak of "Latin decadence" as compared with our
own fruitful energy in money-making; but after all we have to
live, and money-making is at best only one of the more or less
necessary conditions of living. In this matter our acts are more
eloquent than our words. Thirty, even twenty, years ago, London
was a hideous desert, a nightmare city, more lacking in the instincts
and appliances of human living than remote Moscow. Since then—
however great the progress yet to make, and however awkward,
partial and blundering the progress already made—London has been
transformed. Our streets, our parks, our restaurants, our trams
and omnibuses, our public conveniences, our Sunday concerts, have
all undergone an almost startling development which has brought
them considerably nearer both to the ideals and the practices of
French civilization. It may not even be too optimistic to trace some
movement towards French urbanity in the feelings and conduct
of our crowds, when their passions are not aroused. We no longer
see the heaps of excited and groaning humanity fighting and
trampling on each other, not for the sake of entering Paradise but
to obtain slightly better seats than they are entitled to in a theatre
pit; it is true that the *queues* outside our theatres are not yet formed
in the spontaneous French manner, and might not survive the absence
of the stalwart policeman who marshals them, but their existence in
any form is a blow to the old English "every-man-for-himself"

doctrine of social individuality, and a testimony to the power of that conception of "liberty, equality, and fraternity" which was the sentiment of French civilization long before the Revolution set it up on the public buildings of France. It must not be supposed that this progress is largely or mainly a conscious imitation of Paris or any other continental city. It is the result of the fact that French civilization is in its chief lines the inevitable civilization of an urban population, and that as any urban civilization develops it necessarily takes on, whether consciously or unconsciously, the essential qualities of French civilization.

In a remarkable passage of Huysmans' novel, *Là-Bas*, the regret is expressed that Joan of Arc ever arose to wrest France from the Normans, who were seeking to preserve her racial and prehistoric unity with England, and thus handed her over to Charles VII. and his southerners. Huysmans is himself of half Dutch descent, and therefore this lament must not be taken as typical of any section of purely French opinion, and one may indeed doubt whether, in spite of the tendency of the meridional element to float on the surface, it represents any unduly large part of French civilization. Moreover, Huysmans is unjust to the southerner; Taine, certainly, not too sympathetic towards the meridional temperament, has yet (in his posthumous *Carnets de Voyage*) made some very acute observations on the differences observed as one travels towards the south of France; he notes the sense of democratic equality in intercourse, the alert intelligent gaiety, the natural freedom from coarseness, the presence of a sort of instinctive education; he notes especially how the women, while losing the blushing shamefaced modesty of the northern women, have at the same time become the equals, even the superiors, of the men, for "the life and temperament of the south being more feminine, women are on their own ground and command"; here, in short, we see, Taine remarks, the essential elements of the French character pushed to their extreme. Thus we may well doubt whether the meridional temperament has really damaged the balance of French civilization. But if France has lost little, one cannot help seeing how great a loss the destruction of French and British unity has been to England, and, indirectly, to the whole world. The Normans, with their northern race and southern civilization, furnished a bond of union—equally honourable both to France and England—which it only required the growth of tradition to develop. That check on undue individualism which France has ever exercised would have furnished the only possible means of truly unifying the various elements of our land. Our race has no common civilization, and, with all its patriotism, no common country, to which every unit gives allegiance. No man considers that his country is the "British Isles", which is yet the only convenient term available, and only the colonist (and not always he) claims to belong to the "British Empire". The Englishman has the humiliation of knowing that the English crown fell into the hands of Scotch kings; the Scotsman has to realize that his country plays a subordinate part to the country he practically annexed, and that every individual Scotsman has to achieve the conquest of England afresh; the Irishman belongs to a country which is still fiercely rebel at heart; the Cornishman's national motto, "One and all", still applies exclusively to Cornishmen; and the Welshman's aloofness, however silent and sullen, is perhaps the most profound of all. France alone, by furnishing great racial contingents closely akin to each of these separate elements, could have truly unified them. To mention one instance only, though an instance of the first magnitude, the sympathy between the Mediterranean population of France and the Mediterranean population of Ireland (for such, racially, it largely is) would have for ever rendered impossible any "Irish question". The advantage of the union of France and England for the world generally would have been incalculable. The weakness of a civilization based on a broad and human basis of reason is that it is ever too ready to recognize its own limits and to rest satisfied with an epigram in the face of human stupidity. If the humanizing civilization of France had been backed by the energy of England, and held in check by our stolidity and love of compromise, there would have been moulded for the world's civilization the most effective instrument that can be conceived. When the peasant girl of Lorraine, with her hallucinations, galvanized into action the nerveless arms of Charles, she inflicted a blow on the progress of the modern world which, so far as can be seen, has never been equalled.[1]

It would be foolish to recall what has now become an impossible dream, if it had not still an element of instruction. France must always remain the nearest country to Britain, and the French the most nearly related to the British of all European populations. We may admit that our language more closely resembles the dialect of Friesland, and that a certain section of our people, especially in East Anglia and Yorkshire, are more like the people between Holland and Norway. But if we take our islands as a whole, France alone is the European country with which we have any close affinity. Our races have been broken off from their main base in France as truly as our islands themselves have been so broken off. Even yet the line of communication is almost complete; we have but to cross to the Channel Islands to find ourselves, while still on British soil, among people of French race and French speech; again, we step over to the mainland to find ourselves in the Cotentin peninsula of Normandy, surrounded by familiar names, amid faces of familiar type, and scenery that recalls England. Such facts as these have to be recognized even by those among us who are inapt to appreciate the special qualities of French civilization.

That the qualities of the French spirit have also their defects cannot be questioned. It is, however, the reverse proposition which more needs to be emphasized among ourselves. We are quicker to see defects than qualities, unless the qualities happen to be our own. A learned French sociologist has written a book entitled *A quoi tient la Supériorité des Anglo-Saxons*, and recently a brilliant French writer, M. Léon Bazalgette, has written another book entitled *A quoi tient l'Infériorité Française*. However inconclusive these and similar books may be, we might gladly welcome among our British public men and writers any similar sign of a tendency towards that healthy self-criticism and discriminating insight into the characteristics of our neighbours which are among the best signs of a fine

---

[1] While here yielding to Joan of Arc the leading rôle traditionally assigned to her, I am aware that certain characteristic defects of English rule largely contributed to this series of disasters.

civilization. If this popular politician and that popular author—the reader may himself fill in the blanks—were to engage in such tasks at the present moment we certainly should not all agree with them, but their courageous public spirit in insisting on the recognition of those aspects of affairs which we were most in danger of neglecting would be worthy of all admiration. When we look towards France we think we miss that spirit of individualism which we prize so highly in ourselves. We forget not only that the more orderly method of life which is inseparable from urban civilization on its material side removes much of the restless friction which largely drains away our energy, but also the still more important fact that our individualism is only conspicuous on the material plane. In the world of ideas individualism (putting aside eccentricity) is at least as conspicuous in France as in England. We are proud of our physical courage, and of the tenacity with which we fight to the last against immense odds. It may be so, but we have still to remember that, whatever our physical courage, we have produced a fair proportion of persecutors and not by any means a greater proportion of martyrs than other countries. We have invented Mrs. Grundy as the symbol of a power we are all afraid of. We have shown that like the French we are capable of working ourselves up to a fury of wild enthusiasm in the cause of something that seems to us for the moment of immense importance. But we have not shown that like the French we can produce a considerable minority of distinguished public men with the moral courage to face the mob, and accept calumny, ignominy, loss of every kind, even exile. Yet these are the things that make a nation's mission fruitful, and enable it to stand before the world with a good record. It is only the few men of moral courage who ultimately count. *Athanasius contra mundum:* we remember the exiled Athanasius, but we have really forgotten his Arian "world". Again, in the immensely rich literature of France, we find a deficiency of poets; France has not produced one of the world's great poets; that is the inevitable defect of the qualities of mind which have given her a language incomparably fit for prose, but lacking in those large, beautifully, obscurely splendid words which our own poets can use for their emotional ends. The French temper and language lend themselves to rhetoric, which is indeed the "poetry" of a mind attuned to reason and prose; the greatest of French "poets", Victor Hugo, is a superb rhetorician; it is always rather difficult for a Frenchman to distinguish between rhetoric and real poetry. So fundamental is the bias of the French mind to prose that, so far as I know, the only two French poets who are purely poets, as the Greeks and the English have understood poetry—I refer to Villon and Verlaine—are poets by the breaking up of the whole social personality, by becoming outcasts from society. Only by smashing the whole mould of their civilization, it would seem, can the most intense note of personal emotion be reached; whereas in England it has been possible for the greatest poets to live quietly the lives of respectable middle-class citizens. It is the difference between a civilization in which personal emotion, for good or for evil, is traditionally allowed its full swing, and a civilization in which reason and orderliness and the demands of the social instincts are traditionally permanent; the "prose" of such a civilization, it may not be unnecessary to add, is by no means the opposite of idealism, but its ideals are those of impersonal reason rather than of personal self-centred emotion. We have already seen how the much con- temned gaiety of the French, with its tendency to play impudently around the most sacred facts of life, is really bound up with the finest qualities of the French genius, with those heroic or austere qualities which have made France, more than any other country, the land of saints. We speak with contempt, again, of French instability, especi- ally as manifested in politics; but in doing so we not only fail to put ourselves at the point of view of a nation among whom politics, as we understand them, however conspicuous they may appear, are not regarded as the most fundamental matter in life, but we do not realize that that very instability is the sign of a highly-organized and sensitive civilization. In the same way we might pass in review all the defects in the character of the French, or indeed any other nation, to find that they were after all the inevitable defects of qualities, and that nothing in the world is without its compensations for good or for evil.

These things are truisms. But it is the misfortune of popular passions and national jealousies that they impart to the most commonplace matters of fact an almost startling novelty. Anyone who is in touch with French opinion knows how tolerant and how fair towards England is the attitude of educated French people. Yet the opinions of the flimsiest and feeblest of French newspapers—reflecting a vulgar, if not unnatural, reaction against the Pharisaic attitude of England towards France—are reproduced in the most ponderous of our own journals, so to gain a significance and resonance which otherwise they would never reach. Thus the vicious circle is completed, and the English man in the street who takes his opinions, as Englishmen nowadays mainly seem to do, from the newspapers, is hopelessly chained to prejudice and error.

It may well be that the present moment is not the most auspicious even for an attempt to learn something of the secrets of ordinary French civilization, but it is certainly the moment when its advantages are most clearly presented to us. A nation which acts counter to the ideas and sentiments of the civilized world must either succeed in proving to the world that it is animated by motives of unquestionable justice, or, failing that, it must at least be willing to exercise tact and consideration towards other countries. A country which fails to do either must be content to be regarded for the moment as outside the pale of civilization. The latent animosities thus aroused are necessarily strong among a people whose humanitarian ideals and instincts of justice are more developed and widespread than elsewhere. Hence inevitable friction of the most mischievous sort, and the waves of popular passion and prejudice threaten their worst. Yet, whatever havoc they may wreak, the solid bed-rock of the ancient facts on which our race and civilization are founded cannot be permanently shaken. It is well that from time to time we should be reminded of the existence of those facts.

THE GENIUS OF ENGLAND

I

THE ENGLISH are not only, as has often been observed, the most individual of people, but England is also the most individual of nations. That is the natural result of the peculiar position of England as a citadel in the sea. At the outset, the strong and adventurous alone might dare to approach the forbidding shores of this island, to seize and to hold it. A process of selection was thus exercised on all would-be invaders. Only the men of vigorous and original individuality could be tempted to this hazardous enterprise across the waves, only such men could overcome the risks of this dangerous coast and achieve success in their daring task.

When once the island was peopled by a strong race its qualities as a citadel could be utilized. For a thousand years there has been no great hostile invasion of England. The various bands of daring adventurers who seized the land, once firmly welded together, have been free to develop their native characteristics as individualistic sea-faring adventurers, and on that basis to elaborate their culture and display their special genius.

Many of the most marked and the most discrepant traits of the Englishman are accounted for when we bear in mind that he is thus the outcome of a special, perhaps unique, process of selection. That process has made him adventurer and pirate, dreamer and poet, passionately devoted to freedom, independent to the verge of eccentricity, resourceful and versatile, not only a stern moralist peculiarly apt for piety but an aggressive colonizer and a hard-headed, practical man of business. It is necessary to emphasize this factor in the causation of the Englishman because it seems usually to be overlooked.

At the same time we need by no means neglect the influence of race in the making of the English. The races that have their part in the British nation are so various, and the persistence of their characteristics are so visible even to-day, that the crudest theorist in England finds himself invoking the racial factor to explain any puzzling trait in his fellow countrymen.

Roughly speaking, the earlier invasions were of dark peoples and the later invasions of fair peoples. The result has been that, notwithstanding the high degree of amalgamation which has been taking place from the first, the west side of Britain holds a population which is largely of dark pigmentation, while the population of the east side is almost throughout of light pigmentation. These external differences in appearance are associated with equally marked internal differences in temperament. Thus the whole country constitutes a kind of electric battery with an eastern pole and a western pole, whereby a continuous circulation of energy takes place, the two unlike elements forever stimulating, reinforcing, and moderating each other. So are formed vital currents which have often produced friction, and yet largely served to generate the vigour of the English people.

When we come to analyse more specifically the racial elements which make up the two poles of this battery, and to consider what special qualities they may have contributed, apart from the selective process of the sea, to the constitution of the English nation, we are somewhat in doubt as to the earliest recognizable element. We may be certain that it was largely dark, we may assume that it had its chief home in the Mediterranean, and we may choose to call it Iberian, bearing in mind always the influence of the selectional process which has to some extent modified the original character of all the invaders of Britain. This element, combined with more rugged elements of obscure origin, has become closely united with the second main body of invaders, the Goidels followed by the Brythons and both Celts, these uniting with the earlier elements to constitute together what we now commonly call the "Celtic" population of Britain. It is evident, however, that the stocks of earlier arrival than the Goidels and Brythons must count for much; for they imparted to the Celtic blood not only its dark complexion and its robust constitution, but also its stubborn tenacity, its obstinate independence—unchangeable even beneath the mask of a gracious suavity—for these are qualities altogether unlike those of the Gallic Celts whom Strabo has described so well, receptive, versatile, and unstable. The Belgae, however, the modern Walloons of southern Belgium, form the natural links between the Celts of France and of Britain. When one is among the people of Liège and the neighbourhood one has more the sense of being among people with the special air and carriage of the English than in perhaps any other region of the opposite coast.

The well-combined product of these early waves of invasion— all later admixtures in the west being subordinate—which we are pleased to call "Celtic" constitutes a permanent and clearly marked element in the collective whole of "England". These people possess a natural distinction, an inborn refinement, quite inde- pendent of material civilization—the Irish, even of high social class, as Fynes Moryson bore witness, sometimes dispensed with clothing as late as the seventeenth century—which often stamped their features and is marked in their gracious carriage and courteous speech. This is found in every division of the Celtic race in Britain, however variously modified, alike in Ireland and the Scotch High- lands, in Wales and in Cornwall. It seems to testify to the undoubted fact that these people have behind them a much more ancient culture than the later English. They are of alert intelligence and quick wit, democratic in their instincts, ready of response to the appeal of the ideal, impassioned orators, imaginative in vision and impetuous in action, yet with a certain coolness, sometimes even hardness of temperament, which often seems to preserve them from their own excessiveness, and enables them indeed to mock at the excessiveness of others, for they seem too emotional themselves to overrate the value of emotion. The vivacity of their nerves makes them not only dreamers and idealists but apt also for action, and even too readily fighters. In all these respects the Celtic side of Britain has an individuality of its own which distinguishes it from the eastern side in which the elements brought by later waves of invasion remain predominant.

The "Anglo-Saxon" wave furnished what is usually considered to be the Germanic element in the English. Strictly speaking, this came, according to the best modern opinions, from the south of

Denmark and the adjoining region still further south and to the west. It was made up of two or three tribes, the Angles, who seem to have come from Angel in Schleswig, and the Jutes, probably from Jutland, and the Saxons, from the region immediately to the south of Denmark, not identical with modern Saxony, so that we must not too hastily assume that it is from a sense of blood-relation-ship that even in the Great War of to-day there has been more good feeling between the English and the Saxons than with any of the other German peoples to whom the English have been opposed.[1] On the whole this invasion was that of a Low German population, with Scandinavian affinities. The Frisians who occupied, and still occupy, the north-west corner of Continental Europe, seem to have been almost identical with the Saxons, and the language which they speak in Dutch Friesland is nearer to English than any other tongue. The Englishman of to-day can easily understand Frisian, even fragments of Flemish, but the High German tongue has left no marks on England. The High Germans, indeed, were too far east to be attracted to England. They were a vigorous, war-like, migratory race, but the great sweeps of their migrations usually curved in a southerly or south-westerly direction, traversing Italy and Spain and even eastern France, but not expanding further to-wards the west. Of the tribes invading England, the Jutes had various customs of their own which they brought with them to Kent, but the Angles and the Saxons seem much more closely related, in the opinion of some authorities even identical, and it has been argued that the term "Anglo-Saxon" may simply mean "English Saxons".

This Anglo-Saxon invasion was an eruption of savage warriors into a peaceful and civilized population. For we must remember that for centuries the Romans had been in possession, and though we cannot say that the Roman armies made any recognizable contribution to the composition of the British population—for they had long ceased to be recruited mainly in Rome—yet Roman civilization, Roman organization, Roman luxury had permeated Britain. These invaders from Denmark had hitherto come into but

[1] Throughout these essays, the expressions "the Great War of today" or "the present war" refer to the first world war, 1914–18. F. D.

slight contact with Roman influences which had no meaning for them. When they had hewed their way through with fire and the sword, they allowed the beautiful refinements of the Roman villas to fall into decay, until concealed by the grass-land under which we find them to-day, and built their own wooden settlements outside. This wave of invasion thus marked a great gulf in the culture of Britain, and that accounts for the contrast between east and west which all the levelling influence of a thousand years have not effaced to-day.

The Anglo-Saxons extinguished civilization in Britain, although they brought with them a culture of their own which has sometimes been underrated. They constituted, moreover, an element which was destined to be of high value in the final development of the English nation. It is true that early historians have sometimes unduly magnified the part of the Anglo-Saxons in England; they have failed to realize the immense importance alike of the earlier and the later invasions; an England that was all Anglo-Saxon could scarcely have hoped for a larger career in the world than Saxony or Friesland, or so large a career as Scandinavian Denmark. But all the Germanic tribes have possessed, as Ferrero has pointed out, the precious aptitude to act as a cement to other racial stocks, binding together elements which have sometimes been of higher qualities than themselves. They were probably not democratic in the communal or clannish way of the early British, or the individualistic way of the later invaders; like all the Germans, they cultivated caste distinctions, the violation of which was punishable by death. This caste feeling still flourished even when the Anglo-Saxon was overlaid by new waves of invasion. It has so come about that the Anglo-Saxons constitute the solid, persistent plebeian element of the English population; this is expressed even in physical type, and the heavy peasant of a Saxon focus like Surrey and Sussex shows nothing of the distinction of the Highlander or the Cornishman, while these predominantly Saxon regions have produced the minimum proportion of English genius. The Anglo-Saxon has ever possessed a sturdy obstinacy, an independent commonsense, well typified by the south Saxon peasant, William Cobbett. Though "terrible for bravery and agility", the Saxons were fundamentally conservative from the first, the least apt to wander of all Germanic tribes, and in the great Germanic migrations of the early centuries after Christ, Saxons and Frisians and Angles still clung to their old ground on the bank of the Elbe. It is, perhaps, not an accident after all, that England has been named from the Anglo-Saxon. He has not been her brain, but he has perhaps been her backbone, even in an almost literal sense, for the most unmixed Anglo-Saxons run right down the centre of the land, between the earlier British whom they rolled back to the coast, and the later Northmen who have encroached on the eastern shores. Without the Anglo-Saxon England would be impotent; in every conflict of war, in every task of peace, he has been the weapon and the implement.

Before the English people became finally blended and tempered, it seems to have been the fate of each successive invasion to pass through a phase of enervation in this soft mild atmosphere and thus to yield to the onset of the next wave. This happened to the Anglo-Saxons; they lost their sea-power, without being able to transmute it into an effective land power. So they were often helpless before the new generation of Scandinavian pirates who carried out the same methods in an even more vigorous and relentless way. They were not only highly selected invaders—for they came from far to attack a firmly settled land, and only the stoutest could hope for success—but they belonged at the outset to the most individualized of the invaders of these islands. In complexion they were the fairest of all, and in character the most enterprising, the most self-reliant, in their extreme types the most gloomy and the most eccentric. They have left to-day their distinguishable mark all around the northern coast and the outlying islands. In place-names and family-names, in colour of skin and eyes and hair, in traits of speech and character, the Danes thus remain in Norfolk and in Lincolnshire and in Durham and in Cumberland and in Furness, thickly on the coast and islands of Scotland, and sprinkled on the shores of Ireland. It can scarcely be a mere coincidence that it is in the Danish regions of England that I have most frequently met that John Bull who is supposed to be the typical Englishman. He is fair and high-coloured, large of stature, of fleshy texture and rounded outlines, with not seldom the anxious mark on his face of his own physical weight, a little irritable, if not suspicious and defiant, though tender and emotional beneath, and sometimes he may be merely bucolic and sometimes he has the high intelligence and character, the gravity and firm decision of the finest Englishman, but always there is a certain personal consciousness, a burden of responsibility, whether the burden of his own health or the burden of ruling a province. So the Scandinavian influence in England has not been merely local, it has penetrated the national character. There has been no English king with a finer political genius than the Dane Canute, and the spirit of the Northman, with his grave sense of responsibility, primarily to himself rather than to others—the sense of Shakespeare's injunction, "To thine own self be true", and the spirit of Ibsen's hero, who felt that he was most strong when most alone—seems specially associated with the Danish element in the English. Even the plastic force of the Scandinavian tongue has had its marked influence on the structure of the English language, in its simple, concise, direct force, if not in the delicious ripple, as of a wavelet of the sea, which sorts so well with Scandinavian speech and is so remote from the speech of Germanic tongues.

The last great invasion was that of the Normans. It was the most fatefully decisive of all and set the final seal on the genius of England. The Norman was ultimately of the same stock as the Northmen of the preceding wave of invasion. It was that fact which gave so much significance to the Norman Conquest of England. Of all the Norman conquests in Europe, as Freeman pointed out, that of England alone proved permanently effective, and the reason was that only in England were they on a soil over which their own seed had already been plentifully sprinkled. Here alone their potent genius could work on congenial elements and achieve permanent results. Yet the Normans' task of invasion was harder than any that went before, needing all the energies of the great general and consummate administrator who achieved it.

Every fresh invader of England had added to the strength of England. After the Norman Conquest no further conquest seems to have been found possible. England had become what later the French Ambassador to Charles II found it to be, "one vast citadel". The Great Armada, which the world-empire of Spain sent against England, merely served to strew the coast with wrecks, as the Duke of Würtemburg noted twenty years later; the great expedition of Napoleon never even left the would-be invader's harbours; and the recent attempts of the Germans to attack England have only been rendered possible by the cultivation of extreme rapidity in flight. The Normans, it must be remembered, were the most vigorous race of their time. Concentrated centripetal force in combination with explosive centrifugal force—the aptitude to acquire and the aptitude to expand—in them reached maximum intensity. They represented the finest flower of strong northern individuality developed in the favourable soil of the orderly Latin civilization of France. They were, as they remain in France today, narrowly acquisitive, but at the same time they shrank before no extravagance. In all things excessive, as their own ancient chronicler noted, they infused something of that excessiveness into the composite English blood. Yet they were no longer pirates. They were trained in warfare and government; they knew how to found principalities and kingdoms even in the far Mediterranean. They cultivated the arts with daring and brilliant success, and they had a passion for law, even to the extent of contentiousness. Their primitive energy of ruthlessness had become transformed into a genius for organization and an instinct for just, if severe, administration. "A beast, but a just beast," was the schoolboy's verdict on Archbishop Temple as schoolmaster; it has, rightly or wrongly, often been the verdict of the subject races in the east who have come upon this old Norman trait in their English rulers. Justice has been the chief secret of the mystery, as it has seemed to some, of the stability of English government at home and abroad, although it has often been but slowly and pain-fully achieved. It has indeed been said, truly or not, that justice is as peculiarly the trait of the English as reason is of the French or pity of the Russians.

The extent and the significance of the Norman invasion of England has sometimes been underestimated. When we enter the little church of Dives, in Normandy, from which William sailed, and read the list of his companions there inscribed, it may seem to us that we are only in the presence of a select body of great paladins whose influence on the national composition and character could scarcely have been great. The evidence of place-names and the more dubious evidence of family names in England seems to tell a different story. The wave of Norman migration, moreover, continued for a century after the Conqueror's arrival. The Norman and other French elements which thus came over were necessarily less highly selected than the Conqueror's companions, but must have mightily reinforced their influence. The main evidence for the strength of Norman influence in England is written in the course of English history. However well compact the varied elements of the English people may be, and, in so far as they are not compact, however well they may supplement each other, it is throughout the Norman spirit which has dominated England and largely directed English policy in the world. It is the Norman aristocratic dominance, Norman orderliness, Norman administrative energy, which have formulated the English oligarchic constitution and controlled the growth of English dominion in every quarter of the globe.

With the Norman invasion the elements of the English character were all brought together. Nothing further was needed but their permeation and elaboration, their slow development to self-consciousness. There have been minor infusions of new blood since, but these have merely served to reinforce elements already existing. Though small in amount, these later migrations have been precious in quality, for they have been attracted by that spirit of freedom and toleration in England which has offered a home to the finest-spirited refugees from neighbouring lands. Thus it was that England accepted the Germans and Dutch, liberated the Jews, admitted numerous groups of artisans from Flanders who brought both their skill in handicraft and their sturdy independence to enrich the land of their adoption, and welcomed the French Huguenots, who, in the congenial English soil, were free so to develop their high intelligence and lofty character as to take rank among the most typical representatives of the English genius.

The genius of England, the special mark of the higher cultural activities of the nation, has been conditioned in part by the nature of the selectional process through which the country has been populated in successive waves of invasion, and in part by the varying character of the peoples thus introduced.

The result has been that, notwithstanding a slow process of mixture, the east coast of the British Islands has in every field of activity represented one aspect of the English spirit, while the west coast has represented a different and even opposed aspect of that same spirit. The purer representatives on each side have in this way contributed to the vitality of the English genius by opposing and supplementing each other, while the close connection between the two coasts has rendered possible racial blendings which have produced complete and typical representatives of that genius. There are numerous focal spots of genius in the British Islands, each with its own slightly varying characteristics, which we may, perhaps, trace back to the mediæval days when the composite character of the race and its attitude of jealous civil individualism caused the Isle of Wight people to describe Hampshire people as "foreigners", and English towns to display as much hostility to other English towns as though, it has been said, they were in Normandy or Flanders. Such minor variations cannot, however, obscure the wider outlines of the picture presented by English genius.

This complementary opposition, and this racial blending to produce in one individual the union of the two opposites, is seen through the whole of English genius. It is a fascinating task to attempt to trace it out in different fields and to note the varying balance of genius in each field taken separately, for, as we might expect, the method of expression most successfully attained is not the same on both sides.[1]

There are indeed some forms of human activity for which there can scarcely fail to be some degree of aptitude in every region and every race. That is, for instance, the case in politics. Leaders in politics have arisen in all parts of the British Islands. At the same time they

---

[1] It may be mentioned that I have dealt in detail with the distribution of English genius in my *Study of British Genius*.

have always, to a remarkable extent, retained the impress of their race. This remains as true as ever, and among the British political leaders of to-day it is easy to observe how each expresses his own racial tendencies and his own personal heredity. In no field, indeed, is race seen to predominate over environment more clearly than in political genius. That is sometimes, indeed, a factor in political success. Parnell, with his haughty Anglo-Saxon reserve and shyness, his methodical subterranean tenacity, could win from his Irish Nationalist followers a loyalty they could scarcely have yielded to any purely Celtic leader. Disraeli, with his hard brilliance and dazzling Oriental imagination, an adventurer escaped from the Arabian Nights, still attracts, from the most conservative section of Anglo-Saxon England, a degree of sentimental affection never vouchsafed to Salisbury, the genuine and admirable personification of conservative England, and Lloyd George, the complete Celtic Welshman, and as such a natural object of suspicion and hostility to the Anglo-Saxon, is yet able to exert a magic influence over the Anglo-Saxon mind. The really dominating figures in the history of English politics can scarcely be said, however, to belong either to the extreme east or the extreme west. They are intermediate, a mixed race, or else originating in such a district as East Anglia, where the eastern spirit has been specially permeated by modifying influences. Gladstone was of such mixed stocks, as was before him a yet greater Englishman, Oliver Cromwell, and the Pitts, ancestrally spread over various parts of the British Isles, were connected, one may surmise, with the most aboriginal elements of the English people, while the peculiarly typical figure of John Hampden was ancestrally rooted in the Buckinghamshire hills and forests, which have never been thoroughly Anglo-Saxonized. Religion also, like politics, is universal in its appeal, and all parts of the British Islands have produced men of religion, who have displayed one or other of the special characteristics—militant aggressiveness or practical benevolence or orderly ecclesiasticism—which belong to British religion.

In another kind of aptitude, which we might expect to find evenly distributed in a marine citadel, there has been a remarkable tendency to division of labour. Great soldiers belong to the west and great sailors to the east. It is significant that Wellington, the representative English general, came from Ireland, and Nelson, the representative British admiral, from Norfolk. Ireland, Wales and the Welsh Marshes, the Scotch Highlands, Cornwall, with the whole south-western peninsula (though this last region has been also a region of great sailors), have given England the largest proportion of her soldiers and her generals, and all these regions are largely Celtic. The whole eastern and southern coasts have produced great sailors, especially those parts of it where the population is fairest, so that distinguished sailors have been, in a large proportion, blue-eyed. This is a differentiation which seems more marked during recent centuries than it was at the outset of English history, before national feeling had unified Great Britain. It is possible that the military aptitude which through Plantagenet and even Tudor times we seem to find widely diffused in England has become largely transmuted into legal and administrative aptitude. Distinguished lawyers have often come from the northern part of east England, and great administrators from the neighbouring regions of East Anglia, to which both of the two chief builders of modern Egypt ancestrally belong, Lord Cromer and Lord Kitchener, though the latter was more immediately connected with Ireland.

It is when we turn to the arts that we may read in most precise detail the racial characteristics of English genius. Thus, in dramatic aptitude, we find in the British Islands, as in Europe generally, that the fair, blue-eyed population very rarely achieve success. Ireland, Wales, and the English south-western peninsula, have furnished England with actors and actresses; perhaps not one of high eminence has been derived elsewhere. Blue eyes, except in combination with dark hair (which is a Celtic characteristic), one scarcely sees among them. The slow reserved phlegmatic temperament of the Anglo-Saxon is rebellious to dramatic expression. The Celtic qualities, on the other hand, of vivacity, mental alertness, receptivity, and obvious charm, naturally lend themselves to the players' art. They are also qualities that we commonly consider feminine, and it may not be an accident that when we put aside the stage, on which the actress may even outshine the actor, feminine ability, in a numerical estimation of British genius, occupies a relatively larger place in Ireland than in any other region of the British Islands.

The racial opposition of east and west in the British Islands is admirably revealed in English painting. It may indeed be said that nothing shows so infallibly as English painting how profound, and how delicate, yet how unconscious, are the roots of heredity in the English character. The people of the west, as we know, are idealistic, visionary, imaginative; they possess the sense of magic; they worship their own dreams. The people of the east, as we also know, are born naturalists; they are enamoured of reality; they find beauty not in their own visions, but by patiently watching the actual world; they worship Nature. Every English painter has been true to one or other of these deep impulses, however ignorant of it he may have been; it is not easy to find any exception. Reynolds belongs to the west as inevitably as Gainsborough belongs to the east. We could not imagine Richard Wilson in Norfolk or Crome in Wales. Burne-Jones is as emphatically Welsh, the man of the *Mabinogion*, as Constable expresses the whole soul of Suffolk. Throughout we see this radical opposition of temperament between the men of the dark west and of the fair east or north, the men who follow the vision within and the men who brood over the vision of Nature. There is, indeed, one great English painter, perhaps the supreme English painter, whom we cannot clearly place in the one class or in the other, for he seems to belong to both. In Turner we see the faithful realist forever ruthlessly on the track of Nature to catch every subtlest variation of her mood; we also see the extravagant idealist embodying the inner vision of a loveliness never before made visible on the earth; we see them both, moreover, at the same moment. If we investigate Turner's ancestry, we find, as we might expect, that, while on his father's side he belonged to the west, he seems on his mother's side, so far as any evidence exists, to belong to the east. Herein is manifested that vital conflict between contradictory elements which, in the white heat of their fusion, have produced the finest achievements of the English genius.

It is in literature that we may most reasonably expect to read the spirit of a people, and to discern clearly every shade of its racial admixture. In this field the evidence is inexhaustible; the most delicate variations in racial quality, and the strongest contrasts are instinctively expressed by the man who possesses the art to write out of his own nature. The very medium which English writers have been compelled to use, the English language, is a reflexion of the compounded, varied, and tempered nature of the British people, and has thus powerfully aided English literary expression. At the outset, the west, with its more ancient and refined culture, takes precedence of the east. The Welsh *Mabinogion* and the Irish hero tales, with their beautifully embroidered imaginative extravagance, remain to-day far more attractive than the baldly crude narratives of *Beowulf* or *Havelok*, however sincere their simple and intense humanity. For an adequately artistic embodiment, on the primitive heroic basis, of this eastern spirit, we must go to Normandy, to the *Chanson de Roland*, unless, indeed, the final embodiment of that song which Taillefer sang at Hastings took place—as some authorities have supposed—in England. The east, or we may rather say the north, became splendidly fused with the west in the earliest of great English prose books, Malory's *Morte d'Arthur*. Here we see the Anglo-Saxon mind working on the Celto-Welsh stories, so that their variegated tapestry, by force of the emotional human intensity and ethical fervour thus infused, throbs with a poignant inner life. The whole course of English literature is thus typified at the outset in these two tendencies, and in the possibility of their union in a higher manifestation of radiant beauty and thrilling force.

Such blending on the grand scale is necessarily rare. The contrasting opposites are more easily met. Crabbe in Suffolk represents the concentrated and unmixed Anglo-Saxon spirit as certainly as Coleridge and Keats reveal the English south-western peninsula still touched by ancient Celtic glamour. Sir Thomas Browne belonged, like Crabbe, to East Anglia, but in him we hear insistently the magic note of the west, the same note that we hear in Traherne, for Browne was attached by ancestry to the half Welsh county of Cheshire. Everywhere we see that what is in the blood will come out in the spirit and that the subtlest variations of a man's outlook on the world were determined long centuries before he was born.

It would be surprising if Shakespeare, the supreme glory of English literature, were an exception to the rule that English art is the exact reflection of the complex racial elements that make up the English people and the English spirit. In Shakespeare the west and the east, the Celt and the Anglo-Saxon, were fused together with unique and scarcely analysable felicity. Warwickshire is not only, as has often been pointed out, the heart of England, it also represents anthropologically an infolding of the darker people of the west among the fairer Angles, and is thus an admirable centre for a slow and complete process of racial mixture. In surveying Shakespeare's work we may indeed be inclined to think that its Celtic qualities outweigh the Anglo-Saxon. All this vivacity and quick wit, this vivid perception of the sensory aspects of the world, this gay extravagance, this art of weaving a brilliant and variegated tapestry of words, all this is Celtic. Here we are in the world of Cuchullian and the *Mabinogion*. Yet even when Shakespeare is most Celtic he is still also Anglo-Saxon. From this point of view Mercutio and Falstaff are technically interesting, for here we see the Celtic spirit with delightful effect playing through solid fleshy energetic Anglo-Saxon figures. But such figures are merely the by-play of Shakespeare's composite genius. The Anglo-Saxon in him is really fundamental; he is Norse, even Norman, in his oligarchic sympathies, in his fundamental instinct for personal independence and personal responsibility, in the profound melancholy from which his gaiety exhales. In his most visionary outlook he is still on the solid ground of human emotion at its most poignant degree of concentrated intensity. It is from the sharp conflict, the explosive union, of these two elements of the west and of the east, that the flaming splendour of *Lear* proceeds. We may even say that the Anglo-Saxon spirit is the primary element in Shakespeare's character, for we seem to find it almost unmixed in the youthful *Venus and Adonis*, even in the Sonnets, while the Celtic spirit was never more prominent than at the end of his life in *The Tempest*. It is by the vital opposition of these two conflicting elements in the English nation, by the magnificent effect which their fusion may yield, that Shakespeare is in the end so absolutely and completely English. No Englishman of real life ever fully embodied the characteristics of Shakespeare; yet Shakespeare is all England.

II

The movements of peoples within historical times have been mainly from east to west. It has thus come about that adventurous crews of pioneers have been constantly tempted to cast themselves adrift from the Atlantic sea-board of Europe in search of new and perhaps better lands. For those who dared this feat in the north the British Isles lay like a net in the sea which caught them in its meshes.

There were special reasons why this long narrow island of Great Britain, running parallel to the north-western European coast (for Ireland was more protected and in the end suffered in its racial composition from that very protection), proved attractive to the various wanderers from the mainland. It was easy to reach for all bold and skilful seafarers. It was a moist and fertile land, pleasant to live in because its marine climate abolished all extreme rigours of cold and heat, full of beauty and luxuriance to the northerner; "Britain stands like a bride adorned in her jewels," wrote Gildas, the earliest of British historians. There was indeed one peculiar reason, unknown to all these invaders, why they found England attractive. Although migrations tend to be from east to west, what really appeals to the northerner is the warm south. Now, for the northerner, England is a southern land. When we leave in winter the well-nigh semi-tropical Isles of Scilly, we must travel south for a thousand miles before, abreast of northern Spain, we again find a climate as warm as that we have left. The reason is that the Mexican Gulf has sent a shaft of tropical water through the ocean to strike on the edge of this island and bathe its shores in a warm and iridescent mist. The invaders of England, without knowing it, yet felt that they had reached the south. It is, perhaps, a significant fact that on the fiercely piratical Saxons, at all events, England at first had something of the same enervating influence which Italy exerted over the High German tribes, so that they lost their seafaring passion for a while until, reinforced and tempered by other elements, it developed afresh in more orderly forms.

The continental invaders of an island, situated in relation to that continent as England is to Europe, inevitably possess certain characteristic features of mind and temper. Continental migrations are accomplished along lines of least resistance by slow pressure and peaceful inter-penetration, only occasionally exacerbated into acute conflict and actual warfare. Very little selection is involved in such movements of population. Even the pioneers need possess few strikingly distinctive traits of character, for they remain in close touch with the main body of their own people. It is the quality of the social body which counts rather than the quality of the individual unit, and the units, whatever their quality may be, are carried along with the mass.

Migration to an island under primitive social conditions is a very different matter. At the outset the mere desire to leave home and country to cross the sea for a strange land involves some degree of personal idiosyncrasy. The men who experience such an impulse are a little at variance with their environment, restless and uncomfortable, apt to be original, even eccentric. Such is every true-born adventurer. But he must also be bold, self-reliant, capable. If the pioneer of a new world must be something of a dreamer in order to desire a new world, he must be something of a pirate in order to seize it. The men of Columbus's caravels and the men of the *Mayflower* are the eternal types of such pioneers. The invaders of England knew that they would find the shores lined with hostile natives ready to drive them back into the sea, and even the choice of a rugged and uninhabited landing-place itself argued knowledge and skill and high spirit.

Thus it happens that an island, beaten upon by streams of would-be invaders from the neighbouring highly populated mainland, exerts a strenuous selective influence on these would-be invaders. If this selection has been exerted to an unparalleled extent in the case of England, that is because the circumstances themselves happen to be unparalleled.

. . . . .

To understand the essential English qualities we must constantly bear in mind this selective action of the sea, for ever at work on the successive racial masses which surged up against the barrier of the opposite shores.

We see, in the first place, why the invaders were more apt to be dreamers and poets than the people of their race whom they left behind on the Continent. Men who possessed the migratory instinct in the extreme form, adequate to impel them to take the risks of leaving their fellows for an unknown island of the west, must have been, to a greater degree than their kin, idealists, a little out of touch with the social environment, reserved towards their fellows but enamoured of Nature, always athirst for the marvels of the unknown and brooding over joys which for them the world had never known. The men of this temper are predestined to be poets, and it is unquestioned that the English have proved incomparable poets, it may well be the supreme poets of the modern world, as the Greeks were of the ancient world.

The poetry of the common man is religion. The religious spirit is universal but it has been manifested in England in special forms—which were determined by the selective insular conditions of Great Britain. At the outset this selection had in the north special elements to work on. In the writings of a typical Norwegian novelist, Jonas Lie, we may note the obscure depths of religious emotion which seem so often to mark the Norwegian temperament, melancholic, extravagant, for the most part silent; it is the spirit naturally developed under the stress of the perpetual gloom of the northern winter. In Norway this temper seems chiefly to display itself in passive forms; only its more active exponents were driven by their restlessness of soul to take on the semblance of Vikings. On their arrival on British shores they combined with the native stock to produce a still more active, adventurous, even aggressive race of religionists, though retaining a certain melancholic tendency, still plainly to be discerned, and especially marked in parts of Protestant Scotland and Catholic Ireland, in regions, that is to say, against which the Norwegian wave of invasion specially burst and left its enduring mark in physical types and linguistic vestiges. English religion became characteristically English. This is notably so in its close association with personal character and moral self-government. It is this association which has led to a tendency to hypocrisy and cant, a universal tendency, it is true, but one which the foreigner finds to be specially marked in England. Hypocrisy is an unpleasant and socially disturbing vice; it is better, one thinks, to adopt a low code of morals which may be maintained rather than a high code which cannot be maintained, for the victim of this high-strung moral code can admit no human weakness, and must still wave aloft the standard of his ideal in the eyes of the world even though himself wounded to death. Yet we may also remember that so philosophic and impartial an observer as Fouillée remarks that British cant, while easy to ridicule, yet has its good side, and, he adds, the Englishman is here in agreement with the Catholic Church, which has always held that even an external respect for moral order is better than a cynical absence of respect. The Englishman's religion in general remains more practical than mystical. Mysticism is rare in Britain and comparatively undeveloped. We find it indeed among both the Celtic and Anglo-Saxon elements of the population, in Welsh Traherne and Vaughan, and in Anglian Rolle and Juliana, but these are writers unknown outside England, and two at least of them were once forgotten even in England. The reason seems to be that the mystical attitude is that of serene contentment, of a rapturous acceptance of the world as it is, and such an attitude scarcely lends itself to the spirit of the restless adventurer who feels the sting of a whip which drives him into a strange land. The British religious spirit, of which John Knox may be regarded as a typical representative, has been in the highest degree adventurous, aggressive, iconoclastic, more eager for righteousness than for grace, practically benevolent, it is true, but more apt to be stern than tender. It has reappeared again and again, under ever fresh forms: we see it in those daring spiritual pirates, the Irish saints who swooped down, from time to time, men and women alike, on the Cornish and even more distant coasts, to convert the still heathen savages of foreign lands; we see it in the strenuous Anglo-Saxon missionaries, Boniface and the rest, who died in the hard task of converting Germany; we see it in the austere Lollards of the English Midlands; in the fighting Puritans whose zeal for spiritual purity was only equalled by their lust of spiritual loot, so that every beautiful old English church still bears the scars of the wounds they inflicted; in the heroic Jesuit martyrs of a lost cause; in the Quakers who succeeded in making even quietism aggressive; in the Salvation Army of to-day, which has carried out in another form the methods and the achievements of the first Irish saints. Taken altogether, English religion in all its conflicting aspects remains strikingly uniform and characteristic.

On a more intellectual and serene plane it is the same with English philosophy. The dreamer, the adventurer, the individualist, the iconoclast, the Puritan, stalks through the whole of English philosophy. It is the same, no matter whether we date that philosophy from Scotus Erigena or from the superb audacity and insight of the insolent friar, Roger Bacon. Francis Bacon, throwing aside the whole weighty tradition of antiquity with an exalted faith in Nature and in Practice; Hobbes, with his disdain for others and his absolute trust in his own good reason; Locke, with all the zeal of a Puritan, laying bare the *tabula rasa* of the mind; Berkeley, with delicate skill building up a dream world on the site of the material world he had destroyed; Hume, with his solvents to melt away all the venerated faiths of his time; William Godwin, the father of all philosophic anarchism; Thomas Paine, who inspired the ideas of the Constitution of the United States; Herbert Spencer, with his concentrated passion of hatred against every fetter that society seeks to bind on the freedom of the individual; John Stuart Mill, who elevated and enlarged the English conception of individualism to become a rampart against the levelling influence of democracy as much as against the crushing influence of autocracy, who sought to bring women within its circle on the same terms as men, and pointed the way to the conclusion that, rightly understood, there is no real conflict between individualism and socialism—all these were daring and high-souled pioneers who left the old world behind them and steered to new and unknown shores. And the new horizons they revealed have enlarged the scope of the world for all mankind.

English poets have fulfilled the English mission in the same characteristic spirit as English philosophers, although, since poetry is more local than thought, they have not had the same universal influence. Chaucer and Shakespeare, indeed, while remaining essentially English, in large measure transcended the specifically insular English traits. The other supreme exponents of English poetry fall into line with the champions of religion and the masters of philosophy. The sensitive dreamer, Spenser, an adventurer in fairyland whose quest was that of Platonic holiness, and Marlowe, a daring rebel in life and the rapturous conquering Tamerlaine of a new world of beauty, fittingly open the great names of English poetic literature. Chapman, too obscure in his stammering utterance to be among the greatest poets, is yet among the supremely characteristic English poets, alike in his buoyant spirit of heroic adventure and the almost intoxicated ardour of his claims for spiritual independence and moral self-government. Milton, again, not only the devoted lover of Renaissance Italy and the greatest English artist in verse, but a rugged and uncomfortable personality, an original and unconventional Puritan, an impassioned champion of freedom, is a more typical representative of the insular English spirit than even Shakespeare, who moved in a sphere of imaginative extravagance wherein the universe itself melted like a dream. Milton was at heart a rebel—"of the Devil's party without knowing it," as Blake said; and Byron later represented the same insular spirit in a cruder and more obvious form; with the sea in his blood, grandson of a famous sailor, he was a rebel alike in life and literature, a voluntary exile from his own land who died on his way to fight for the freedom of another land, and became in the eyes of all Europe the most typical, and indeed the most influential, of English poets. Scarcely less typical was another and grander spirit, Landor, also a voluntary exile, with the fascination for the south which has inspired so many English poets since Chaucer—as though England was after all but a stage in the wanderings of the northern sailor-dreamers—a rebel who stands only below Milton in the combination of artistry with impetuous even eccentric originality and the consuming passion for freedom. William Blake, again a daring rebel, who in his concentrated genius carried eccentric originality to the point of insanity, a man who was prepared to be aggressive in his violent independence, a political revolutionary—even sagacious in his political insight—and at the same time the daring seer of obscure universes, was as quintessential an Englishman as his namesake the famous republican Admiral. Scarcely less so was Shelley. The exponent in verse of the doctrines of Godwin, that extreme type of self-governing English individualism, he soared on skylark's wings of flame to pour forth in a supreme song the whole of the dreams and aspirations which lie concealed beneath the disguises of the English heart. Keats, who as an artist ranks scarcely below Milton, is typically English in the union of his worship of sensuous beauty with a profound almost Scandinavian melancholy which he never lived to harmonize with that worship. Herein Wordsworth was one of the foremost and most characteristic figures in English literature. The most patriotic of English poets and the most passionately enamoured of English freedom, purely as an artist, however fine his quality, he would hardly rank with Herrick, scarcely in the first line at all. But a subtler rebel than the rest, Wordsworth found the way to harmonize, rather to transmute, his restless discontent into a new and glorious vision of the world which embraced the lowest things with the highest things in one common rapture. Thereby he ceased to be poet and artist to become high-priest, revealing the rites of a sacred mystery which has been so potent to heal the restless English soul that for many he is even to-day the greatest of English poets, and in that "Golden Treasury" which is held to be the impeccable anthology of English verse Wordsworth seems to lead the whole choir. One other and later figure must be named. William Morris, a poet in the copious and essential spirit of Chaucer himself, a man of inexhaustible practical energies, the most versatile of artists and craftsmen, was at once a successful business man and a hard-working enthusiast in a political revolutionary cause that might well be termed Utopian and to him became a religion. No child of England has better summed up the Englishman.

It may indeed seem that to put in the foreground the religion, philosophy, and poetry of England is to overlook that hard-headed practicality and relentless acquisitiveness in the world which the foreigner often regards as the real mark of the Englishman and sometimes views with jealous gnashing of teeth. It is not so. Men

THE GENIUS OF EUROPE

were poets and magicians, even philosophers, long before they were much enamoured of business or even of piracy. These are both alike secondary. But piracy, which has the same acquisitive object as commerce, and was indeed almost as honourable and legitimate an avocation until the sixteenth century, was, as we know, in the blood of the English even before they reached England, being indeed an essential condition of their arrival, for it was as pirates that the lure of England selected them from among their tamer home-abiding fellows. They were, above all, sailors, and seafaring involves numerous related qualities, not only adventurousness and self-reliance but the inventiveness and the aptitude to become a "Jack of all trades", as every sailor is even to-day. These qualities were no doubt latent in the race but they were quiescent. The early history of England is no record of growing acquisition but rather of the slow and steady loss of hereditary possessions, culminating in the expulsion of Queen Mary's garrison from Calais when England lost her last patch of Continental land; it was not till then, in Elizabeth's days, that England's real career on the acquisitive territorial side began, and it began, we may remember, in the days of Shakespeare, the supreme moment of England's poetic efflorescence; it began, moreover, in poet's dreams of new worlds, the Utopian El Dorado, Spain and England, often akin and alike led by the same ideals, being almost abreast in the adventurous quest—Spain, indeed, a little ahead, though putting forth her Cervantes at the same moment as Shakespeare arose. In commerce the English lagged still further behind. The English temperament being primarily adventurous, could not easily feel attracted to avocations so tame and pedestrian as those of commerce in their earlier and lower stages. So the Hanseatic Germans, patient and plodding and honest, not disdaining the pettiest profit, and ready to adapt themselves to every market, established a great centre in London to do business for the English. It was not till larger lures were attracted to commerce that the English, who could be rapacious as well as indolent, were greedy to swallow the bait. Hakluyt brought together the records of the daring and the suffering of these pioneers—half of them often "gentlemen desirous to see the world"—who first carried English wares into remote lands. They endured endless hardships on sea and on land, sometimes shut up by the caprice of oriental despots, sometimes duped by rival merchants, driven from their ships by pirates, slain by barbarians, the victims of disease in strange cities. Yet persistently they made their way, dined with the Emperor of Muscovy, extorted concessions from the Sophy of Persia, sought to outwit the Venetians, and even dreamed of discovering by God's grace the far country of Cathay. Hakluyt's *Voyages of the English Nation* is, beyond all other books, the English "Odyssey".

This kind of commerce soon became combined not only with adventure but also with patriotism, and the whole amalgamation was lifted on to a higher plane in the imagination of more magnificent pirates who felt that they had risen above piracy. "Who was ever a pirate for millions?" as Raleigh, the type of these super-pirates, asked of Bacon. A century later the possibility of carrying on the old spirit of high adventure in the new careers of business had become generally realized by Englishmen. For the old Greeks, as for the modern Japanese, business was low and degrading; even for the devotedly shopkeeping German the rigid rules of caste still draw a line between the noble and the trader, but in England, after the triumph of Cromwell, the sons of the lords ruined in the Civil War turned naturally to trade. The English shopkeeper thus easily became the English merchant prince; Constantinople and Smyrna and Alexandria soon saw scarce any but adventurous Englishmen in their harbours; and to-day it is the complaint against English business that its methods are aristocratic and haughty. It was not until the eighteenth century, however, when their Dutch rivals on the sea were overcome, that the English acquisitive and practical qualities became developed and seriously organized in colonization and commerce and manufacture, soon to assume a vast expansion through the new eruption of mechanical inventiveness.

Therewith the English established political economy, and it is significant that the theoretical foundations of that science were laid, in the *Wealth of Nations*, not by a prosperous man of business but by an absent-minded Scotch professor, a philosopher and a moralist, who elaborated the fruitful conception, already divined by the

French physiocrats, that in the mechanism of society the prosperity of all is best attained by the utmost freedom of each to seek his own prosperity unhampered by the whims of ignorant legislators. The great British men of business and the great colonizers of new territory have often been adventurers in whom the spirit of piracy still survived, but, at the same time, dreamers and moralists. The apparent contrast in the English mind between its practical materialism and its poetic idealism has been a mystery even to the English mind itself. But when we place ourselves at the right point of view we see that there is no mystery at all and scarcely even a contrast.

In reality the gradual process of marine selection which produced the English could only select elements that were fundamentally harmonious at the outset, however apparently dissimilar. Moreover, new elements were always welded by intermarriage into the existing stocks, for each successive war of invasion usually reached the same eastern shore of the island and was free to mingle with the elements of the previous wave. Some early writers, like the British Gildas, speak in their rhetorical indignation as though the invaders exterminated the population they found. That was scarcely the case and we may certainly be sure that the women were not killed out. We may also be fairly certain that those historians are mistaken who have imagined that the invaders were usually accompanied to any extent by their own women. Even the Normans, the latest and most civilized of these invaders, brought no women, and when some years afterwards some of the high-spirited and irate ladies left behind sent over to declare (to the scandal of many churchmen) that unless their husbands returned at once, they would take other husbands, it appears that only a few of the Conqueror's companions responded. We may be sure that most of them found the daughters of the people of whom the Pope had said *Non Angli sed angeli* sufficiently pleasant in their eyes. We may thus account for that high degree of anthropological unification which has taken place in the British Islands. It is true that pigmentation of hair and eyes increases as we go westwards, with, also, areas of heightened pigmentation in sheltered easterly regions, but head-shape, as tested by the cephalic index, is remarkably uniform all over these islands. Very few stocks arrived save by stringent selection of the sea, and the stocks that by force of the possession of certain uniform but unusual complexes of qualities succeeded in arriving, were firmly blended together.

.   .   .   .   .

What is the worth of England's contribution to the genius of Europe and the civilization of the world? The most discrepant judgments on the English are pronounced by foreign peoples; never more so than to-day when such judgments are still edged by the enmities or the friendships of war. The English, we are told, are loyal and honourable, always daring in enterprise and prudent in action, the patterns of wise moderation and firm stability, the champions of the oppressed and the upholders of freedom in the world. The English, we are also told, are brutal and egotistic, sullen and cruel, the supreme representatives in the world of hypocritical cant and stupid self-conceit.

It would be hopeless to attempt any complete justification of these judgments, either on one side or on the other. No nation always lives up to the eulogy it may deserve at its finest moments, and every nation is the mark for scornful epithets which are often flung at random. It is possible, however, that there are reasons for the marked contrast in the characteristics ascribed to the English. The pronounced individuality of a highly selected people has inevitably led to the exhibition of great qualities balanced by the great defects of those qualities.

The process of insular selection which made England, while it has introduced into the English nation many unexpectedly correlated characters, has also unexpectedly excluded other characters. It is in this way that, though they have always been very religious, the English have never had any genius for religion. That is the more notable since the Netherlands, with a population out of which the English have been in some measure selected, constitutes one of the chief centres of European mysticism. But the qualities of daring combined with prudence which the piratical invader needs exclude "The Imitation of Christ". English religion has been, on the one side, militant and missionary, on the other side philanthropic and practical; beyond this it has been compromisingly worldly, that is to say, infused by the cautious political spirit of England, always occupied in finding a middle path amid its own extravagances. The history of the English Church has been throughout that of a steady and perpetual effort to maintain a balanced compromise between the conflicting ideals of doctrine and ritual which threatened to rend it asunder.

The same influences which have prevented the development in England of the finest manifestations of otherworldliness have equally impeded the more worldly manifestations of self-satisfied earthly philosophy. The art of living may have had its philosophic recognition in England, notably in Shaftesbury, but it has never been embodied in the life of the people as it has in France. Nor, on the higher plane, have massive and receptive personalities, complacently and genially sociable, ever flourished in England as they have, in more or less attractive forms, however unlike, both in France and Germany. There is no English Montaigne and no English Wilhelm von Humboldt. The refined social grace of eighteenth-century France and the enlightened cosmopolitanism of eighteenth-century Germany were alike hard to attain by the English, who yet played so large a part in inspiring the ideals of both lands in that age. Even that pantheistic earthliness which has sometimes so magnificently inspired and almost intoxicated the art of the closely related Flemish has never crossed the narrow sea. It has been transmuted into mist or into flame. Turner is the English Rubens and Swinburne the English Verhaeren, and there is no English Jordaens at all.

The English lack of initiative in the art of living has been accompanied by a comparative lack of genius for great art generally, except in the sphere of poetry, the only art which is apt to ally itself with adventure. The reason clearly seems to be that the artist in life, or in material, like the man of religion, demands stability and serenity, he is not usually embodied in a personality of the migratory and predatory kind. The Netherlands was an intensely active focus of musical development, and its activity has continued to some extent until to-day; but the English school of music never attained high importance and reached its climax in Purcell two centuries ago.

There has never been any great original architecture in England, notwithstanding that the neighbouring region of France is the home of Gothic and that the Normans were mighty and even original builders in their own land. English architecture is indeed abundant, endlessly varied, of inexhaustible charm. It appears to have been produced by a practical and versatile people who especially sought convenience and comfort, were admirable craftsmen, and probably at their best in domestic building. But of architectonic power to conceive great buildings, such as we find in so many regions of France as well as in Spain, we find no trace anywhere, except when the architect was manifestly a foreigner, and even the most admired fragments of English building—such as the west fronts of the cathedrals of Peterborough and Wells—sin flagrantly against the simplest canons of art. There has, again, scarcely been a single great English sculptor, notwithstanding a wealth of excellent anonymous carving. In painting there are no great schools such as may be found on the opposite coast, alike in Holland and Flanders and France, only a few great individual figures, and of these not one that can be compared in universal significance to Van Eyck or Rubens or Rembrandt, who were yet all so closely akin in race. The English have been less artists than amateurs of art, and that, indeed, on the grand scale. From Holbein onwards great artists were attracted to England, and, earlier than any other people, with a touch of the predatory impulse of their seafaring ancestors, the English swarmed over Europe and with the finest taste gathered up all the beautiful things they could acquire. England is still rich with the artistic wealth thus obtained, and but for the reckless dispersal of so much of it in the Puritan revolution would now be the envy of the whole world.

The English have always been great amateurs, not only in art but in science, even in life itself. That is the natural method of the individualist. It involves the spirit of adventure, a love of risk, a fine relish for the unknown, an immense self-reliance, and the caution, the diffidence, the perpetual self-questioning without which all the other qualities would merely point the road to destruction. Schools, universities, even traditions have played a comparatively small part in the production of English genius. Everywhere we see pioneers setting out, often alone and unaided, hampered by difficulties on all sides, for the conquest of some new world. The type of the men of this race—the remark has been made before—is set forth in the one English novel which belongs to universal literature. Robinson Crusoe is the complete Englishman. A supreme amateur, cheerfully facing immense difficulties, endlessly versatile in aptitude and resource, joyously exploring a new earth and patiently building up a new civilization from the simplest and most unpromising materials, Robinson Crusoe is the type of every Englishman who has sailed to find the Poles or penetrated the heart of Africa, ruled provinces in India or founded colonies in Australia or painfully sought out the secrets of Nature. Isaac Newton or Charles Darwin, the Englishman is still Robinson Crusoe.

The defects of a man of such make-up are obvious. The original process of selection which tended to exclude the supreme sedative influences of mysticism, and art, and the cultivation of fine living, and to emphasize the pursuit of adventure and risk, was still further heightened by the insularity that process culminated in. The energy of the English has always been associated with insularity. It has been almost as difficult for ideas as for armies to enter the citadel of England. Any vital movement on the Continent, the manifestation of any great new personality, have only succeeded in crossing the Channel after long years. It was the insular stupidity of England, and no enmity on the part of France, which delayed the Channel Tunnel, a stupidity for which a heavy price has had to be paid in the Great War. "The inhabitants are magnificently apparelled, and extremely proud and overbearing," wrote the Duke of Würtemberg's secretary on entering London in 1592; apt to scoff at foreigners, he added, because they seldom go into other countries; "superb, haughty, and suspicious," said the French Ambassador in 1666. Although politically, as the list of Governments from the Reform of 1832 until to-day shows, England is predominantly Liberal, beneath political distinctions the spirit of the people is fundamentally conservative. Thus, timid through his imaginative intuition of remote dangers, yet valiant to the point of rashness and even cheerful in the face of real risks, haughty, reserved, yet irritably aggressive, with roughnesses and angularities which tend to become exaggerated even to eccentricity, the Englishman has always been to the foreigner an object of mixed astonishment, amusement, and admiration. How many there must be of whom it has been said, as the Italian said of Landor: "All Englishmen are mad; but this one——!"

Yet the most original, the most individualistic, the most reserved of peoples, however greatly prizing the sanctity of the person and the privileges of the home, must still find among themselves a social medium of intercourse. It has thus come about that some of the most precious and distinctive qualities of the English have been slowly evolved in reaction against those primitive qualities by which they won England. In this way we may explain English formality, the English clinging regard for all the conventions, the respect for red tape and the reverence for "good form". So has arisen the "English gentleman", a phenomenon which has often attracted attention. He is the direct outcome of all the irregularities of the English character and the heterogeneous nature of the English popu- lation. In a homogeneous population, like that of Russia, such a phenomenon could not have been produced, it would seem too intolerably irksome, if not inhuman. English gentlemanliness is analogous to French politeness, which is a highly polished surface absolutely necessary for the avoidance of friction among a people of very mixed racial elements with strong social impulses and tense nervous systems. The English gentleman has, however, only been very slowly evolved. He is startlingly absent, even in the highest circles, in the fifteenth century, and we are surprised at his lapses even in the seventeenth. It is because he is so recent that the English- man cherishes him so reverently and associates with him his highest ideals of conduct, even at the cost of more intellectual acquirements. "We shall never be gentlemen and you will always be fools," said the German officer to the Englishman in the course of the present war; the flattered amusement which that oft-quoted epigram has caused to the diffident pride of the Englishman is itself a trait of national psychology.

The spirit of the English "sportsman" is, on a lower plane and in wider diffusion, comparable to that of the English "gentleman". Sport in the shape of games is the ideal of the ordinary man in England whose education and social status do not enable him to cherish the ideals of the gentleman. But it is fundamentally the same thing. It is a sublimation of the crude energies of the race; it is a transformation into orderly and socialized play of the predatory contests of the ancestral invaders. It is a training and a discipline. It invigorates the body and balances the mind. Above all, it cultivates the sense of "fair-play" into a national possession. It is this spirit of sport which animates not only the English politician but even the modern English soldier, who thus comes to approach war in a spirit of adventure and good-humour, even of gaiety, which has often astonished the onlookers by its contrast to that of the German and especially Prussian soldier who, ever since Frederick William I introduced the obligation of universal military service, has been taught to regard war as a solemn patriotic duty to be carried out obediently as the State may direct in the service of the Fatherland. The Englishman hides his sense of duty behind a mask, whether of phlegmatic stolidity or good-humoured indifference, and in that concealment places his pride. "No race," it has been said, "not even the Chinese, shows less what is going on inside."

It is also as a secondary reaction, and not as a primary quality, that we must regard another characteristic of the English, already manifested in sport, the tendency to moderation and compromise. The primary English quality resulting from the selectional process that made England was rather of excessiveness, crudely gross in the Saxon, more finely transmuted in the Norman. That excessiveness seems long to have prevailed unchecked; in politics and religion alike it was so even in the Civil War of the seventeenth century. The extremity of the evil of conflicting extravagancies seems at that culminating point to have led to a general reaction which before had only been manifested in isolated personalities like Falkland. Then in politics we have the final establishment of the English Constitution, with King and Lords and Commons holding each other in mutual check and balance, while government is carried on by the alternate play of opposing parties as in a game; and in religion we have the development under the late Stuarts of toleration, which meant the practical recognition of the right of the individual to form, and act upon, his own opinion in the great issues of life generally, as against the claim of external authority to prescribe limits to thought and practice. Both these very English characteristics, it must be noted—that towards compromise in action and that towards toleration in thought—can only arise in a developed social consciousness seeking to meet the dangers by which it is threatened; they are based on reflexion, and directed, not by primitive impulse, but by the controlled effort of will. Thus the ideals of compromise and toleration in English public life are strictly analogous to the ideal of the "gentleman" in English private life, both alike secondary results of the same primary characters; they are not, like the mutual help of the Russians, the outcome of a simple and instinctive feeling of brotherhood; they involve a high discipline, not often completely attained and needing to be perpetually reinforced. This reinforcement is effected by the play of the primary impulse against which they are a reaction. The violence of the early Stuarts was the stimulus to English political compromise, and the violence of the Quakers the stimulus to English religious toleration. The same process continues to-day. Every violent outburst of primitive English individuality tends to lead to a readjustment by which a greater number of individualities are more harmoniously enabled to expand, by the neutralization of their own destructive and negative aspects in favour of their constructive and positive aspects. Even Socialism is thus in England a development of Individualism. The process is not always effected without confusion and conflict, as we see in its recent extensions in the sphere of women's activities, but it is the method through which England's part in the world's civilization is progressively evolved.

When we bear in mind these considerations it seems difficult not to conclude that the English qualities have had a real value in the world. It may be said that even their defects have heightened these qualities. Taken altogether, we see here a primitively adventurous, even piratical people, independent, self-reliant, sometimes self-confidently reckless, yet with inexhaustible reserves of energy and

resource, and throughout a jealous regard for the rights of individuality. We see, too, how these qualities became secondarily evolved
into an aptitude for caution and compromise and moderation, the
element of the English genius for self-government. The form of
government which has naturally arisen among people of this
temperament is an oligarchy on a democratic basis sufficiently free
and robust to expand progressively while still constantly growing
more vigorous and more self-conscious. England passed through her
brief period of "Prussianization", once and for all, at the firm hands
of the Normans seven centuries before the Hohenzollerns conceived
the task of moulding the tough Germans of the Mark into a docile
State, and even in the days of the Plantagenets, in one of the earliest
books of English prose, the English Chancellor, Sir John Fortescue,
was laying down the modern English doctrine that the King is
simply the delegate of popular power, and that "the laws of England
in all cases declare in favour of liberty". The English political genius
for self-government, thus slowly and solidly evolved, has influenced
the political methods of other countries, for which it may or may
not have been suited, so that it has sometimes seemed to the foreigner
that "England has taught freedom to all the world". Voltaire
remarked, two centuries ago, that the English were jealous not only
of their own freedom but of that of other peoples. With whatever
conspicuous aberrations, the policy of England in her over-sea
Dominions—a policy embodied by such typical Englishmen as the
Lawrences and Sir George Grey—has not been one of mere exploitation but rather of a firm and just guardianship which has
recognized self-government as the ultimate goal. In this way the
alienation which the Englishman's reserved and haughty temper
tends to produce is often converted by his firm justice and strength
into a loyalty which has perplexed the enemies of England. This has
been so even in Ireland where yet the record of England is seen at
its worst, the outcome of evil traditions belonging to a time when
the incongruous elements of the English genius had not yet been
harmoniously amalgamated. The history of England and her great
administrators in regenerating Egypt and slowly educating the
population to freedom is a less sullied page and even typical of

England's civilizing function. But this mark is clear even on the earliest English colonizing efforts from the days of Elizabeth onwards. We see it in the wise leadership of Captain John Smith in Virginia, and in the enlightened ideals, ahead of the world even to-day, which inspired Penn at Philadelphia, while most Englishmen now recognize in Washington a far truer exponent of the English spirit than in the benighted Government he opposed. The modern Rome, Professor Sergi has termed England, comparing her mission in the world to that of ancient Rome, and others have made the same comparison. Rome is supreme and unique. And it seems profitable to compare the career of England to that of the Great Republic on the sea which was indirectly ended by England's rise. Oligarchic, proud, adventurous, and free, with the genius alike for self-government and for the government of others, Venice founded a mighty empire which for nearly fifteen centuries attracted the loyal devotion of its citizens and its subjects, prefiguring in a smaller but more beautiful shape the yet mightier career of England. It was by a happy inspiration that the architect who embodied the spirit of England in the Houses of Parliament, on the banks of the Thames, combined in that delightful pastiche of buildings the memory of Canterbury Cathedral with the echoes of Venetian palaces.

Yet England, however, falling short in Roman solidity or Venetian beauty, has always stood for one great quality of supreme human value. England represents the original initiative of personal individuality. Among no other people has there ever been so emphatic an insistance on the self-reliant qualities of the individual, with all his rights and all his duties. Only in the United States has it ever been seen in the same degree and then through the same selectional process acting on much the same racial elements. This extreme individualism has certainly been on one side a defect of national character. It has induced an unwillingness to help those who will not help themselves, and an indifference to the resulting sordidness of life which have only been in some measure corrected by the concerted social activity of recent times. The observant Swiss traveller, Muralt, at the end of the seventeenth century, noted the ugly side of this individualism in its disregard of those who incompetently fell out of the social ranks, and though Voltaire, on his famous visit to England a few years later, was impressed by the high general level of prosperity among English peasants, Hogarth was at the same time depicting a less attractive aspect of English individualism. So typical a patriot as John Bright opposed factory legislation and the sacred name of Freedom was misused to delay the establishment of universal education. But if on the negative side English individualism has often been harsh and stupid, on the positive side it has been the impetus to an endless series of achievements in the physical and spiritual worlds. For it is not only as adventurers and sailors and explorers and administrators—Drake or Clive or Nelson or Cook—that the English spirit of self-reliant individualism has displayed its ardent force and audacity. Notwithstanding that timidity in the intellectual sphere which seems so often to mark the Englishman—as though all his firm valour were of that immediately practical kind which the primary selectional process had evoked—the adventurous and revolutionary spirit of English individualism has nowhere been more conspicuously displayed than in the region of science and philosophy. Hostile to tradition and rebellious to authority, fundamentally Protestant, we see Roger Bacon and Francis Bacon, Hobbes and Locke, Hume and Spencer, spiritual vikings and sublimated buccaneers. The men of this temper were yet constructive as well as destructive; Newton was not only destroying Cartesianism but making the physical universe afresh, and Darwin was not merely tearing up the first chapter of Genesis but writing a more wonderful story of creation; Newton and Darwin together have inspired the main currents of modern scientific thought all over the world, yet even in the absence of these two supreme figures the achievements of English science stand easily beside those of any land, and they have nearly always been reached by methods of personal initiative and original insight which contrast strikingly with the Teutonic methods of elaborate combined organization and national plodding thoroughness, systematically testing in sequence every possible solution of the problem in hand until success is achieved, methods well typified by Ehrlich's progress to 606. The German in science is minute but short-sighted; the

Englishman overlooks much, but he still possesses the long-sighted vision of his sea-faring ancestors.

It is not only in the higher ranges of life and thought that these methods have dominated England. They have permeated the whole activities of the people and moulded the shape of national development. In Prussia, where it has sometimes seemed possible to find points of contact with England, it is the State which dominates the individual; within a very few generations a succession of strong rulers, acting on a rugged, recalcitrant, and yet docile population, has here swiftly constructed an artificial State system which insists on setting its seal on the entire activities, material and spiritual, of the people. But in England we find an ancient and independent community which has slowly worked out its own natural ways of self-government without any notion of what a State is. The ordinary educated Englishman is unconscious of the State, he never gives it a thought; if it should happen that the idea is presented to him he usually reacts to it in violent opposition. His instinctive voluntaryism, the outcome of a spontaneously energetic individualism, leads him to organize, when organization seems required, on a basis of freedom which insists that each unit in the organization shall be inspired by the same voluntary energy. No pressure from above is tolerated. The mighty development of the Labour movement in England and the countries largely moulded by English influence, together with the early development of power and stability in trades unions, have been directly due to the free play of this voluntaristic impulse. The military system of England has grown up on the same basis. The high qualities of the British soldier are due to the fact that he is thus the outcome of selection by voluntary choice. Methods of conscription or national service, which are adopted almost as a matter of course in other countries, are altogether alien to the English temper. They find their advocates in the heterogeneous population of England, but such advocates are rarely of pure English breed. The true Englishman hotly resents the mere suggestion of compulsory military service as an insult. No doubt this attitude is compatible with indolence and intellectual narrowness which might easily lead to disaster; and with the characteristic tendency to compromise and to hypocrisy which while remaining a method of English tenacity has often gone far, as we may see to-day, to nullify or to prevent the finest tradition of the English spirit. So it is that with an explosion of virtuous indignation we would "cast out the Devil of German militarism by the Beelzebub of English militarism". That is what the foreigner means by "British Cant". Yet in the long run the tradition prevails; the English resourcefulness and stability, an unlimited reserve of energy, justify indifference to emergencies which may never occur, and should they occur can be resolutely met. In every field of social activity the same attitude is manifested. Thus in the case of the sick and the destitute, where it might seem that even the extreme individualist could well accept a central State activity, the English have clung as long as possible to methods of individual philanthropy and freely organized charity. The claim of Socialism can only be commended to the Englishman by the argument that, by the removal of social friction and economic oppression, we may enhance and expand the forces of individualism.

It has been possible in England to defend the worst abuses in the sacred name of an individualism that was false because it meant the freedom of some individuals to flourish at the expense of other individuals. Yet the qualities of adventurous energy and restless aspiration, of original initiative, of personal self-government, of free and spontaneous organization, which have specially stamped the English genius, possess an incomparable value. Whatever other qualities may be required, these qualities, certainly, are indispensable to every fruitful and civilizing movement which humanity may undertake.

N O ONE who has seen on the stage *The Golden Cockerel* is likely to forget that delicious fairy-tale. To one who knows something of Russia it has, however, a more special significance. He would recall how in 1553 the great English navigator, Richard Chancellor, who was seeking a northern route to the East, accidentally discovered Russia and was received in Moscow by Ivan the Terrible, seated on his great gilded throne, in a long garment of beaten gold, with his imperial crown on his head and his sceptre of crystal and gold in his hand; and how, during the space of five hours, during which the Tsar changed his crown twice, dinner was served to the vast company in vessels of fine gold and bowls of silver which held, at the least, six gallons apiece.[1] He would recall, too, his own wanderings in the Russia of to-day amid the vestiges that yet remain of that colossal sumptuosity. And Rimsky-Korsakov's opera-ballet becomes, more than a modern fairy-tale, a fantasia on the essential theme of Russia.

That is to say that Russia is still a little barbarous, and perhaps to define the quality of its barbarism. From the German point of view the Russians are barbarous, just as the Germans are from the English point of view, and the English from the French ("English barbarism is well known," remarked Rousseau). But, it must be remembered, rightly used, the term "barbarous" implies no depreciation. To suppose that "civilization", "barbarism" and "savagery" represents a descending hierarchy of moral values is as unreasonable as to suppose that "man", "woman" and "child" represents a

[1] Both Chancellor and Anthony Jenkinson, who followed four years later as Ambassador for Queen Elizabeth to Ivan, insist in their vivid and precise narratives on the gorgeous and sumptuous display of the Court of Muscovy as exceeding anything to be seen elsewhere in Europe although, as he mentions, Chancellor was acquainted with the French as well as the English Court. Chancellor and Jenkinson described the people, their social condition and the laws they lived under, as well as they described the Court, and altogether these early narratives constitute the best introduction that could be found to the study of Russian psychology. Hakluyt included them in his great work. An account of the first travellers to Russia, from Ohthere onward, is given by R. H. Major in his lengthy introduction to the two volumes of early visits to Russia published by the Hakluyt Society.

similar hierarchy. "Russians produced on Europeans of the seventeenth century the same impression as Persians do on us to-day,"
remarks Brückner. But to say that a community is more civilized
or more barbarous than our own primarily means that it is a little
older in culture, or a little younger: it says nothing as regards its
superiority or its inferiority in other respects.

Among the nations of Europe we may find perfected examples
of all three stages of culture—savagery, barbarism and civilization—
through which a nation is supposed to pass in the long course of its
development. Some nations, one is inclined to think, never completely pass through all these stages, but reveal from first to last
the predominant traits of one stage only, carrying it onwards to the
highest point of refined development. Thus the French have ever
represented civilization. From the time that we first hear of them,
through Roman contact with Gaul, they have exhibited those
qualities of sociality and courtesy, the instincts of temperance, the
sense of justice, that alert, receptive, versatile intelligence, which
are of the very essence of the finest civilization. Spain, again, seems
to present—and in no evil sense—the typical and idealized traits of
savagery. A severe asceticism, combined with mystic exaltation, the
subordination of useful work to active enjoyment, a profound sense
of the supremacy of personal qualities, indifference to pain, suffered
or inflicted—these are characters which have often marked the best
type of savage life in various parts of the world, and they are the
characters which have always distinguished the Spaniard. But
between these extreme forms of human culture there is room for
the ideals of barbarism, and it is these which Russia seems to
supply in a highly typical form. The monarchs who dominate
the history of Russia—Ivan the Terrible, Peter the Great,
Catherine—have all the colossal and exuberant qualities of a state
of culture which has lost the narrow ideals of savagery, and has
never attained the finer ideals of civilization. All the traits of the
Russian character and of Russian life—the hospitality of the
people, their copious repasts, the profusion of colour in their
costumes and their cities, the bizarre incoherence of their architecture, the mixture of tenderness and cruelty in their dispositions,

74

their expansive frankness and emotionality—these are all traits which are strictly barbarous.

It is not difficult to trace the temperamental barbarism back to its sources. We have not only to remember the powerful tincture of Eastern blood which has been infused in Russian veins, but the environment of Russia. Russia has been in the closest touch with nearly all the great oriental empires most typically barbarous. It has absorbed them, or is about to absorb them; it has at some time received homage and tribute from them. We may realize this in the Treasury of the Kremlin at Moscow, where crowns and thrones and sceptres and swords, gold, jewels and ivory, all the richest and most extravagant spoils of barbarism, have been profusely piled up during five centuries as in no other place in the world. Russia is not a barbaric power, but circumstances have given her a temperamental barbarism just as they have given France a temperamental civilization and Spain a temperamental savagery.

Germany, also, seems a little barbarous from the English standpoint, and Russia, being still younger in culture, still more barbarous. The remarkable point is that Germany and Russia are so unlike each other. The reason is not obvious, for they occupy contiguous regions:[1] they are, roughly speaking, compounded of the same two races, and they have both for long periods been dominated by the same sort of ferocious and autocratic rulers. But when we look a little more closely we see that there are differences alike in the nature and the nurture of the two peoples. There is a masculine and a feminine element, alike in the German and the Russian—using these terms in the conventional sense without reference to the actual qualities of men and women—but Germany thrusts forward her masculine quality and Russia her feminine quality, and, moreover, the feminine quality of Russia is more massive and less docile than that of Germany, while the masculine quality of Germany is more aggressive and more disciplined than that of Russia. The environment of the two racial conglomerates has, moreover, been unlike. Germany has been surrounded by vigorous foes and has thus been

[1] Milyukov remarks that Prussia is the country most resembling Russia in geographic and economic respects.

forced to assume an alertly offensive attitude. Russia is so vast that she has never been conscious of the necessity for that attitude. She has usually been able to repel her foes, or to assimilate them, with little effort.

This sense of vastness we cannot easily lose in Russia. For it is not only the country which is vast but often the products of the soil and the productions of the people. Russians are not above the average European stature, but one seems to find a notable number of immense people among them,[1] and other living things, even the cats, are sometimes larger than one has seen elsewhere. The Russian drum as described by Giles Fletcher three centuries ago, seems a characteristic instrument, for it required four horses to bear it and eight men to beat it. The psychological implications of this characteristic of Russian things is what concerns us here, and the chief of these is gentleness. We are told of that very typical Russian, Turgenyev, that he was a man of enormous build and extremely gentle manner, almost feminine in his impressionability and delicacy. This is the typical combination presented by Russia itself, like the elephant, enormous and delicate.

There is another characteristic of Russia which, it is possible, has had a repercussion on the national psychology, and that is the uniformity of its vast extent of soil. The great "Russian Platform", as the geologists term it, has permitted a degree of movement and expansion impossible in more impenetrable countries, so that nomadism has been from the earliest times in the genius of the race.

[1] No country has among its great men so large a proportion who have been literally great in bulk and stature. This was notably the case with one of the most typical and prominent of Russians, Peter the Great, who was a giant, nearly seven feet high. Turgenyev, the greatest artist in Russian literature, was also a man of colossal bulk, and his brain, which was entirely healthy and well-proportioned, is the heaviest (2,012 grams) that has ever been found in any man of intellectual eminence (it is interesting to note that the smallest, Smetana's, also belong to a Slav). Nor is this tendency found only among intellectual men of upper class, but equally among those of lower class. Lomonosov, the versatile and encyclopaedic peasant from the north who pioneered the Russian intellect in the eighteenth century, "looked like a Hercules", tall and broad. Chelyshev, a peasant with the instincts of a great statesman, the pioneer of temperance reform and of education, was "a man of almost Herculean size and strength". Varlamov, the great actor, possessed an almost gigantic figure. It would be easy to multiply instances. One is inclined to think that the very moderate average of stature in Russia may be due to an excessive proportion alike of very tall and very short persons.

To the same cause we may, no doubt, in part attribute that absence of dialect in Great Russia which has been of such significant importance in the diffusion of Russian literature. Thus also we may explain the curious anthropological fact that, roughly speaking, the broad-headed population both to the east and to the west of Russia is more broad-headed than in Russia. The brachycephalic stream that flows across Europe seems in passing through Russia to have spread out and mingled harmoniously with the earlier population, so that, anthropologically, Russia may be said to be more "European" than much of Western Europe. This same tendency marks the genius of Russia, the character of the Russian. It flows out and it lacks clear outline; it is attracted to the mystically vague and has difficulty in concentrating its will-power. On this basis we have Russian idealism, Russian religious devotion, Russian indifference to conventional moral rules, often so distressing to the Western European, and Russian resignation, the *nichevo*, "it doesn't matter", which is as characteristic of Russia as the postponing *mañana* is of Spain.

Associated with these qualities, and further developed by the hard natural conditions of Russian life, which have rendered mutual service essential, there is the most profound of all Russian traits, humanity. The wanderer through Europe finds that he encounters the most disinterested human kindliness, among all classes of the population, in two countries, Spain and Russia, a surprising fact to the Englishman at home who meekly accepts all that he has been taught concerning the land of the bull-fight and the land of the knout.

The prominence of the whip in Russia remains an interesting fact. It is asserted that the knout was introduced by the Northmen (including Angles) who dominated Russia. It is the English "knot", with corresponding words in allied languages. So that, far from being Slav, the knout would thus have been inflicted on the Slavs' long-suffering back by their Teutonic masters. But that by no means settles the question. The whip flourished in Russia long before the Northmen arrived and assumed special developments then. It was, indeed, an important implement among the ancient Scythians because they were a nomadic people with large herds; they also used these whips as a punishment for their slaves. Herodotus tells us (bk. iv, ch. 3) that a serious rebellion once took place among these slaves, and the Scythians at last bethought themselves of their whips, whereupon the slaves fled. Collas suggests probably the use of the *nagaika*, as a recognized weapon of war among the Cossacks of the Don, even in the Russian army, may be a tradition from Scythian days (G. F. Collas, *Geschichte des Flagellantismus*, vol. 1, p. 387).

It is certain that the whip has played a considerable part in Russian social history, severe flogging having only been abolished in 1863. In part this is due to the fact that the general level of Russian culture and social civilization corresponds to that of a couple of centuries earlier in Western Europe, when the whip still flourished in Germany and had not died out in England, though it was disappearing in France. Thus, speaking of England only about a century ago, George Ives states with many references in proof (*History of Penal Methods*, pp. 147 et seq.): "The children were beaten at home, the boys were flogged and birched in the schools; the servants were frequently thrashed in the country districts; the prisoners in the gaols, both men and women, were commonly whipped; and all disciplined men of the fighting forces were knocked about until their skins became as red or blue as their jackets." But flagellation in Russia has gone beyond this, and even the first English discoverer of Russia, Chancellor, four hundred years ago, speaks much of the flagellation commonly practised there, evidently as of something quite unfamiliar to him. It has not only been carried to a brutal extreme as a punishment, but there appears to be a sort of predilection for the whip, an almost abstract admiration for it, a satisfaction which is passive as well as active. Wiener refers to the Russian's "native spirit of self-castigation", and while he is speaking metaphorically of the satisfaction which the Russian finds in facts usually regarded as humiliating, and of his preference for depreciation over laudation in national affairs, there is yet a more literal truth in the statement. The ancient Russian practice of the vapour bath still includes the use of little, supple birch rods to promote the circulation.

This custom dates back for a thousand years or more. Nestor describes it in his *Chronicles*, putting the words into the mouth of the apostle, St. Andrew, on a supposed missionary visit to Russia: "They whip themselves so severely that they are hardly alive when they come out; they throw cold water over themselves and so revive, and they do it every day; no one inflicts this torture on them; they inflict it on themselves, for bathing and not for torture."

There seems to be a marked tendency to algolagnia in Russia, not only in its sadistic but also in its masochistic aspects. It is noteworthy that Sacher-Masoch himself was a Slav. Of the women of Galicia (to which Sacher-Masoch belonged) it is said that they either rule their husbands or become their abject slaves, and it is possible that such a tendency may be found in the Slav feminine character generally, for in Russia we find on the one hand a pronounced traditional subjection of women to men, and on the other a tendency (well marked in the great Russian novelists) to represent women as energetic and strong-willed in opposition to the weak and irresolute men; the great and heroic part played by women in Russian revolutionary movements is also well-known. A Russian lady of apparently sadistic temperament, though not represented as peculiarly abnormal, is brought before us in Danilov's *Memoirs*, written in the eighteenth century. When a child, Danilov lived with a pious widow. "The widow," he tells us, "was very fond of cabbage soup with mutton at dinner. As soon as she seated herself at the table before her favourite dish, she would have the servant who cooked the soup dragged into the dining-room by other servants who would put her on the floor and mercilessly beat her with rods. The widow never stopped eating so long as they beat the cook, who would scream with pain. It evidently served to heighten her appetite." At a later period, early in the nineteenth century, Turgenyev's mother, after her husband's death, dealt out perpetual punishment and beatings to her five thousand serfs. Though her conduct was a source of much distress to her son and heightened his opposition to serfdom, she was generally regarded simply as a woman of great energy and intelligence, but eccentric. More usually we hear of the masochistic tendency of Russian women, and various writers have referred to the disappointment said to have been experienced by Slav women in and out of Russia when not beaten by their husbands. Baron Herberstein came across an example of this during his stay in Moscow in the sixteenth century. "There is at present," he says, "a certain German, a blacksmith, who married a Russian woman. After she had lived some time with her husband, she one day thus lovingly addressed him: 'Why is it, my dearest husband, that you do not love me.' The husband replied: 'I do love you passionately.' 'I have as yet,' said she, 'received no proofs of your love.' The husband inquired what proofs she desired. Her reply was: 'You have never beaten me.' 'Really,' said the husband, 'I did not think that blows were proof of love, but I will not fail even in this respect.' So not long after he beat her most cruelly; and confessed to me that after that process his wife showed much greater affection towards him." Finally, while Herberstein was still in Moscow, the black-smith cut off his wife's head and legs (Herberstein, *Notes Upon Russia*, ed. Hakluyt Society, vol. i, p. 94). It is evidently difficult for a German to enter sympathetically into the Russian spirit; less of an artist in emotion, his idealistic excessiveness outruns his humanity and even his affection, and impels him to drive an idea literally to death. The craving for physical violence as a proof, if not symbol of love, is found arising spontaneously among the women of all countries.[1] But among women of the Slav race it seems to be specially marked, even to-day, and recognized in social custom. This becomes evident when we read Kovalevsky's account of the Slav wedding. The bridegroom while leading his future wife home gives her from time to time light blows from a whip. When they enter the bedroom he says: "Take off my boots," and she finds in one of them a whip. This is an indication how he is entitled to correct her when necessary. The beneficial effects of chastisement, adds Kovalevsky, are still accepted by the country people, and in more than one popular song the wife is represented as complaining bitterly of the indifference of the husband who never gives her a good beating (M. Kovalevsky, *Modern Customs and Ancient Laws of Russia*, p. 45).

[1] See Havelock Ellis, *Studies in the Psychology of Sex*, 2nd ed., vol. iii, pp. 78–82.

As already indicated, however, in Russia this complacent acceptance of the whip has not been confined to women. It is interesting to note the experience of so highly intelligent and much-troubled observer as Casanova, who at one time spent some time in Russia. He was far from cruel, but after mentioning that he had as his mistress a remarkably beautiful Russian peasant girl whom he was sometimes compelled, according to custom, to beat, he adds some general remarks on the necessity of the whip in Russia among soldiers, servants, and women of the people as the only way of obtaining obedience. "The servant here, whose soul is still more servile than his body, only reasons after receiving blows, and then he reasons thus: 'My master has not dismissed me, he has beaten me; then he loves me; in consequence I ought to be attached to him.'" Casanova narrates an incident, coming under his own observation, which seems to indicate that even the horses in Russia reasoned similarly. His coachman found that one of the horses would not eat and was reduced to despair, for there was a long journey ahead. Casanova accompanied him to the stable where the coachman harangued and caressed the dispirited animal, with tears in his eyes, imploring him to eat, but all in vain. Furious at last, he led the obstinate animal out of the stable, fastened him up, and belaboured him with a stick for a quarter of an hour, till Casanova's heart bled. Then, on being led back to the stable, the horse calmly began to eat, while the coachman danced with joy. Casanova's astonishment was extreme. "Only in Russia," he remarks, "could this have happened, for here the strokes of a stick seem to fulfil the conditions of panacea" (Casanova's *Memoirs*, ed. Garnier, vol. vii, ch. 7). Such incidents as these recall Baring's remark (*The Russian People*, p. 39) that the Russian inflicts pain with the same stoicism with which he accepts it, and we may do well to remember also the remark which he adds concerning Russian peasants in general: "I have never witnessed on their part any single example of brutality."

There is thus a tempered hardness in the Russian as in the Spanish character. Directly one leaves Germany to be faced at the frontier station by the Russian soldier one feels thankful if one possesses no guilty conscience for those serious and fearless eyes to search. In

Germany, indeed, one has seen much disciplined obedience to duty, but it has been an externally imposed duty, and here one is confronted by men on whom duty is internally imposed. Yet it is not possible to be long in Russia before seeing the elements of ruggedness in the Russian character melt into harmony. Describing a typically Russian face in one of his stories, Chekhov remarks that, separately, all the features were rude and heavy; taken together they produced the impression of singular harmony and beauty. Such is the typical Russian face, a peasant's face, even sometimes among the aristocracy, yet still clearly an aristocratic peasant. Such also is the effect of the whole Russian character, the strength that brings forth sweetness.[1] All modern Russian literature, from the days of Gogol, bears the seal of this mingled temper, variously proportioned, but always this same seal of ruggedness which finds its issue in an infinite sweetness, a revelation of human tenderness never before seen in the world.

The old saying: "Scratch the Russian and you will find the Tartar", is not now generally accepted. We are more inclined to say, with Walling (*Russia's Message*, p. 4): "Scratch the Russian and you will find the New European." The old saying seems to have been suggested by the impression produced by the spectacle of Peter the Great's sudden introduction of a superficial Western culture on contemporaries who were aware that, when this progressive Tsar left the house he lived in during his stay in London, it was found that the valuable furniture was destroyed and covered with filth, the pictures riddled with bullets, the windows broken, the whole house ruined, and William III had a big bill to pay. It was the same impression which produced Rousseau's remark (in *The Social Contract*): "The Russian will never be civilized because he has been civilized too soon." The Russian, however, has scarcely been adequately epigrammatized at any period by calling him a veneered savage, if that was what was understood by "Tartar", for, as a matter of fact, the Tartar element, as revealed in the ancestry of men

[1] Merejkovski, referring to Tolstoy's "peasant look", remarks (*Tolstoy as Man and Artist*, p. 159): "It is worthy of note how in the faces of great Russian writers, as of Turgenyev when old, there is this mixture of plebeianism with the look of the noble, the look of European high-breeding. This union seems splendid and natural, as if one did not interfere with the other."

of genius, is associated with refined and ideal qualities. It may possibly be true that, as Sarolea believes (*Europe's Debt to Russia*, p.115) if the Russian noble is scratched, there is often revealed the Byzantine, by which he means a spirit of evasion, an elusive mass of contradiction.

Indolence, apathy, resignation, mystic fatalism, are noted by all as the weakness of the Russian.[1] They are associated with impressionability, for to understand the Russian we must never forget that he is allied in temperament to the Celt. These traits are, indeed, fostered by the physical and social conditions of Russian life. They are not incompatible with latent energy; they usually indicate that energy has not been adequately stimulated. One may remember that when the English were in a social stage somewhat similar to that of the Russians to-day, they, too, were said by foreign travellers to be indolent. The mighty subconscious energy of the Russians has largely manifested itself, one may say, in orgiastic forms, that is, not by deliberate will-power but by spontaneous impetus. This is so even on the lowest plane, as we see in the Russian use of alcohol, and it is hard to picture a Russian without vodka. But Russian religion, especially in its sectarian forms, is equally orgiastic. It is notable also that music and the dance, which of all forms of art are in primary impulse the most orgiastic, are precisely the arts in which the Russians have exhibited most superb energy and skill. In England there is a prejudice against organization by emergency, perhaps out of modesty since it happens to be our English method; we admire organization by deliberate mechanical routine; yet the former method is better, and for obvious reasons: it demands the intelligence which routine kills and it evokes the energy which routine dissipates. The Russian temperament especially lends itself to the illustration of the splendid achievements thus attained. Volcanic eruptions from within and violent shock from without have always been the stimulus of the great manifestations of the Russian spirit. Russian apathy is, in another aspect, Russian elasticity. There is a Russian national game in which the conqueror is not the

[1] Even in Tolstoy's novel, remarks Merejkovski (*Tolstoy as Man and Artist*, p. 223), there are "no persons, no characters, no personalities, but merely contemplative victims who do not struggle or resist".

one who floors his adversary outright, but he who receives most blows without giving in. The Germans who, in the present war, have rejoiced over Hindenburg's smashing blows at the Russians were not acquainted with this game. The modern Russia, which we know in literature, may be said to date directly from the war of 1812: a yet more modern Russia will date from the present war.

For the past two centuries Russia's vigorous neighbour, Germany, has often had an active hand in her affairs, not always with the best results. There has been, of late, a growing and profound divergence, for the new materialistic organization of Germany on the Prussianized basis has subordinated spiritual culture, while in Russia by national temperament that culture has dominated the recent expansion of materialistic civilization. It has thus come about that Russia has succeeded to the spiritual hegemony which at the beginning of the nineteenth century Germany exercised over the world. It may even be said that Russia has been the heir of Germany. A century ago Germany and Russia were spiritually akin, and Germany was the teacher. Fichte had an immense influence on Russian thought, and his centenary last year was especially celebrated in Russia. Solovyev and Lopatin, no doubt the most typical and the most distinguished of Russian thinkers, are marked by a large idealism, and tendency to accept direct non-sensuous intuition, which allies them to the great thinkers of old Germany, and to the modern Bergson, the most Russian of Western philosophers. The Russians have also succeeded to that spirit of internationalism, the spirit of Lessing and Goethe, which the Germans have lost, though no doubt only temporarily lost. It has implanted itself on the Russians peculiar spaciousness of mind and on his pliant receptivity, his feminine massiveness of temperament. One notes the youth who provides himself for the long railway journey with a supply of the best reviews in three or four languages; one scarcely meets him outside Russia, even in the land of most self-conceited culture, whichever that may be.

It is sometimes said that there is an affinity between the Russian and the English minds which the war will tend greatly to develop. That is a statement to be treated with circumspection. Certainly

Russia exerts a peculiar fascination on those Englishmen who have entered into her spirit. Only Spain has exerted anything like the same influence. Highly uncomfortable countries, both of them, for the foreigner, oppressed by opposing extremes of climate, in all respects superficially alien, they yet both reveal—and especially, it seems, to the English mind—the exalted mystery of a spiritual yet human beauty, and the vision leaves behind an undying home-sickness of the heart. The fascination works also in the reverse direction. English institutions and English character for generations presented to progressive Russians an ideal to strive towards. At the same time, Shakespeare has been a great force in Russian literature, our English Sterne, so mighty an influence on Europe, affected the beginnings of Russian literature, and Dickens, in whom Sterne's emotional unrestraint was associated with modern humanitarian ideas, has naturally been also an influential and popular author in Russia, while Darwin and Spencer have been the chief formative elements among Russian intellectuals. But it is also true that when the Russian "intellectual", who often cherishes warm admiration for English freedom, English self-discipline and English political institutions, visits England his enthusiasms are apt to become qualified, just as they have also been qualified by the Russian Revolution[1] which has presented England for the first time to the Russian as not only a conservative but a reactionary land. The Russian finds that English freedom can subsist with a vast amount of rigid moral and social convention; he not only discovers that he cannot go into good English society in his shirt-sleeves, however high the thermometer, but he realizes that English democratic institutions are impotent to create that democratic feeling which in Russia is inborn. He learns in England to appreciate Russia.

Very soon after the English discovered Russia Queen Elizabeth and Ivan the Terrible were on excellent terms through the medium of their ambassadors. Ivan was indeed so sympathetic towards England that he was called "the English Tsar", and the English carried on a more profitable trade in Russia than anywhere else, thus receiving the market of the Germans at Novgorod (Alexinsky,

[1] The Kerensky Revolution, for Ellis wrote this essay in the summer of 1917. F. D.

Russia and Europe, p.26). It was not alone the autocratic rulers of the two lands who agreed so well together. At a much later date the great Russian revolutionary, Alexander Herzen, who knew many countries, preferred England, and during his residence in England, in 1858, in a pamphlet called *La France ou L'Angleterre?* advocated an alliance between Russia and England rather than France. Disclaiming either Anglomania or the desire to injure France, he declared that "the English school is the only school for Russia—a country without centralization, without a bureaucracy, without prefectures, without gendarmes, without revolutions and without reaction". At a later period, likewise, Homyakov (*Russian Review*, 1912, No. 2 p.19) remarks that while "the culture of the Englishman finds repose in the primitive natural characteristics of the Russian people, its native breadth of mind, and its own expressive soul", conversely the Russian, with his "charming indiscipline", is wholesomely attracted by English discipline. Struve, also, the distinguished Russian economist, considers that twentieth-century Russia peculiarly needs "the most precious thing in English culture, the moral and religious education of individuality which can be traced through the whole history of the British nation".

But the successful revolutionaries of 1917 were disillusioned. They felt that the war which had brought emancipation to Russia had brought servitude to England. In an interesting interview with Chkheidze—not a solitary dreamer, it must be remembered, but the leader of the Petrograd Committee of Workmen's and Soldier's Delegates and considered at the time as the most powerful man in Russia—this is clearly brought out. Becoming himself the questioner, Chkheidze asked his English interviewer: "Is it not true that the war has destroyed English liberalism? Is it not a fact that you have surrendered all those liberties for which you profess to be fighting? What has happened to your right of public meeting, your free speech, your liberty of the press, even your right of trial by jury? Has not this war forced you to abandon your democratic principle of government which has been Britain's glory for so many years, and obliged you to adopt the Prussian system of a military dictatorship which you denounce?" (*Daily Chronicle*, 17th May 1917).

It may be noted that the mixture of enthusiasm and incompatibility in the Russian's attitude towards the English is not of recent date, nor, it may be added, is it felt towards the English alone, but probably, in a still higher degree, towards Americans, and we may recall the enthusiasm which drew Gorky to the United States and the impression left on his mind when he was practically driven out of the country.

Karamzin, who may be regarded as the father of Russian literature and found his inspiration largely in England, has himself recorded his enthusiasm for the English and their achievements long before he ever visited England. In 1790 he came over, and we find him writing from London, in his *Letters of a Russian Traveller*: "Now I see the English at close range, and I do them justice and praise them, but my praise is as cold as they themselves are. . . . 'It is a snow-covered volcano', a French *émigré* said of them, smilingly to me. But I stand, watch, see no flame, and meanwhile freeze. My Russian heart loves to bubble in a sincere lively conversation, loves the play of the eyes, the rapid changes of the face, the expressive motions of the hands. The Englishman is reticent, indifferent, and speaks as he reads, without even expressing the sudden mental convulsions that electrify our whole physical system."

Since Karamzin's time the external aspect of the English temperament has to some extent changed on account of the great degree in which the population has been urbanized during the past century. An urban population acquires much of that nervous mobility and expansiveness which Karamzin regards as natural to the Russians who were not, and even to-day are not, in any large degree urbanized. But the incompatibility in other form still exists. On this point I will quote at some length the remarks of a Russian correspondent—a man of noble family and intellectual endowment who had spent much of his life in various countries—in a letter written some years before the Revolution: "The Russian Liberal frequently attaches great value to the salutary influence of the laborious environment of Western Europe, so different from the morbid and unbalanced condition in Russia. In spite of this theoretic eulogy, however, the social life of Western Europe is antipathetic to him. This, I remember, was the case with my father, a convinced Liberal. He attributed everything to politics. France had been his favourite country, as of other Russian liberals and radicals, but the alliance of the French with the Tsar caused these sympathies to grow cold, and England became the admired land of my father and of his compatriots, the reason being that they knew little about it. Russian educated society differs profoundly from the corresponding class in all other countries, but it is from English society that it differs most. I said this to my father, but he would not agree, asserting that there was much analogy between the English spirit and the Russian spirit. Later we went to England together, and he was obliged to admit I was right. In London he talked with many Russians who had lived long in England, and they all declared that it was impossible for them to adopt the manners of English society. The Russian is indeed essentially democratic in character, even when he belongs to the aristocracy; Kropotkin, Tolstoy, Prince Khilkov are not very exceptional characters in my country. There are among us counts and princes, even of reactionary views, who talk to lower-class people with entire familiarity, as to equals. The Englishman, on the contrary, is aristocratic by temperament, even when his opinions are democratic. He never forgets the sub-division of the social hierarchy, which in Russia it is the easiest thing in the world to forget. Rich Russian princesses will ride on the top of a tram-car, mixing familiarly with the women of the people they meet there. This absence of caste feeling is common to Russia and to the Turkish and Tartar East. The Russian holds in horror the social conventions which play so large a part in English life. In the richest and most refined Russian society you may meet people in flannel blouses with leather girdles, and these people, dressed like peasants, are doctors, engineers, authors, like Gorky or Andreyev, known all over the world; and, believe me, it is not *pour épater le bourgeois* that they do this, out of love of singularity, for nobody notices their costumes; anyone, rich or poor, may dress thus, and may go to a social reunion in a frock coat or in his shirt-sleeves, if he pleases, without attracting attention. Of all people on earth Russians respect tradition the least. There is nothing of that worship of the

past which rules in England. Old things do not appear to us vener-
able, but rather the reverse. In England, the respect for property and
legality is developed to the highest degree; the Russian is communistic by instinct. Among us quite honourable people will borrow
large sums of money from their friends and not concern themselves
about repaying it, not from dishonesty, but because they attach
little importance to money, and, in their turn, are quite willing to
lend money to others, without expecting its return. Such was, for
example, the revolutionary Bakunin, an eminently Russian
character. Scrupulous precision in money affairs seems to a Russian
a ridiculous middle-class virtue, not far from sordid avarice. As to
legality, I have often heard my fellow-countrymen, and by no
means merely those of extreme views, say that the tyranny of the
law is worse than that of despotism, for the despot may at least
possess a heart: 'We do not want an autocracy, but Heaven preserve
us from European legalism!' That is a saying often heard in Russia.
The stiffness of English social relations, again, has no existence
among us, and a certain simplicity and easy-going familiarity makes
it easy for people with even a very dubious past to enter an aristocratic circle, and makes it difficult to shut out the importunate. It
may be added that Russian ladies, even the most virtuous and
those moving in the best society, have broad notions of sexual
morality and show little severity for the weaknesses of their own
sex. An unmarried mother in Russia need lower her eyes before no
one; she is received everywhere, and, if necessary, she will state
without embarrassment that she is not married and has a child. I
know the case of an unmarried lady who has had four children by
four different men; this has not interfered with her position as
professor in a government college for girls, although all her pupils
are acquainted with the circumstances. A woman who has deserted
her husband and lives openly with another man can be received
everywhere in Russia. Russian women laugh, not only at the rigid
and terrible puritanism of English women, but at the worldly and
hypocritical decorum of the women of the European continent
generally. Family life in Russia, often in practice involving free
love, is thus totally opposed to English puritanism. In this matter

Russian society has even recently made a step forward. Formerly, without compromising her social position, a woman could leave her husband and live with the elect of her heart. To-day one often sees two or three women openly living in the same house with their common lover, and two or three men with the same woman, and that in the best intellectual society (I could mention names of celebrated literary men). Everyone regards such unions as natural, and the women who form part of such households are everywhere received and enjoy general consideration. The Russian cannot understand the English method of living; he cannot understand, for instance, how educated people can sing psalms and listen to sermons. And he views with astonishment the English passion for sport. Many Russians love physical exercise. But that sports should be organized, and governed by rules, that they should be transformed into pretexts for competitions, with which journalists fill columns and pages, that a whole nation should be excited by the results of a football match or a yacht race, that there should be newspapers devoted to sport, and that sportsmen should be professionals—to a Russian this is unheard of and monstrous, and even indecent and idiotic; in our eyes it is an indication of softening in the brain of a nation. To us it seems that the best energies should be devoted to the bettering of social conditions and the removal of economic inequalities and the struggle against oppression and injustice. It is wrong to devote so much time and thought and energy to games when one lives under such conditions as are presented by English society, so full of wrongs, prostitution, alcoholism, capitalistic exploitation, landlordism, colonial oppression, criminality, prisons and gallows. In Russia only the *canaille*, aristocratic or plebeian, are occupied with sports, and in this respect the English seem to Russians as mediaeval as the Spaniards with their bull-fights. A Russian cannot understand how an intelligent Frenchman should admire Napoleon, nor why Nelson, the assassin of Caraccioli and the instrument of European reaction, should be so persistently popular in England. In Russia the heroes of war are only popular among the military. A soldier, however great, says nothing to the soul of an educated Russian."

How true this statement (written in peacetime) is of the Russian's estimate of war may be realized from a corresponding statement by Chkheidze in the interview already quoted, spoken in midst of the World War: "War is the most dangerous enemy of freedom. Rights are surrendered which may never be regained. The man of thought is displaced by the man of action. Reason gives way to force. With the soldier in power no one knows what may happen, no one is permitted even to discuss what ought to happen. The soldier only thinks in slaughter and destruction. He has no political instincts, no sense of statesmanship. His own business is to kill. He kills, and keeps on killing, till there is nothing more to kill. It is not safe to trust the world to such a man."

The remarks of my Russian correspondent may perhaps help to show how it is that even English enthusiasm over Russia sometimes arouses in the intellectual and cultured Russian a little amusement, if not even irritation. He is moving away from the antique beauty and simplicity which the foreigner can most easily admire, and he is moving towards an ideal which is scarcely that of his visitor. Stephen Graham, for instance, has through a long series of books emitted a gushing stream of warm and delicious sentiment over everything Russian from the Tsardom downwards. It is characteristic of the Russian temperament that Russians are inclined to treat Mr. Graham's sentiment with mild sarcasm, while (Wiener tells us) they will say, with a smile, that by far the best book ever written on Russia is the scathing attack of "E. B. Lanin" (Dr. Dillon) on Russian incompetence and corruption.

We have no occasion to be ashamed of our English methods and achievements. The English, as Ferrero pointed out years ago,[1] created the first real republic in Europe by continuously scooping out the vital pulp from the monarchy and conserving intact the beautiful desiccated rind. This scooping process occupied some six centuries, and Ferrero foresaw that the English would apply the same wise and skilful method to capitalism. The English feel a deep repugnance to revolution by programme, and prefer to exercise an art based on a natural and leisurely wisdom they are unable to put

[1] G. Ferrero, *Europe Giovane*, 1897.

into words. But this is hardly the impulsive Russian method. The Russian Revolution was effected in a day, without bloodshed, almost without opposition, by the unanimous will of the whole people. Moreover, it was not merely a political but a social revolution. Never before has any nation achieved revolution so swift, so complete, so comprehensive. Yet the bulk of the Russian people live in a stage much more primitive than that of the Victorian age. That is why the spectacle which Russia presents is so interesting, because so full of developmental possibilities. We see this great people with a psychology in most respects so youthful, so sensitively receptive, so pliant, even sometimes, it seems, so weak, yet so vigorously and impulsively spontaneous, so massively powerful, so firmly resistant. And our interest is deepened because these possibilities of development are presented to us in a people whose achievements have already made them in some respects the chief representatives of the world's culture of our time.

.   .   .   .   .

No European country presents so many surprises to the traveller as Russia. We go to Russia furnished with a large supply of miscellaneous opinions derived from various excellent sources, from the conversation or the writings of anarchists and diplomatists and statisticians, from Russian novelists, from the newspapers. Yet none of these suffice to convey those great and dominant impressions which are gained by actual contact with the people and their land. Partly, it seems, this is due to the fact that these various sources of information are mostly too specialized, that each presents us with but a single aspect, even when that aspect is not over-emphasized or distorted. So vast, it would appear, is their land, that few can focus to a point the really salient characteristics of its genius.

The first novelty that surprises the traveller in Russia is its landscape. He has heard of it as largely a barren land of forests and steppes and plains, devoid of beauty. Travelling from Warsaw to Moscow, through a vast expanse of distinctively Russian scenery, one finds oneself in a country which, in its own way, possesses an exquisite beauty. The same mistake has been made about Russia as about Australia, and for a somewhat similar reason, the presence of monotony and the absence of cultivation. Yet both these characteristics may often be among the very elements of beauty in landscape. The characteristic tree of Russia is the birch, one of the most beautiful of all trees, and though the birch indicates poverty of soil—the great belt of fertile Russian soil lies further south—this very poverty of soil chastens the crude luxuriance of vegetation and imparts to the landscape a parsimony which emphasizes all its gracious outlines. In these ever-present slender silver drooping birches, in the occasional sheets of still water, the bright and variegated wooden cottages with their patches of sunflowers, the rare human figures, men and women at work in the fields with their sickles, and now and then a town with its blue and gold domes shimmering through the mist, we have the finest elements of a scenery of exquisite sylvan beauty, an endless succession of Corots. If the world is not yet sensitive to the beauty of the Russian landscape it can only be because the Russians themselves have never seen it. When we walk through the Tretyakov Picture Gallery at Moscow and note the chief works of the best Russian painters we find historical and religious works, gorgeous architectural views, exotic landscapes, vigorous portraits, scenes of war, death and execution, lurid catastrophes of blackness and flame, but little indication anywhere of a sensitive aesthetic vision of the beauty of their own land.[1] It seems that the Russian is still too youthful and too self-conscious to perceive the delicate beauty of the world in which he himself lives. It needs something exotic, something tremendous or pathetic, to stimulate his crude and undeveloped aesthetic sense of vision. In literature he has expressed himself, but not yet in painting. There he has the same barbaric craving for horrors which in the region of drama we find among Elizabethan audiences.

A further surprise awaits the traveller when he comes to contemplate the people themselves and their lives. The Russian population —I speak of the days before the Revolution—certainly may well be

---

[1] Harold Williams remarks that it was left to Levitov, at the end of the nineteenth century, to "discover the beauty of Russian scenery". But Levitov was a Jew and a writer.

the most resigned in Europe, but it is not the least free, nor, in its own way, even the least cheerful. Shaggy, uncouth, bewildered—recalling the early pictures of the English peasant as well as the representations of his own Scythian ancestors on the famous Nicopol vase in the Hermitage—for all his air of passive resignation the Russian is yet energetic. Very robust, very healthy, it seems, sometimes, of almost colossal dimensions, on holidays radiant and sweet, with their shining, good-natured faces, and clean feast-day clothes, men and women alike are marked by their quiet strength, their simplicity, their frank honesty, singularly often with the imprint also of a stern sense of duty, and above all a profound and unfailing good-nature. There is no hint of servitude in their expression. For centuries Russia has not been a free country for the man who thinks for himself. But there are not many men who really think for themselves, and the ordinary Russian could exert himself freely within the circle of his own activities without meeting with any social or governmental fetters. I know no great city where the peasants occupied so large and so prominent a place as in Moscow; they constituted the markets, they crowded the churches, they roamed unquestioned and unwatched even into the private apartments of the Imperial Palace as it then was; they were the fitting inhabitants of a city which has itself well been called a huge village. City life here was lived at so low a degree of tension that it had not sharply marked off the rich from the poor, the townsman from the countryman. There was a general air of freedom and unconstraint which contrasted not only with Germany but with France and with England. Even in Poland, notwithstanding the melancholy air of ancient distinction which brooded over the land and the people, repression had ceased to be a marked feature of daily life long before the World War.

Patient and resigned as the Russian might appear, he had his weekly Saturnalia. Every Sunday, in any great city like Moscow, a rumour of festivity began slowly to fill the air, the silent leisurely streets of the vast village became animated, the melancholy resigned Russian was transformed, caught out of himself to become a gay and jovial being. Towards evening the restaurants of all classes were crowded, on every hand one heard the solemn strains of the mechanical organ, often large and expensive, which the Russians loved so much that no decent restaurant could afford to be without it; voices broke out into singing; little bottles of vodka circulated freely and at frequent intervals a small glass of fiery liquid was swallowed, always undiluted, at a single gulp. It may well be that this potent stimulant was required to stir the Russian into animation, to break through the passive Eastern elements in him and to call out the boisterous European element.[1] Yet there was little tendency to turbulence or disorder; one was simply conscious of an atmosphere of unreasonable, almost childish joyousness, and, as evening came on, the more helplessly drunk were tenderly and sympathetically led home by less intoxicated friends. Habitual drunkenness was comparatively rare; the impulse to intoxication—closely associated with such criminality as was to be found in Russia—occurred only in these primitive orgiastic outbursts, nearly always associated with festivals, as Beauplan described it in Ukrainia three centuries ago.[2]

---

[1] It is noteworthy that the consumption of alcohol, which before the war was in Russia about the same as in England, was thus very much less per head than in England, being only 0.95 gallons proof as against 3.42 gallons in Great Britain; though it must be added that the Russian drank twice as much raw spirit (in the form of vodka) as the English. The Russian consumption of alcohol was indeed the smallest per head in Europe after Norway. Nor can it be said that the deaths due to disease from alcoholic poisoning were large in number, when the vast population is taken into consideration, being only about 1,000 per annum. The prohibition of alcoholic drink took place in 1914, but was not so sudden as it might have seemed, for the Duma had for some time been working in the direction of temperance legislation, especially under the stimulus of the vigorous propaganda of Chelyshev, a self-made business man, who died just after prohibition was proclaimed. The introduction of prohibition was, however, even if desirable in itself, far too sudden to be effective, for there were no adequate compensatory interests and excitations to substitute for alcohol. It thus happened that the very same district which had petitioned for prohibition would, when prohibition had been introduced, petition for its abolition. Moreover, the drinking of methylated spirit enormously increased, not merely among habitual drunkards but among elements of the general population of all ages and professions previously accustomed to the use of vodka. The result has been that deaths due to alcoholic diseases have increased instead of diminishing.

[2] The drunkard is dealt with tenderly and sympathetically, even with admiration, throughout the course of Russian literature, and notably in the literature of the people from the epic songs onwards. Very popular is the story of how the toper, who had drunk his whole life long but always praised God for each flagon, succeeded in making his way into Paradise, in spite of the refusal of St. Peter and other saintly door-keepers to let him in. He reminded each of them in turn of his own greater sins, and in the end they were silenced and the gate was opened.

To a similar cause—the instinctive craving for orgiastic moments of self-forgetfulness—may be due that strange proclivity to unconscious impulsions and outbursts which Dostoyevsky noted among Russian convicts, in that volume of Siberian reminiscences which is so fascinating and illuminative. We realized the true character and disposition of the Russian—made manifest in his abandonment —as we wandered on Sundays and feast-days among the childlike people of this, as we often inclined to call it, primitive race.

.　　　.　　　.　　　.　　　.

When we contemplate the map of Europe we can scarcely fail at first to find Russia a rather disconcerting part of the picture. It is a disparate element, a huge mass of smooth equable space against which all the concentrated varieties of Western Europe stand out in violent contrast. Yet at the same time we realize that without Russia Europe will hardly hang together. At the worst Russia appears still as a huge air cushion perfectly adjusted as a buffer to protect the back of Europe from the extravagant commotions of Asia. This is why it often seemed so difficult to decide whether Russia is European or Asiatic. Every shock that passes through this vast space becomes changed and tempered as it moves, and as we move eastward we become more and more conscious of Asia, as we move westward more and more conscious of Europe. Yet fundamentally, as the geographic picture clearly suggests, we are always in Europe.

At the same time, with these special traits, Russia is a geographic unit, a clearly defined and singularly uniform unit. Its natural boundaries are inevitably fixed in Europe between the Arctic region and the Caucasus, between the Ural Mountains and the beginnings of the tormented lands of Western Europe at the Carpathians. It is true that the Russian State, while roughly corresponding in Europe to these natural limits, is not exactly conterminous with them at every point. Russia fails so far to reach the Carpathians, although the Ruthenian population here belongs to the Little Russian Group, and political reasons have prevented Russia hitherto from extending to Constantinople, although natural regions cannot be said to stand in the way of this extension, while historical, religious and economic reasons have strongly impelled Russia. On the other hand, pressed back here, the Russians have overflowed beyond their natural boundaries south of the Caucasus. At one point, in the north-west, the natural frontier of Russia is not quite clear; here the frontier is mainly racial, for the expansive Russian finds himself west of the Vistula against the solid wall of the Prussian State which ever tends to diffuse eastwards, so that there is even a claim of Prussia to the possession of Courland which has undoubtedly been in part colonized by Germans.

Yet Russia seems all of a piece. The last of European lands to emerge from the Glacial Drift, it has never been lifted and broken, displaced and folded, by the great influences which have crushed and crumpled the whole of the tormented surface of Western Europe. Russia lies everywhere in smooth and flat strata and con-tinues on to the east of the Urals, through Siberia, in much the same manner. Even hilly regions in Russia are not due to displacement of strata but merely to the eroding action of the slow but mighty rivers.

There is the same uniformity in the climate as in the soil. This is a climate of continental type, and it is so throughout its vast extent, with a small rainfall and with extremes of temperature. Everywhere in Russia the summer is fiery and the winter is icy. We commonly regard Russia as a land of snow and biting frost where the people are habitually smothered in furs, and the Russians themselves seem to regard their land as a land of cold, just as the Spaniards regard their land as a land of heat, and are as exclusively preoccupied in guarding against cold as the Spaniards are against heat. Yet, as is the way of continental climates, Russia can be as burningly torrid as Spain, and I have nowhere in Europe felt so hot as in Moscow, for against this heat the Russian has no protection; having expended so much energy in fighting against Nature in winter, the Russian seems to feel that in summer he may abandon himself to an instinct which is even more congenial to him, and fling himself into the arms of Nature, to wallow shamelessly and indolently in meadows and streams. There is only one region of Russia where the intem-perate continental climate grows comparatively mild and mellow, and that is on the Black Sea, the miniature Russian Mediterranean, and indeed an inlet of the Mediterranean, but still a northern inlet, and from the central Mediterranean standpoint, as Ovid long since found, not altogether desirable. There can be no doubt that the Russian climate has been a factor of the first importance in the formation of the Russian temperament. A climate that was more exclusively cold or more exclusively hot might have exerted a hardening of the fibres and a steeling of the will. But the Russian, a helpless victim of opposing extremes, has become firmly resistant indeed, yet softened rather than hardened; the receptive impulses have predominated over the impulse of energetic action, and massive emotion has often swallowed up the decision of the will.[1]

This land is, for the most part, not luxuriant, so that Russia is in general only thinly populated. It is only in the south-west, in the land of the Little Russians, that we find luxuriance, for here is the rich black belt of earth passing eastwards below Moscow. Hence the population is here thicker, and during the last half century has become still denser, as on the old agricultural activity a new industrial activity has been superimposed and the factory life of Western Europe established. But for the most part there are not only no mountains in Russia, but even forests are confined to special regions. Thus it is that on these flat, bare, thinly populated and far-expanding plains we have, as nowhere else, the sense of space. The Russian has a passion for space (with a corresponding dislike of fresh air often found in bleak country regions) and he has invented untranslatable words to express his appreciation of illimitable horizons and his desire to clasp Nature to his bosom.

There is no doubt, in any case, about the huge amount of space covered by Russia. It is even vaster than our impression of it as we traverse the country. The greatest plain in the world, Russia is larger than all the other states of Europe together, while, if we include arctic Russia, it is four times the size of Europe and covers a sixth part of the total land area of the globe. If we try to distinguish

[1] Baring (*The Russian People*, p. 39), who attaches importance to the Russian climate as a factor in moulding Russian character, considers that it has made the Russian, on the one hand, tenacious, strong and hard; on the other hand, patient, resigned and kind.

a central core in the vast Russian plain, I think we may fairly select the roughly circular or heart-shaped space—itself larger than any Western Europe country—almost completely enclosed by the Volga, the Dnieper and the Don. Petrograd, indeed, is outside this heart of Russia, but Petrograd is merely the modern bureaucratic capital, artificially established in modern times by Peter the Great. Within the core, or on its periphery, and all dominated by Moscow, we find Kiev, Nijni-Novgorod, Kharkov, Tula and Yckaterinoslav; through it runs the great Black Belt of rich agricultural land, and within the girdle of these mighty rivers are the industrial areas of Russia, the mines, the coal-producing fields, the centres of manufacture and commerce, the focus of progressive thought, and the chief region of expanding population; here in the south-west is the outlet by the Dnieper to the Bosphorus and the Mediterranean, and on the opposite farthest eastern side is Kazan, where we touch the variegated and bewildering groups of semi-Asiatic peoples. Yet this central core, which has always been central in the history of Russia and is now becoming of even more predominant importance, is, so far as elevation is concerned, an indistinguishable portion of the vast Russian plain. In the history of Russia, in the constitution of the Russian people the whole of the plain has taken a moulding part. Just as the growth of England has been conditioned from the first by the fact that it is an island, so the growth of Russia has been conditioned throughout by the fact that it is a plain, a land of nomads from the first, a medium of perpetual diffusion and racial expansion, the elected land of colonization.

Who are the Russians? They are the largest and most easterly group of the Slavs, one of the main divisions of European peoples, other and smaller groups being the Poles, now divided between Russia, Germany and Austria, the Czechs of Bohemia, the Wends who are melting away in Saxony, and the Serbs, Croatians, Bulgarians, and some other peoples in southern Austria and the Balkans. Most of these peoples speak a modification of the same fundamental speech, and most of them are obviously related in physical type and psychic character. The word Slav is of proud significance, but the Slav peoples have on the whole, notwithstanding their nomadic and colonizing tendencies, been of peaceful and unwarlike temper; they early tended to become individually subjected to the Germans to whom we owe it that the word "Slav"—changing its significance, as Gibbon remarked, from glory to servitude—became our word "slave". The name Russian is now applied to three closely related but distinct peoples occupying a huge part of the vast plain to the east of the Vistula and the Carpathians: the Great Russians, the Little Russians, and the White Russians. Although closely related and not fundamentally unlike in physical type, it is evident that these three divisions of the Russian people have long been separate, for though they all speak dialectal variations of the same Russian speech, they cannot understand each other. It must be remembered that even these three groups of true Russians only account for about half the population even of European Russia; to make the account fairly complete we should have to deal with Poles, Letto-Lithuanians, Jews, Finns and Asiatic Mongols, not to mention German colonists.

The Great Russians, who are by far the most numerous and approach 90,000,000 in number, occupy the larger part of the central core of Russia of which Moscow is the centre, and, moreover, they extend northwards towards the Arctic region. They are of medium height and of medium pigmentation (40 per cent blond, 20 per cent brunette and 40 per cent mixed), with a tendency to chestnut or auburn hair, light complexion and "beer-coloured" eyes. They are rather broad-headed, with a cephalic index averaging 82, but in this respect differ little from other Russians, a moderate broad-headedness prevailing all over Russia with a remarkably slight range of variation. They are usually regarded as in the mass a phlegmatic, stolid and stubborn people. Yet they possess a practicality and opportunism, a dislike of general ideas, and resourcefulness and tact, which Fouillée regards as due to the fusion of Norse and Slav elements and compare to the rather similar combination of qualities produced by the fusion of Germanic and Norse with Celtic elements in England and America. Peter the Great, the typical

Great Russian, was a mixture of Slav and German, and the Romanov family has been largely Germanic, susceptible to Germanic influence down to its fall.

The Little Russians, or Ukrainians, who number some 40,000,000, occupy the south and south-west, including the region of the Don Cossacks, and their centre is the ancient seat of Russian civilization, the early capital on the Dnieper: Kiev.[1] Their territory is milder in climate and more fertile in soil than are other regions of Russia; it is, moreover, not only a great agricultural region, but in recent years a great industrial region also; the population is increasing rapidly and cities are growing in size. The Little Russians are decidedly taller than the Great Russians (though still on the average much shorter than the English or the northern Germans) and slightly darker, in as much as they show a smaller proportion of blond people and a larger proportion of mixed type; they are also rather more brachycephalic. They differ in temperament from the Great Russians; they are of more southern type, more emotional and genial, more open-hearted and hospitable, fonder of pleasure and games, and dance, song and music. The musical and poetic genius of the Slav elements in the population of Austria and Saxony are un-questionable. When we bear in mind the rich and deep vein of folk-music among the Little Russians, their geographical position and their anthropological traits, it is difficult not to believe that we have in Ukrainia the roots which have branched and flowered in some of the finest musical artists of the West.

This difference in temperament is the indication of the social and economic characters which separate the Little Russians and Ukrainians from the Great Russians. Thus they stand outside the communal system which is sometimes regarded as purely Russian. Shidlovsky states (*Russian Review*, 1912, p. 24) that if we take a diagonal line through Russian Europe, pointing north-east and south-west, communal land tenure, which is extensive along the north-east end of this line, is completely absent along the south-west

---

[1] Kostomarov, in 1861, set up a theory according to which the Little Russians are alone purely Slav, the Great Russians being Finns, etc., slavonized. But it is highly improbable that the modern Little Russians are unmixed.

end, while, reversely, population is most extensive along the south-west end. The direction of the line also indicates a progressive falling off of productive agricultural methods in passing from the south-west to the north-east. Shidlovsky believes we may conclude that communal tenure, which may be good in a low stage of culture, is unsuited to higher and more populous stages. These differences may help us to understand the anxiety of the Ukrainians after the Revolution to set up a separate state of their own.

The White Russians, perhaps so called from their light-coloured homespun garments,[1] are few in number, only about 5,000,000. They occupy the territory to the east of the Poles and Lithuanians and to the west of the Great Russians. Their land is poor and unproductive, in some parts covered with forests, and others marshy. They are the fairest of Russians, with only 11 per cent brunette people, and the tallest; by some (Leroy-Beaulieu, for example) they are regarded as nearest to the original type of the eastern Slav, having been protected by their forests and swamps from racial admixture. In language they closely resemble the Great Russians, the tongue of the Little Russians having been much modified, probably because their southern position laid them open to the Tartar and other invasions.

This picture presented by the Russians is anthropologically simple, and fairly easy to understand. But when we turn to the question of origin the simplicity disappears and the best authorities speak with hesitation. What was the original type of the Slavs? What relation have the ancient Scythians to the Slavs? What is the part of the Finn in the modern Russian? What that of the Scandinavian? How far is the Russian a Tartar?

The initial difficulty arises that the original Slav, far from being an eastern broad-head, seems to have belonged to the totally unlike long-heads. One of the oldest known Russian skulls of the Stone Age has been described in detail by Virchow as large, heavy, broad-

---

[1] I may add that this seems confirmed by the narrative of the early German traveller from Strasbourg, J. D. Wunderer, who in describing in 1590 this tall primitive population, humble in aspect and superstitious in beliefs, says that the men wore but little clothing (the women less) of coarse grey stuff, while at Moscow the women (as still to-day) wore garments of all colours.

headed and broad-faced, and belonging to an individual of "Tura-
nian, or, if one will, Finnic population" (*Comptes-rendus Congrès
International de Médecine*, Moscow, 1897, vol. ii, p. 85). But the
kurgans—which are funeral mounds of immense number belonging
to the Russian Stone and later ages and scattered all over western,
central and southern Russia—reveal a population predominantly
long-headed, not so very dissimilar (as Sergi insists) from the
neolithic population in Europe generally. They were a peaceful
folk, however, and there is a notable absence of weapons of war
in their graves. But in Moscow cemeteries of the sixteenth century,
according to Sergi, who examined a very large number of these
skulls as well as from the kurgans, the dolichocephalic, long-headed,
or, as Sergi would term them, Eurafrican, type of skulls, have
fallen from 56 per cent to 44 per cent, while the brachycephalic,
broad-headed, or Eurasiatic types, have risen from 44 per cent
to 54 per cent. Anutchin of Moscow makes the difference still
greater, estimating the population of long-headed in the sixteenth
and seventeenth centuries as only 15 to 20 per cent, while at the
present day it is still smaller (Sergi, *Europa*, 1908, p. 265).

These facts are undoubted, but their interpretation opens the
path to the widest divergencies of opinion, even among the best
authorities. What names can we give to these peoples? Or were
they really one people? And when can we begin to apply to them
the name of Slav? Sergi regards the people of the kurgans as
identical with the Stone Age people of Europe generally. For other
authorities, not necessarily contradicting Sergi, they are definitely
Finns. The Finns, now mostly brachycephalic, are by some (notably
Ripley) regarded as originally mostly dolichocephalic. So that it is
not clear whether we are to consider them as in early days Mongo-
lians or true Europeans. But whatever may be said for their original
European character, unless we regard them as very thoroughly
permeated even at an early period with Asiatic elements we cannot
attribute to them the Mongol elements in the Great Russian's
features which so become difficult to account for, while the gentle
and unwarlike character attributed to the Finns by Tacitus and
Jordanus seems to fit better an Asiatic than a European temperament.

In any case, it seems that the Slavs, especially the Great and White Russians, largely absorbed the Finns. "We are all ready," remarks Pavel Milyukov in his *Sketch of Russian Culture,* "to recognize the Finnish facial features in the Great Russian, but we can give no exact scientific definition of the physical marks of mixture," though the early Slav is commonly regarded as tall and blond and the Finn as short and brunette, with high cheek-bones and squat nose, while the Great Russian represents a compromise between these two opposed types. The same authority (as well as Klyuchevsky, *History of Russia,* vol. i, ch. 13) points out that the suffixes *ma* and *va* in Russia mean river, and these names are spread from the north towards the south-west (including Kostroma, Vladimir, Moscow, Kaluga), as also is the legendary and popular worship of water, rocks and trees, derived from the Finns. To-day there are to the east of this region two Finnish peoples, the Cheremisses and the Mordvins, who have been in their present seat for five hundred years. Moreover, Jordanus mentions the Meri as occupying precisely the country just described as delimited by these river names, and the Cheremisses still call themselves Meri. There seems little doubt that the Finns were the most ancient known inhabitants of Central Russia, whoever they were originally and wherever they came from. There is thus a Finnish substratum in the Great Russian, and it may be added that the Lithuanians, formerly much more to the east than now, were blended with the Finns (as regards some of the ultimate problems of the origin of the Finns, who must not be considered, as was formerly common, of low type, see W. Z. Ripley, *The Races of Europe,* pp. 363–7).

Many competent anthropologists, like Bogdanov and Anutchin, regard the kurgan population as, on historical and archaeological grounds, Slavs. (Anutchin expressed himself in this sense, though stating that the question is difficult, at the International Medical Congress at Moscow in 1897, but, according to Ripley, a few years earlier he had expressed a contrary opinion.) So that the question would arise how the Slavs came to change their physical type. Bogdanov believed that the change took place in part, though not entirely, without fresh racial admixture. This is in accordance with a belief as to the possibility of change in head-shape long maintained by Adolph Bloch, and more recently shown actually to occur in the children of American immigrants who are found to be of different cephalic index from their parents, under the influence of environment. Most anthropologists, impressed by the fact that where a population remains in the same spot and unquestionably unmixed with new racial elements it retains its head form through vast periods, view with suspicion the claim for spontaneous variations. Thus Arbo of Christiania, considering that to regard the early Slavs as long-heads throws all Slav craniology into confusion, would settle the matter by regarding the people of the kurgans as North Germans or Scandinavians, aristocratic invaders not necessarily representative of the general population who were probably too poor to erect kurgans as funeral monuments (*Comptes-rendus,* International Congress of Medicine, Moscow, 1897, vol. ii, p. 42). There is no doubt that the energetic and enterprising Scandinavians, at the great Viking period of their development, radiated, not only to the west, south-west and south—to Iceland and the British Isles and France and Germany—but also to the north-east, to Russia, and the name of Rurik is famous in Russia as the counterpart of the great Norman chieftains in the West, who founded aristocratic hegemonies in the lands they invaded. But it is decidedly hazardous to identify the kurgan graves with the Scandinavians.

Whatever may be thought of the people of the kurgans or the precise moment at which the Slavs originated, there is less doubt among competent authorities as to the chief Slav centre in early times. This is placed by Niederle as probably between the Oder and the Dnieper (or, as Milyukov states it, south of the Niemen and west of the Dnieper), and Niederle believes that even in prehistoric times the Slavs at places had reached the Elbe, the Saale, the Danube, the Niemen and the Baltic. (Kunik, however, states that the Slavs were not on the Baltic before A.D. 150.) Klyuchevsky, the distinguished Russian historian, again considers that the eastern Slavs entered the Russian plains from the slopes of the Carpathians —the Sarmatian mountains of the classic writers—and thus entered an entirely different environment from that of the Germanic Slavs,

who settled in more confined regions, amidst old-world civilization, and in the sphere of Roman influences, while the eastern
Slavs on their great plains led a nomadic life, constantly migrating,
colonizing and fighting, in later times extending northwards over
a large part of Russia.

This view fairly corresponds with that of Nestor, the earliest
serious chronicler of Russia, who states that the Slavs were descendants of Japheth who established themselves on the Danube,
some years after the Deluge, in what was later the land of the
Hungarians and Bulgars. Long before, in Greek days, Herodotus
had placed the Neuri, whom he described as related to the Scythians,
not far from the river Bug where we should expect to find Slavs.
Pliny the Elder, in the first century (*Natural History*, bk. iv, ch. 97),
and Ptolemy, a century later, first mentioned a people we can quite
definitely regard as Slav, the Venedi, dwelling on the banks of the
Vistula; these are the Wends, the name the Germans have always
applied to the Slavs, and they still linger in eastern Germany under
that name and retain some of their ancient characteristics. The name
"Slav" itself is said to occur first in the early sixth century in
Pseudo-Caesarius's *Dialogues* (Migne. P. G. xxxviii, 985) while
the earliest definite account of the Slavs is by Jordanus, as "Sclaverii".
A name of honour and by some supposed to mean "glorious",
the European word "slave" dates from the times when the Germans
supplied the market with Slavonic "slaves". Klyuchevsky, in
summing up this question of the emergence of the Slavs in the
early part of his *History*, concluded that about the second century
A.D. the Slavs were swept by surging currents of racial migration
into the region of the Lower and Middle Danube. Here they began
to stand out from the Sarmatian mass, but, defeated by Trajans'
Roman army, they abandoned the Danube and during the next
five centuries the eastern branch engaged in the migration, at first
sojourning in the Carpathians, then on the Dnieper. Until the
seventh century, however, they remained united with the
western Slavs whose descendants are to-day found in Austria
and the Balkans. The origin of the Slavs by the Danube seems
confirmed by the fact pointed out by Zmigrodzki, that in the

legends of all branches of the Slav races that river is regarded as holy.

It thus appears that the Slavs emerge at a comparatively later period, and then in the West. By what name or names they were known before, and whether they had previously come from the East by the paths along which later they moved towards the East, it is highly probable that they were blended of peoples who were known earlier under other names. Southern Russia, previous to our era, was overrun by successive tribes of nomads from Asia, as later by the Huns and the Tartars. There were, first, the Cimmerians, then, in the days of Herodotus, the Scythians, and later the Sarmatians. These last, Milyukov states, corresponded to the Alans (as shown by their proper name preserved by the Greeks) and to-day are the Ossetes on the slopes of the Caucasus, a people with long oval heads, regarded as more or less definitely Aryan in speech, but closer to the Persians than to the Western branches. They gave their names to the Danube, the Dniester, the Dnieper, and the Don. Zaborowski seeks to connect them not only with the Kafirs of Kafirstan but with the Kymri of northern Europe. It seems hardly hazardous to suppose that they have left their blood as well as their names among the people who occupy the land that was once theirs.

Of the Scythians this may be said with even more assurance. The Scythians, who had been preceded in southern Russia by Greek colonists, are believed by Zaborowski in his study of the southern Slavs (*Bulletin, Société d'Anthropologie*, 1895–6) to have come from the east of the Caspian. They were not an unmixed race (speaking seven different languages in the time of Herodotus) and they dominated a large area of south-west Russia and the regions westward, until in the second century A.D. they were subjugated by the Goths from the north, the Goths, two centuries later, being in their turn overwhelmed by the Huns.

The Scythians—who seem to be related to the Goths, Massagetes and Dacians—had acquired a considerable degree of culture by which we recognize their presence in the furniture of their graves. They were interestingly described by Herodotus (bk. iv), Lucian and others, and their manners and customs not only agree with the results of archaeological investigations in southern Russia, but are clearly the source of many practices of the modern Russians, who are probably, in part at least, their descendants. When we see the Scythians represented on the ancient Nikopol vase we at once recognize by their costumes the modern Russian peasant. The classical writers from Homer on idealized the Scythians—though they recognized that they were apt to be drunken, dirty and perverse—and admired the men of wisdom and high character which Scythia so specially produced, the type of these being Anacharsis, referred to by Herodotus (bk. iv, ch. 46).

Scythian antiquities, as found in the kurgans of southern Russia, are well known. They are often of gold and show a considerably high degree of culture. While Greek influence is plainly discernible, these objects, in accordance with the conservatism of the Scythians, preserve a definite character of their own, and the archaeologist has little difficulty in recognizing them wherever they may be found. It is an interesting fact that they have been found at various places in Europe considerably to the west of Russia; in Roumania, in Galicia, in Transylvania, in Hungary, in Lusatia (a Slav centre amid the surrounding Germans even to-day), and even as far away as Baden. Near the Carpathians they are very numerous. There is some doubt as to the age of these objects and as to the significance of the more remote finds. Furtwängler places some of these as far back as the sixth century B.C. Paul Reinecke, in a careful and detailed study ("Die Skythiscken Alterthümer im Mittleren Europa", *Zeitschrift für Ethnologie*, 1896, Heft I) comes to the conclusion that the Scythian period in Europe (lying in about the middle of the La-Tène culture) belongs to the last two centuries B.C. and disappears during the first two centuries A.D. Our knowledge of this region at this period is extremely vague and confused, but Reinecke believes it is reasonable to conclude that the Scythian boundaries to the west cover the regions in which we find Scythian remains numerous, though when they are less numerous we may be merely concerned with intrusions into another sphere of culture, that of the Germans or that of the Celts of the south of the Danube.

He further believes that the presence of characteristic Scythian objects—short swords, special type of mirror, etc.—shows that a uniform Scythian population extended, just before the Christian era, from the south Russian steppes towards the Altai and Yenisei. This Scythian population, he holds, was not (as Müllenhoff held) Iranian, nor, as commonly held, in part Indo-Germanic, but ultimately of north Asiatic origin, whether Ugro-finnic or Turkish or otherwise Mongolian, he leaves undecided in view of the imperfection of our knowledge.

The distribution and character of the Slav populations are discussed by L. Niederle of Prague in *La Race Slave* (translated from the Czech), 1911. Ripley, in the chapter on "Russia and the Slavs" in his *Races of Europe* (1900), brings together many of the puzzling facts and makes a valiant attempt to co-ordinate them. He regards the Slavs as brachycephals of the Alpine race who blended with pre-existing Finns, the Finns being northern dolichocephals who were ultimately of Mediterranean race. Linzelbach ("Geography in Russian History", *Popular Science Monthly*, January 1915) gives a slight but intelligent sketch of the development and distribution of the Russians.

It is yet necessary to refer to the element contributed to Russian nationality by the Scandinavian Norsemen. This element, as has so often happened wherever Norsemen and Normans penetrated, is probably much more important than its mere numerical size would indicate. Even the very name of Russia is Scandinavian. Various origins have indeed been assigned to the word. Thus Ripley states that it is "undoubtedly derived from a root meaning red", and so indicating a rufous tendency in Russian pigmentation. There is nowadays a fair amount of agreement on the part of the best authorities with the distinguished Danish scholar, Vilhelm Thomsen, in finding for it an entirely different origin. It appears that the Finns, who were seated between the Slavs and the sea, and therefore nearer than the Slavs to Sweden, termed the Swedes Ruotsi. But this term cannot be explained from Finnish and was therefore probably used by the Scandinavians themselves, as meaning rowing-men or sea-farers, and later learnt from the Finns by the Slavs (V. Thomsen, *The Relation Between Ancient Russia and Scandinavia*, 1877, pp. 92 et seq.). Thus a term used by the Slavs to indicate the Scandinavian invaders who founded a state only then became totally changed in meaning and eventually signified not a Scandinavian but a Slavonic nationality. The Russ (Swedish) Rurik founded Ladoga (then outside Slav territory) in the ninth century and afterwards took possession of Novgorod; later, in 882, his successor Oleg seized Kiev. The name "Russ" then vanished from Novgorod and became exclusively associated with Kiev. It was gradually applied to all the territory acquired by the Russian crown and so came to stand for a Slav nationality of which the earliest state-builders had been Norsemen; the fusion of Norse and Slav elements being completed, according to Klyuchevsky, during the eleventh and twelfth centuries. Just in the same way, Thomsen remarks, a tribe of Germanic Franks gave the name of France to a land that in the main was not Germanic. In connection with the Norse element in Russia we hear much of the Varangians. This name is most commonly applied to the military bodyguard of the emperors of Byzantium which was composed of Norsemen, at first Swedish but later on mostly English. The word has, properly speaking, however, Thomsen states, no military sense, but geographical, signifying Sweden (op. cit., p. 110). It is in this sense that we must understand it in connection with Russia. The names of the early Russo-Varangian princes were nearly all Scandinavian in origin—Rurik, Oleg, Olga, Igor, Askold, etc. But the Varangians of Russia were quite different from their Danish kinsfolk. That is to say that they were not so much pirates as merchants travelling to wealthy Byzantium (we may recall the prominent part played in the epic songs of Russia by Sadko the Merchant). To this day, Klyuchevsky remarks (*History of Russia*, vol. i, p. 59), *varyag* means in Russia a pedlar or retail trader. Wherever the Norsemen went they carried with them a spirit of independence and energy, a width of political imagination, and great constructive energy. It was these characteristics which give them an influence in Russian history, far beyond that which they would otherwise possess. "It is the Norsemen," says Thomsen (op. cit., p. 130), "who laid the foundation on which the native Slavs have raised a colossal superstructure." The petty Varangian principality, founded at Kiev by two Vikings, Askold and Oleg, Klyuchevsky similarly remarks (op. cit., vol. i, p. 73), was the primal form of the Russian State.

After the Russian people had become constituted as predominantly, if not fundamentally Slav, Russian life flowed in an undivided stream up to the twelfth century, being concentrated in the south round Kiev—which still retained Norse traditions brought by the *Varyag* warriors, an intellectual atmosphere, and some degree of relationship with the external world—and thence sending out more or less feeble branches to east and north. Then came the last important racial disturbance, the invasion of the Asiatic Tartars who captured and destroyed Kiev in 1240, compelling the Kiev Metropolitan to migrate northwards to Vladimir in 1299, and after to Moscow, which in the fourteenth century became the leading state, the political and spiritual heir of Kiev. Moscow and its princes, remote from the civilized Western world, became narrow and hardened in the prolonged struggle with the Tartar oppressors, who ruled from a distance, making raids when they deemed it necessary. In this way the princes of Moscow, with no higher culture than that of a degraded and barren Byzantinism, acquired a spirit of cunning, cruelty, and tyranny which constituted the germ of the power of autocratic Tsardom. Finally, the Tartar yoke was thrown off, and the Tartar racial elements in Russia became diffused in the general population, and perhaps, as Leroy-Beaulieu believes, more generally separated out in special districts, but in the end Europeanized. Notwithstanding their importance for Russian history, their part in the promotion of Russian nationality, Milyukov and other authorities hold, has been insignificant. Ripley considers that this Asiatic element has perhaps been more powerful in determining the Russian character than the physical type, but this is doubtful.

When we are content to avoid any minute discussion of the probable meaning of such terms as Scythian, Slav, Tartar and Finn, the problem of the racial elements of Russia becomes simple, and owing to the activities of Russian anthropologists during recent years it is easy to outline the main racial features of the country. The earliest known population of Russia, as disinterred from the kurgans or burial tumuli which exist over a large part of the land, is nearly always found to be mainly long-headed. Whether these people corresponded to the tall long-heads now inhabiting Sweden, or whether they belonged to that primitive stock of long-heads which, according to a theory now tending to prevail, then occupied nearly the whole of Europe and had not yet become separated into fair and tall northern long-heads and dark and short southern long-heads, is not quite clear. In any case the Russian long-heads were closely related to the Neolithic people of Europe and Northern Africa. Before historical times, however, these conditions had long begun to change; dark broad-headed people from Asia—some with, some without Mongolian affinities—had begun the slow migration by which they eventually succeeded in reaching Great Britain and in placing large and permanent colonies throughout the whole of Central Europe. Russia is for the most part a vast plain, and these Asiatic peoples had every facility not only in reaching Western Europe, but also in spreading themselves over the whole extent of Russia itself. These three leading facts—the early possession of Russia by the long-heads, the great wave of immigration which has gone on throughout nearly the whole of historical times, and the special configuration of the Russian soil —explain all the main ethnic characteristics of Russia. At the present time Russia is inhabited by a moderately broad-headed (brachycephalic and sub-brachycephalic) population, varying only to a very slight degree over the whole of its vast extent. This population is not only less broad-headed than the Asiatic peoples to the east, it is less so also than the European peoples of the Central European highlands to the west of it. At the first glance this state of things seems anomalous; we might have expected the immigrants to show a constantly decreasing broad-headedness as they approached the Atlantic and mingled with the long-heads of Europe. The different conditions of the soil, however, suffice to explain this anomaly. There have been no natural boundaries to confine the eastern migrants in Russia and enable them to preserve their racial characters in purity; the broad-heads at once spread far and wide over these thinly populated plains and were interspersed among the earlier population.[1] Those, however, who pushed on into Europe found themselves enclosed within well-defined natural boundaries. On every hand the fertile plains were here largely occupied by vigorous long-headed population; the central heights were comparatively unoccupied, and though the broad-heads also overflowed into the plains and mingled with the existing population, in these central regions they were able to entrench themselves firmly; here their mental qualities enabled them to flourish; they have been well guarded by nature from invasion, and have never been displaced. Thus it is that the Savoyards and the Swiss are to-day as broad-headed as the tribes—probably while parent-stock—who dwell to the north of the Hindu Kush, while the vast intervening plains of Russia are inhabited by a more mixed race, whose roving disposition and fondness for living on their horses have been noted from the dawn of history. When we realize this we may realize also in what sense and to what extent the Russian is, as he is sometimes called, an Asiatic. From the narrowly European point of view he is Asiatic, from the Asiatic point of view he is European; in reality he is a well-tempered mixture of both the great racial stocks, European long-heads and Asiatic broad-heads.

This conclusion harmonizes with the impression which we receive in travelling through any large extent of Russian territory. Long faces of European type, grave and energetic, are scarcely less common than broad Mongolian faces with somewhat flattened noses, humble, good-natured faces. It rarely happens that either type, as found among the common folk, is beautiful; beauty seems usually to be a late acquisition in the history of a race; the related Pole, whose civilization is ancient, possesses it in a high degree, but Russia is still young, and the vigorous colossal forms one seems to see here so often have something of the crudity and shapelessness of the child. This contrast between the Pole and the Russian is indeed

---

[1] It is probable that the process was not really quite so simple as I have here stated it, but it would be unprofitable to enter into details concerning a migration which is still very imperfectly understood.

striking, and alone suffices to account for the antagonism between them. To wander in the charming Saxony Gardens at Warsaw and to see the women strolling along its alleys with their proud, sensitive carriage, their beautiful hair, their refined, intelligent faces, or else sitting on the benches or at their windows reading—for there are many women in Poland, and they have a notable love of reading—is a delightful experience which can nowhere be repeated in Russia. The refinement of the Poles has penetrated even to the lowest stratum of the population, and the gracious beauty of the women in the market-place at Warsaw, the Zelazna Brama, wholly different from the dazzling superficial beauty of southern women, witnesses to a fine nervous texture matured through ages of civilization. Here we feel the pressure of a race that has lived and suffered, and is even too conscious of the proud dignity that comes of living and suffering. Almost equally remote from the attitude of the Russians is that of their neighbours, the Hungarians, with whom they have some affinity. The Hungarians are also youthful, but they form a compact people which has gained national self-consciousness, and are possessed by a tremendous energy, a great capacity of enjoyment, an eager greediness for life. Everything at Budapest testifies to this: the swiftness of the boats on the Danube and of the silent electric trams fleeting along the streets, the rapidity of the Hungarians' walk, the full bold stare with which men and women alike seem to seek to master your secret with the least possible delay—so unlike the Russians, who intuitively divine you but never stare—the gorgeous display of the ballets in their theatres, the brilliant cafés, the hurried impetuosity of their music, even the fiery dishes they love. Here is passionate energy of life, at full tension, but it is far from the grave, quiet unaroused strength of the Russians. The humble, strenuous, laborious Russians are indeed alive, but they have never yet awakened to more than a dim consciousness of life. They still possess the terrible earnestness of children.

The Russians, as we often fail to realize, are essentially an artistic people. They are artists whose impulse has not tended, like that of the French, to be diffused through the whole of life, but has mostly run along special channels, leaving whole fields of human activity

114

untouched. In that, we may probably say, the Russians reveal that they are still in close contact with a barbarism from which they have only imperfectly emerged. By barbarism, let it be clearly understood, is meant, in the strict sense, a stage of culture, and not a stage of mental and moral inferiority. In the popular sense, it has often been pointed out, the Russians of the last century were the reverse of "barbarians". The most competent and penetrating critics of the Russian character all insist, often indeed using the same words, on the elasticity, the ductibility of the Russian temperament, the complete absence of anything like "German phlegm", its agility of mind and fertility in ideas, its aptitude for assimilation and imitation, its impressionable sensibility and nervous mobility, as of a more barbaric Celt.[1] We have here, it will be seen, a people possessing in a predominant degree the innate aptitudes of the artist. The modern Russians have been barbarians in the same sense that we may say that Shakespeare and the men of his age were barbarians.

The great flowering period of the Russian genius was the nineteenth century. At no earlier date is it possible to find a single Russian whose achievements in any field of art were of European significance. Pushkin was born in 1799, Glinka in 1804. At the end of that century a few Russians of the great period, like Tolstoy and Rimsky-Korsakov, still survived, but the period itself was over. It had given place to an age in which capable and accomplished men flourished in abundance, but not a giant among them all. The nineteenth century, more especially the central portion of that century, is the Russian analogue to the English Elizabethan age.

There are, indeed, instructive points of resemblance, and of difference also, between the great flowering period of England and that of Russia. They both sprang up suddenly on what seems, to a casual glance, a poor and bare soil. They were both very close to a background of barbarism which made itself felt in some of their most characteristic and splendid productions. It is thus that they were both most potently attracted to the artistic medium of words, and both, though inheriting an admirable popular decorative art,

[1] So, for instance, Leroy-Beaulieu (in *L'Empire des Tsars*, vol i), Fouillée (in *Psychologie des Peuples Européens*) and M. Baring (in *The Russian People*).

were indifferent to painting, the English genius for painting only appearing during the second half of the eighteenth century and becoming eccentric, almost extinct, before the end of the nineteenth century, while all the extravagant effects of its artists have not even yet secured for Russia any pictorial art of originality and perfection.[1] For painting is not a democratic art, and both Elizabethan England and nineteenth-century Russia on the artistic side were, in a sense, democratic, slowly developed from the depths of the people's heart. Just as the splendour of Elizabethan drama had slowly germinated during centuries in popular passion plays and mysteries and farces before it was vitalized by Renaissance germs from Italy, so the subtle and daring realism of the modern Russian novel had been prepared by a people with a singular genius for story-telling whose earliest literature is indeed the earliest popular literature in Europe that has survived. So it came about that, as the Elizabethan dramas appealed to the whole Elizabethan population and Elizabethan playhouses were the largest and most sumptuous in Europe, so nowhere has the novel been relatively so largely read, so influential, of such seriously deep import in the public estimation as in Russia, while the operas of the great Russian masters can be sung by peasant choirs to appreciative peasant audiences. There is indeed one respect in which the great period of Russian genius contrasted flagrantly with the Elizabethan period and brings home to us the fact that while both these periods were democratic in origin and expression, they were by no means equally so in the political framework of the states within which they arose. The sturdy English had already won a large measure of self-government from the autocratic Tudors; in Russia the days of self-government belonged to a remote past, and the nineteenth-century outburst of genius arose under conditions of despotic repression which were gaining rather than losing force. In this way it happened that the Elizabethans were free to develop at home with but the slightest official repres-

[1] This can hardly fail to be clear to any intelligent visitor to the Tretyakov Gallery in Moscow. Brückner, in his *History of Russian Literature*, remarks that even in literature the Russians have shown little feeling for landscape and suggests that they have a feeling for man only, and not for nature. But the feeling for man has found no memorable manifestation in Russian painting.

sions; their struggles and their impassioning interests, the battles they fought and the influences they underwent, were in the great world, in France, in Italy, in Spain, in America. The Russians were cut off from the world as they had been cut off for centuries. In place of the fortifying struggle without they were compelled to a more cruel and depressing struggle within, against their own rulers; exile, if not death, has been the most common lot of the finest Russian spirits, and while it may sometimes have given poignancy to their genius it has yet been a terrible calamity.

In no country have the manifestations of genius in art, and the operations of the intellect in general, been developed under such a crushing and almost continuous oppression as in Russia from the date of their earliest manifestations down to the Revolution of yesterday. In all countries men of original genius and pioneers of intellectual progress have been liable to suffer from poverty and neglect, and this has happened in Russia. In most countries also, at some periods, the champions of religious freedom or of political freedom have been persecuted without mercy, and that has happened in Russia. But in most countries the artist has usually found a way of escape from direct persecution by finding his home in a larger world of the spirit beyond religion and beyond politics. But in Russia, with all its vastness, this has not been possible, for Russia has been cut away from European culture, and there has been no world of the spirit, untouched by oppression, for the Russian artist. Therefore he has, by necessity, been revolutionary. Only those artists have been immune who used a medium like music, which could avoid revolutionary interpretation.

The melancholy, resignation and sadness which scarcely seem a prominent part of the primitive Slav character, yet have so deeply marked the artistic productions of the Russians, from their most exalted to their most popular manifestations, that it was possible for Herzen to say that "Sadness, Scepticism and Irony are the three strings of the Russian tale". These characteristics are sometimes ascribed to the climate. The climate may have been a predisposing factor, but it is probable that a still more potent and direct factor has been the crushing oppression of a despotic Tsardom which regarded that whole population as actual or spiritual serfs, and a rigid Church intolerant of any deviation from orthodoxy.

The manifestations of nineteenth-century Russian genius remained, nevertheless, a connected whole precisely as were the manifestations of Elizabethan genius. The Elizabethans remoulded the drama, transformed it into a shape almost like that of opera, in order to bring it into relation with the other forms, and especially music and song, in which their genius was being manifested. In the same way the Russians, developing that popular genius for story-telling they already possessed in the twelfth century produced a prose literature which, while by its simplicity, sincerity and realism it rarely transcended the bounds of prose, was yet adapted to unite with the national genius of music and song and the dance. It is significant that Pushkin, who inaugurated the great period of Russian art, wrote his novel, *Eugene Onegin*, in verse, and the composers of Russia have been constantly inspired in their operas and ballets by the Russian novelists.

This orientation of the art impulse towards song and music, alike in the flowering times of English and of Russian genius, points to a common emotional temperament. The man who makes music is not necessarily a man of emotion, though he often is, but the man who feels music, to the extent that his activity is guided by it, is necessarily emotional. It is probable that a genius period which emerges from a background of barbarism is always emotional. The restraint and repression of emotion is often a mark of savagery, and always of civilization, but it is scarcely a mark of the intermediate stage of barbarism. Among savages the necessity for individual resistance leads to stoical fortitude; among the civilized the social necessity of consideration for others leads to a rather similar attitude; but among barbarians the first motive is no longer insistent and the second is not yet highly developed. In France, where civilization is old and barbarism lies in a remote past, emotionalism has never been a dominating feature of any great art period. But it became possible, even inevitable, in England for Shakespeare in a supreme degree and in a less degree for his followers who were truly representative of their time. Their superb art could easily, as it seemed recklessly, take the form of an overwhelming stream of magnificent emotion.

Intoxicated barbarians, they seemed to the French, and in a sense were, though the wine they had drunk was of the finest vintage of genius. When we find among them a poet, like Ford, who is concentrated in emotion and parsimonious in its expression, we realize that we are in the presence of a modern born out of due time.

It is not surprising that Shakespeare has been a powerful influence in Russia.[1] Pushkin, who inaugurated the great period of Russian genius and remains in some respects its most representative figure, felt the impress alike of Shakespeare and of Byron, a belated and therefore rather wayward and artificial representative of Elizabethan emotion and energy. In many Russian novels, and supremely in the novels of Dostoyevsky, we are restored to a true Elizabethan world, a world of surging emotion, grave and gay, a world with unfathomable inner depths, a world of crime and madness, full of all the terrors of conscience. *Hamlet* is of all Shakespeare's plays the most popular in Russia, the most frequently translated and acted. The nineteenth-century Russian found in *Hamlet* something intimate and familiar. "Hamlet stands nearer to us than any other of Shakespeare's characters," remarked Professor Arabazhin. Of all Shakespeare's characters Hamlet presents the supreme dominance of emotion. Others might, in special circumstances, be swept by mightier waves of emotion, but in Hamlet the dominance of emotion was a fact of his organization. Acute yet not massive in intellect, finely receptive, nobly ideal, infirm of purpose and will, struggling impotently in a political world that was, as he said, "a prison", and throughout all a temperamental artist, every Russian of the nineteenth century who sought to stand upright and be himself felt that he was a Hamlet confronting a Hamlet's fate.[2]

[1] André Lirondelle has written a volume on this influence at the formative time of Russian literature, *Shakespeare en Russie*, 1748–1840, 1912.

[2] Many distinguished Russians have written about Hamlet. Turgenyev, who wrote a characteristic story entitled *Hamlet of Shtchigry*, remarked in an essay on *Hamlet and Don Quixote* that everyone belongs to one of these two types, but that in his time there was a predominance of Hamlets. Herzen was taken by his countrymen, at one time or another, it has been said, for both a Hamlet and a Don Quixote, though Beltov, the hero of his own admirable and largely autobiographical novel, *Who is to Blame?*, is mainly of Hamlet type. The Russian Hamlet is necessarily a special kind of Hamlet, who has been best described by Goncharov in *Oblomov*, so that Russian Hamletism has been appropriately termed *Oblomovschina*.

A great flowering period of art can never arise from a rootless soil. It was not so in Elizabethan England, and it was not so in the nineteenth-century Russia. So far as any great manifestations of art are concerned, Russia was indeed absolutely barren before Pushkin and Glinka arose. Yet no country in Europe had for long centuries been so rich in the nebular folk-elements of great art, and Pushkin began his literary career by retelling folk-tales he had learned from his nurse, while Glinka brought the folk melodies within the sphere of art. We may perhaps even go back to the earliest historical times and to the first emergence of the Slav. The Scythians seem to have been unique among barbarians of their time for their combination of receptivity and originality. The special trait of their original work seems, as we examine its manifestations, to be energy of emotion; this is well illustrated by the outline and attitude of the animals they loved to represent and it is indicated by that passion for song and dance which has marked the Ukrainians of this region even to the present. It must be remembered that modern archaeological research shows that Scythian influence and Scythian culture prevailed right across Russia into Siberia, and that, as Reinecke argues, in the five hundred years before Christ a race uniform with the Scythians extended to the Atlas Mountains and the Yenisei River in central Siberia. We are thus brought towards the River Amur and to the confines of Mongolia, a region in which Russian influences are beginning to prevail now as formerly, it may be, Scythian influences prevailed. Now, the art products of this region have been studied with great care and penetration by Laufer, and he shows (though without stating) that these Siberian Tunguses and other peoples of the Amur in their representation of motion, and in their especial lines for the cock and the fish, show exactly the same springing motion as we may detect among the animals represented by the Scythians, while it is unnecessary to insist on the important place of birds in Russian folklore and art down to to-day.[1] Laufer believes that the love of

[1] Viollet-le-Duc in *L'Art Russe* represent figures of winged women firmly gripping horned animals, of fantastically energetic griffins, etc., as found in the tumulus of Alexandropol in the Ykaterinoslav district.

motion and the attachment to the spiral are primitive in the Siberian mind, not a degeneration from conventionalized animal forms, but more often developing into animal forms. The ability to watch motion is highly developed in the east Asiatic mind. The conception of a fish in the form of a spiral, and more obviously that of the cock, is based, Laufer contends, on a true observation of these animals in their living state, their capacity for motion appealing to a people who were fascinated and irresistibly drawn to motion in art.[1] We may perhaps dispute the views of Laufer as to the exact relation of these peoples' love of motion to their art, but we cannot put aside the evidence this searching and thorough investigator brings forward as to the reality of the Siberian's impulse to express, above all, motion in his art. And what Laufer says of the Siberian we may also say of the primitive Russian.

Nor is it necessary to go as far back as to the days of the Scythians, nor to limit the inquiry to the artists of design, in order to trace a possible, if not probable, relationship with Asia. The delightful and unique folk-stories of the Russian epic cycle, with their mingling of the spirit of the East and of the West, present the same problem, and such distinguished authorities as Stasov and Potanin have been able to maintain the view that these stories came with the Tartars direct from Asia.

The Russian treatment of the essential art of architecture is very instructive in this connection. It cannot be said that the Russians have shown any real originality in this field. But they were surrounded by all sorts of types of architecture, and they have very characteristically affirmed their own temperament in the selection and development of the architectural motives, Eastern and Western, which lay around them. The foundation was Byzantine; that indeed was the inevitable result of the fact that their Church has its home in Byzantium, and was by no means the result of deliberate choice. The low, massive and heavy Byzantine construction presented a superb style, but it was not a style that appealed to the Russians. They rapidly moulded out of it, by the application of light and gay

---

[1] Berthold Laufer, "The Decorative Art of the Amur Tribes", *The Jesup North Pacific Expedition* (*Memoirs* of the American Museum of Natural History), 1902, vol. iv, p. 77.

Eastern motives, a style of their own of a totally different complexion. To the European eye, trained on Greek, Roman and Gothic types of building with their orderly and harmonious development, this Russian architecture seems fantastic and bizarre, scarcely a style at all. We seem to see St. Sophia trying to grow into a Chinese pagoda. Yet in this process the Russian artistic temperament was really affirming itself. We may say indeed that it was losing hold of the central aims of architecture, but, in contrast to the contemporary architecture of France, and Italy and Germany, the Russian architecture of the twelfth century was emancipating itself from heaviness, soaring up into variegated slender shapes of elegance and novelty, instinct with movement, and adding to its external decoration the new charm of brilliant colour. We see that this architecture has lost the expression though not the form of European Byzantine, and yet it has not become entirely Asian; it has been moulded into something distinctively Russian.[1]

In the selection of the arts in which he excels and in the nature of his excellence within those selected arts the Russian alike shows the artistic fascination of motion. The Russian is drawn to all the dynamic arts; the static arts make no appeal to him. Dancing and song, music, story-telling and drama,[2] these are the arts in which he excels. For sculpture, for painting, for the arts of design generally, the arts which hold motion in suspense on balanced equilibrium, for all the arts which offer him no opportunity to be carried out of his fatalistic apathy into a stream of powerful emotion, he has little aptitude and no originality.

This Russian selection among the arts is, indeed, fundamental. Unless we realize it clearly we not only fail to understand the Russian temperament, but the special meaning and fascination of

[1] Milyukov gives a brief but instructive account of the development of Russian architecture, *Skizzen Russischer Kulturgeschichte*, vol. ii, ch. 2, section 2; a more extensive account will be found in Viollet-le-Duc, *L'Art Russe*. The latter author considers that the tendency of Russian buildings to be raised to a height out of proportion to the cramped space they frequently enclose is due to the fact that they arise from plains.

[2] We might have expected to find the drama coming before story-telling. It seems probable that the special circumstances of Russian history and Russian environment have prevented the drama from attaining a development for which there has been no lack of aptitude and inclination.

Russian art must remain a closed book to us. Above all, we shall fail to understand why it is that within their own limits the Russians are a race of artists. To the Russian, for the most part, with all his zest for life and his passion for motion and emotion, real life under the conditions which climatic and social circumstances have combined to prescribe seems pale and wearisome, deceptive and often painful. It stirs his latent possibilities of energy, but the stimulus it offers seldom reaches the intensity necessary to bring him to the point of great action. The Russian of his time, remarked Chekhov in *The Steppes*, has to remember, but he does not love to live. So he remains passive and resigned, finding his consolation either in the idealization of the past or the mystic promise of the future. It is the essential temperament of the artist.

It is this aptitude for emotion—alike for mystical religion and for art in all its forms—that alone offers the key to the Russian's apathetic temperament. Motion and rhythm—from the crude stimulus of vodka and the vigorous iteration of the *trepak* to the subtlest appeals of the ideal dream—stir the indolent Russian more profoundly and more massively than they have ever stirred other people. The Russian language itself is powerfully rhythmic and the Russian system of versification is rhythmic and not syllabic. How fundamentally this characteristic is based on the physical love of violent motion we may realize by remembering how that attraction of crude rhythmic motion has always prevailed in Russia. It is illustrated, for instance, by the ancient delight in swings which four hundred years ago attracted the attention of the German traveller, Baron Herberstein, as a remarkable novelty, and he describes how the women in Moscow go on holidays to the meadows and seat themselves on a sort of wheel of fortune, and are moved alternatively up and down, or they fasten a rope somewhere with a seat to it in which they sit and are swung backwards and forwards as they otherwise make merry with clapping their hands.[1] In this sort of wheel of fortune we seem to have the origin

---

[1] Herberstein, *Notes upon Russia* (Hakluyt Society), vol. i, p. 94. Herberstein added that there was no dancing; in explanation of this it must be remembered that the Russian then sought pitilessly to repress anything "pagan".

of the "Montagnes Russes" which have now spread over the world under such names as "switch-back", and are still much appreciated in Russia itself; I recall being invited by a highly cultivated Russian and his wife near Moscow to enter a switch-back with them, and their enjoyment of the experience.

It is, however, not only in the selection of the arts in which he excels but in the nature of his excellence within these selected arts that this characteristic is clearly to be seen. It marks modern Russian literature from the start. In Pushkin motion, rapidity of movement, the dramatic spirit, are in the highest degree marked. The same characteristic is in Russian architecture as it developed out of the heavier Byzantine; "a delightful effect of free movement characterizes Russian architecture," Harold Williams has well said. In the ancient folk-music, as we should expect, this special emphasis of motion is noted, and by musical historians who seem never to have suspected that they were in contact with a profound Russian characteristic. Russian musical authorities speak of the "fantastic leaps and bounds" in Russian folk-music, its "graceful decorative outline", its "opening up of distant horizons", the "tireless leisurely stride of its rhythms". It is interesting to find experts making these statements as to Russian folk-music, since, from a broader standpoint, we may find precisely these characteristics, on the one hand in the general activities of the Russian when released from the bondage of his daily life, and, on the other hand, we scarcely fail to note that these same characteristics have continued to mark Russian music even in the most splendid phases of its nineteenth-century development. We find, indeed, not only the same poignant and haunting melancholy of the folk-music in the great Russian composers, but all the characters of that primitive music which its students have noted—its energetic dance rhythm, the masculinity of its sweeping melodies, its march-like procession through immense space, its orgiastic intoxications—come to us again, exalted into shapes of magnificent splendour, in Musorgsky and Borodin and Rimsky-Korsakov and Tchaikovsky; for Tchaikovsky, whatever may be said of his international tendencies, is Russian, characteristically Russian, as even is Rubinstein, and we can scarcely find the tramp of people over vast plains, which is the whole history of Russia, so well represented as in Rubinstein's *Tower of Babel*.

This continuation of the spirit of ancient Russian folk-music in modern Russian music is probably well recognized and is certainly fairly obvious. There is another extension of the spirit of primitive Slav music which is less obvious and less recognized. Nietzsche long since pointed out that many of the great German composers are really of Slav origin, having sprung, that is to say, from districts in Germany or Austria where an ancient Slav element predominated.[1] He never developed the point in detail and he never argued that the Slav origin of these composers could be traced in their work. It is highly probable, however, that Slav traits could be traced by a competent investigator in the great German composers of Slav origin, although we should expect such traits to be usually too deep-lying, and too highly transformed, for easy recognition. I will only refer to one case, that of Handel. Long before I had even thought of Handel in this connection, in listening to his music it would happen that the instinctive mental image would come before me of a giant painting frescoes upon a vast wall with a swift and sweeping brush. It is the kind of impression which Russian music produces upon us again and again; that in Handel's case the visual image should be particularly clear is merely due to the fact that he was himself, far beyond what is usual in musicians, a visualizer, who saw the world in pictures, and in his music is constantly descriptive. Handel's work seems to show, indeed, all the characteristics of primitive Slav folk-music; his sanguine temperamental attitude was remote from the resigned and melancholic Russian's, but in music they were at one. Here are the same leaps and bounds of emphatic rhythm, the same large melodic outlines, the same senses of space, the same orgiastic excitation. We may indeed, say that Handel carried the genius of Slav music to a height

[1] Brahms is usually reckoned as the most conspicuous exception to this rule, and certainly it would not be easy to find the Slav characteristics in his work. But while Brahms mainly belongs by blood to the north-western and most purely Germanic corner of Germany (see May Florence, *Life of Johannes Brahms*), it must not be forgotten that his great grandfather came from Hanover, into which the Slav element which covers Silesia and Saxony at many points penetrates, as is, for instance, indicated by Ripley's map of the relative frequency of brunette types in Germany.

never attained by the Russians, who seem but inspired amateurs by his side. Yet he is moved by their spirit and, like them, he also, instinctively and deliberately, rejected church music and always clung, so far as England allowed him, to the theatre and the atmosphere of the theatre, even in his oratorios. Now Handel was born a German, but his paternal grandfather had come from Silesia, a province permeated by Slav blood, to settle in Halle, which is one of the most profoundly Slavonized districts of Saxony, and his mother belonged to Halle.[1]

We must not, however, suppose that the developed Russian music of the nineteenth century arose directly out of primitive Slav music any more than out of the trivial operatic music of the French then fashionable in Russia. The great Russian composers of that century were indifferent to the Church, but without the Church they could scarcely have existed. For centuries the Russian Church had fostered and developed liturgical music, though, as in other arts, its inspirations were foreign and not native. This church music lent itself to adaptation by the secular composers through the very fact that limited it, the fact that it was purely vocal, the Eastern ecclesiastical tradition not allowing the use of instruments. Hence its splendid choral effects and the magnificent manner in which it has utilized the deep rich Russian bass, and its incomparable accents of emotional appeal and persuasive command. This liturgical singing of the male voice, when heard at its best in Moscow and Petrograd, it has been truly said, "surpasses in dignity and grandeur any church music in the world". In the great Russian composers, and notably in Musorgsky, we clearly realize not only the indirect results of the ecclesiastical development of music, but the direct chromatic inspiration which comes from that liturgical music.

It is not out of place to remark that the rites of the Eastern Church, even apart from their musical aspects, can scarcely have been without significance alike as a manifestation and an inspiration of the Russian aptitude for art. The Russian Church has no conspicuous spiritual

[1] The characteristics of Handel's work are well brought out in the attractive little monograph devoted to that composer by Romain Rolland, who, clearly, never realized the Slav element in Handel. Nor, so far as I know, has anyone else.

function; its priests are men of humble social rank and they are seldom called upon to act as directors of conscience. But the sacerdotal impersonal function of the Russian priest is enormous, and his almost magical incantations are omnipresent. In every circumstance of life he is called upon, and the Russian people are constantly overshadowed by a shimmer of gold, the waving of rich vestments, the vision of variegated ikons, the red glimmer of smoky candles, the echo of deep liturgical chants—all the mystery of these hieratic rites which Byzantium inherited from the sombre Orient. To anyone moderately familiar with the Mass of the Western Church the liturgy of the Eastern Church can scarcely fail to seem a revelation. The Mass, it is true, is the development of an ancient drama still full of mystery and beauty and the haunting appeal of antiquity, but that development has taken place in a centre exposed to many streams of influences and perpetual modifications; accretions and worldly compromises have so affected it that its unity has become complicated and its dramatic meaning can often only be clear to the initiated spectator. The Eastern liturgy is also full of ancient symbolism, so ancient that the Church itself is not always clear as to its meaning, but the rigid orthodoxy of the Eastern Church, for which the Pope of Rome is merely a heretic, and its conservative traditionalism preserve the primitive Christian rites which came to it from Byzantium a thousand years ago. The result is that the liturgy remains in a high degree a Sacred Mystery in which the two elements of Drama and Worship are alike emphasized. These effects are heightened by the Eastern church building with its raised stage on which the singers stand at each end, while the reader's ambo is in the middle and behind the ikonostas, the richly ornamented screen with its holy doors, through which the priests pass to consummate the rite at the altar concealed from the worshippers in the church. They are heightened also by the romantic appearance of the long-haired and bearded priests and the erect or kneeling attitude which is obligatory on the worshippers, by the absence of the sermon which is always an element of weakness in Western ritual, and, above all, by that pervading element of deep and vibrant choral music which suits so well this liturgy, alike as

Worship and as Drama. There are no people in Europe so devoted to primitive ritual as the Russians, and in their churches, we may be sure, they were unconsciously training themselves in the elements of that art centuries before that art took place.

It is universally acknowledged that this efflorescence began with the performance of Glinka's *A Life for the Tsar*, in 1836, and his masterpiece, *Ruslan and Lyudmila*, in 1842. Glinka was born (in 1804) into a pale and thin musical world nourished on feeble imitations of fashionable French composers like Boieldieu and Grétry. It was, by a kind of religious communion, that when past the age of thirty he found the new path. Against the background of his time his operas glow with a new vitality and brilliance which has now grown dimmer, so that his work seems conventional and old-fashioned compared to that of his followers. He not only worked on a larger scale but with original melodic outlines and new orchestral colour. He introduced the Russian folk-melody, and, going beyond even Slav elements, he also utilized those oriental elements which have ever since had an attraction for Russian composers. Glinka's work was, it has been said, a palace erected in the desert, and, while it caused considerable sensation, its reception was by no means altogether favourable: it seemed too vulgar and plebeian for fashionable and refined people. Italian opera, then coming into favour, received more applause, and the discouraged Glinka wrote no more and died in 1857. How little impression he had made on his unfavourable environment is shown by the fact that it was not until the year before Glinka died that Dargomyjsky, who was only nine years younger, took the next forward step with his *Rusalka* (Undine), and that also was received so coldly that, like Glinka, he was discouraged, and wrote no more for twenty years. Yet with *Rusalka* the pioneering work of the national Russian school of music was completed. Glinka had brought in the lyrical and epic elements; Dargomyjsky introduced the dramatic and comic elements. "I wish the sound to express directly the sense of the words," he wrote. "I seek truth." Russian music, like all other Russian arts, Milyukov remarks, seeks to be realistic. Inspired, like Glinka, by popular music, and lacking Glinka's melodic aptitude,

Dargomyjsky triumphed in his recitative and his choral movements.

The way was now prepared for the great national masters of Russian music: Musorgsky, Caesar Cui, Borodin, Rimsky-Korsakov. They grouped themselves towards the middle of the century round a man of deep artistic feeling, fine critical insight, and much musical erudition, Balakirev. This group of highly educated men, interested in art and literature and philosophy as well as in music, were bound together by the same sympathy and admiration and sometimes even composed in common, yet each respected the individuality of the other. One name, and the best known of all, is missing—that of Tchaikovsky. He was educated, as later was Glazunov, at the Conservatoire of St. Petersburg, which was under the direction of Rubinstein, and there was a certain amount of hostility between the new group and the conservatives of the Conservatoire. But Rubenstein, himself, stood aloof from polemics, and Tchaikovsky was always sympathetic towards the Balakirev group. It is as an echo of that old dispute that we still find it sometimes stated that Tchaikovsky was not really of the Russian school at all. That can by no means be accepted. However closely his training may have brought him in touch with the traditional methods of Germany, any instructed person, if we could imagine such, who had never heard of Tchaikovsky could not fail, on listening to his music for the first time, to be aware that he was in the presence of a composer deeply and distinctively Russian. His intimacy, his complacent abandonment to melancholy, the outlines of his melody, his sudden outbursts of reckless violence, even his superb Fifth Symphony, all reveal the Russian. Yet it is undeniably true that the complete and authentic voice of Russia is heard not in Tchaikovsky but in Musorgsky and Borodin.

The men of this group come before us in their splendid strength, not out of any tradition, but rather as daring amateurs of genius, much in the same way as at the same time the English Pre-Raphaelites were creating a school of their own in painting. Like the Pre-Raphaelites, the Russians chose their own traditions, and it is significant that among all European composers they chose for special admiration precisely those two, little known at the time, with whom they had most affinity, Berlioz and Liszt, and thereby marked also the emotional romantic character of their school. They were largely amateurs in a literal sense, men not trained to music or men whose mind and racial origin hardly seemed to indicate them as fitted for a severe training in art. Glinka was a Government official, as for a time also was Dargomyjsky. Musorgsky began life as a military officer with the reputation of an elegant dandy who would gracefully play fragments of *Il Trovatore* to an admiring feminine auditory. Rimsky-Korsakov was a naval officer. Tchaikovsky, whose mother was of old Hugenot family, was educated to be a lawyer (as later was Cherepnin). Borodin was a distinguished chemist and with only very remote musical associations, being the illegitimate son of a Georgian princess whose family claimed to be the descendants of King David and quartered the harp and sling in their arms. Caesar Cui was of mixed race, being the son of a Frenchman by a Lithuanian mother. He rose to the rank of lieutenant-general in the army, and was a professor of military engineering, the author of various important works on fortification. But with all their difference of training and race these men attained completely a harmonious blend of musical production which by its direct force, its realism, its sincerity, its intimacy, and the national elements from which it drew its vitality and character, became not only one of the chief glories of Russian achievement but a pinnacle in European art.

Between Musorgsky's *Boris Godunov* and *The Golden Cockerel*, the last important work of Rimsky-Korsakov, less than half a century elasped. Within this period all the great music of Russia was produced. Glazunov, Rimsky-Korsakov's pupil, became the chief representative of Russian music, an accomplished representative, but European rather than Russian in character, and certainly not of the race of the giants. The other recent Russian composers have, for the most part, been of still narrower calibre, however interesting and attractive sometimes as experimentalists on a small scale. Not of these men could Nietzsche have written: "I would exchange the music of all the West for the Russian way of being sad."[1]

---

[1] Nietzsche, *Werke*, Bk. xiv, p. 142.

Thus we see that, alike in music as in literature, the two great fields in which the Russian has chiefly revealed his genius for art, energy has fallen to a lower level and a superb flowing period has come to an end. It is a phenomenon which is invariably witnessed, for it lies in Nature, and the great period of Russia in art has lasted much longer than the singularly brief though more splendid Elizabethan period in England. Such a phenomenon is not evidence of fundamental failure. We may be sure that the Russian genius for art will take new flights. In the meanwhile there are other tasks which—as we may agree with Gorky in believing—must be regarded as more immediately urgent.

Although the drama has not in Russia reached the same height or the same extension as music and the novel, it yet remains an important, interesting and, indeed, characteristic link between them, beneficial in more than one direction, for the great Russian composers have constantly been inspired by drama and, in turn, produced dramatic operas, while the great novelists, from Gogol to Chekhov, have written dramas. There seems, indeed, to be really a special dramatic aptitude in the Russian, and his emotional depth, his sincerity, his naturalism, his psychological insight, his artistic temperament have all combined to make the Russian drama popular and successful, while there have been a succession of powerful Russian actors, down to Varlamov and Madame Savina, who might have attained to European fame had they possessed the opportunities which Chaliapin has owed to the fact that his dramatic ability was manifested in opera. How native and natural the drama is in Russia is shown by the fact that the first permanent Russian theatre arose not in the capital by court patronage, but in a provincial town, Yaroslavl, in the middle of the eighteenth century. How admirably the drama lends itself to the artist in the Russian is shown by the achievements of the Moscow Arts Theatre—the Rebels' Theatre, as it was formerly called—which was founded in 1898. Its moving spirit was Stanislavsky, whose grandmother was a French actress, a fact to which we must certainly attach significance although this institution remains primarily Russian. It may well have been that the Arts Theatre of Moscow was suggested by the Théâtre

Libre of Paris, where Antoine was working for the ends of art in the same high spirit and the same thoroughness. Stanislavsky, also, like Antoine, at first devoted much attention to Ibsen. The chief success of the Arts Theatre has, however, been with the plays of Chekhov. Here the Moscow Arts Theatre was enabled to become completely and genuinely Russian and to combine the delicate interpretation of characteristically Russian works of genius with a patient care for the technique which disregarded all money-making aims, although worldly success was, in due course, attained.[1] Notwithstanding the dramatic aptitude of the Russian people, and the facility with which the great Russian writers seem to have produced dramas, there are yet few Russian plays of the highest class, mostly comedies, and there is no great Russian dramatist. Ostrovsky is usually regarded as the most conspicuous dramatist of Russia, and his vigorous and copious dramatic power is undisputed and easily to be traced in the translations of his plays. But not even Russians seem inclined to claim for Ostrovsky any place among the great dramatists of Europe. It would seem that it was to the form of the novel that the Russian imaginative writers of the nineteenth century first and instinctively turned, and only in the second place to the play, exactly the reverse of what we find among the Elizabethan imaginative writers for whom the play was everything and the novel scarcely had an existence at all.

The ballet in Russia may claim to take a place beside the drama in a higher degree than in any other country. The best Russian composers have written ballet music, the stories on which ballets are in Russia founded are largely definite and coherent, sometimes national stories, and the whole conception of the ballet has been developed, broadened and vitalized to a greater extent than elsewhere. It is sometimes said that, however marked the Russian aptitude for dancing may be, the Russian ballet is an imported product. It is true that the ballet was in the eighteenth century brought into Russia from France, as at an earlier period it had been brought into France from Italy. But in the soil of the Russian spirit ballet has

[1] Many accounts of the Moscow Arts Theatre have been published; see, for instance, *Russian Review*, 1912, no. 3.

developed into a highly artistic transformation of those special qualities of simplicity, sincerity, dramatic realism and natural emotion which mark the other finest manifestations of Russian genius. Although as a medium of art it has not sprung out of the popular Russian passion for dancing—any more than the classic and Renaissance forms of the Elizabethan drama sprang out of the popular English love of play-acting—yet it has been vitalized by that passion, and we are justified in regarding the Russian ballet as specially Russian and its ultimate developments as the most exquisite form of ballet yet attained. The Russian Ballet Theatre of Diaghilev and Fokin and Bakst is comparable to the Moscow Arts Theatre of Stanislavsky—the best in Europe in the opinion of many —both alike bearing witness to the prime adaptability of the Russian artistic temperament and the exquisite perfection of the results it is able to achieve.

We reach at length the art of the novel in which the Russian genius finds at once its largest and most concentrated expression, summing up here indeed all those manifestations which elsewhere are more impartially distributed over a variety of literary forms: its poetry, its philosophy, its religion, its morals, its social theory, its politics, its history. "Literature," it has been said—and by "literature" is here meant mainly the novel—"has been in Russia the field in which all the battles of progress have been fought." That has come about partly through natural aptitude and temperament and partly through the conditions of life in Russia, which for three centuries made it highly dangerous to express real convictions in any form but that of fiction. The combined result of these two factors has been that nowhere else has the novel ever been so influential a factor in a people's life as in nineteenth-century Russia. In considering the Russian special aptitude for fiction it is interesting to note the high degree to which in Russian literature poetry has become embodied in the novel. Certainly there are Russian poets. There are, to name the best-known, Pushkin, Lermontov, Nekrasov. At the outset one may note that not one of these poets was by race pure Russian. Not only were they themselves partly foreign, but they were for the most part considerably influenced by foreign models. It is remarkable again that the works of these poets are often really versified novels, notably Pushkin's *Eugene Onegin* (which is commonly regarded by the historians of Russian literature as "the first Russian novel"). Both Pushkin and Lermontov also wrote real novels in prose, and those of Pushkin are, indeed, of such importance that he is often regarded as the real founder of the Russian novel. It may be added that the position of Nekrasov is still disputed, even in Russia, and it is admitted even by his admirers that he wrote verse with great difficulty and is a very unequal writer. We have to recognize that even, as Brückner, the historian of Russian literature, admits, the Russian is by temperament sober, realistic, sceptical; he laughs at German enthusiasm and exaggeration; he is profoundly interested in man but not in the visible world of Nature; compelled by the severe conditions of his climate to be Nature's enemy during the long winter and Nature's slave during the brief summer, he has little time to become Nature's poet.

We are not called upon, however, to dispute the quantity or the quality of Russian poetry; the beauty and inspiration of much of it, from the impassioned lyrics of Pushkin onwards, may be more or less appreciated even in translation. Yet we may well maintain that it is in their prose that the Russians have shown themselves to be most truly poets. In every one of the great Russian novelists of the nineteenth century, down to Chekhov, there was a poet, and often a profound, exquisite and subtle poet. To the discriminating reader the poet in these novelists is all the more remarkable because reserved and seemingly unconscious, never reduced to the trickeries of "poetic prose", never even emphasized, except possibly in Sologub, the latest of all and the most remote from the great tradition.

The novelists, certainly the English novelists, who have most influenced the Russians are—often Scott who influenced the whole European novel—Sterne and Dickens. But the Russians rarely or never exhibit the extravagance of the sentimentalism which marks the English writers. Even when clearly of no greater genius than the English writers, and much less original, they yet possessed a sense of measure and harmony which the Englishmen lacked, the outcome of precisely that instinctively artistic temperament which we have to recognize as characterizing the Russian. It is manifested indeed in the most primitive traditional stories of Russia, in the epic songs, where we find, for instance, that the young Indian prince proudly refers to the sweet mead and old liquors in his mother's vaults at home, so beautifully ventilated that "the silver casks rock in their chains and murmur like swans at play upon the bosom of quiet boys".

The great efflorescence of Russian literature of the nineteenth century began a few years earlier than that of music, as we should expect in the case of an art which requires less preliminary technical training. Pushkin was born in 1799, five years earlier than Glinka, and *Eugene Onegin* appeared in 1831, five years earlier than *A Life for the Tsar*. Before Pushkin there is not a single figure in Russian literature to arouse general European enthusiastic admiration. Yet it would be a mistake to suppose that the way had not been prepared for that nineteenth-century outburst. The tedious pioneers of Russian imaginative literature were just as important as the humble pioneers of Russian music. Not indeed that they were all tedious, for the folk-literature of Russia is the most vivacious and fascinating of all Europe. We feel in it, as we feel in the Russia it expresses, both the East and the West. On the one hand it touches the *Arabian Nights*, on the other the *Mabinogion* and the *Morte d'Arthur*. Yet it remains throughout unique, essentially Russian, with the special qualities of the Russian genius, its latent poetry, its imaginative vivacity, its movement and spaciousness, its democratic feeling, its humanity and tenderness, its underlying mystery and melancholy, even its idealization of the joys of drink.[1]

The *byliny*, or epic songs of Russia, celebrating the great achievements of the ancient Russia heroes or *bogatyrs*, are not only unique

[1] See, especially, Isabel Hapgood's delightful *Epic Songs of Russia*. Rambaud's *La Russie Epique*, though not recent, is an interesting study of this literature. It is interesting to compare the epic stories of the Northern Slavs of Russia with the rich and beautiful traditional stories—entirely distinct though with much of the same fundamental character—of the Southern Slavs of Serbia, as revealed in Petrovitch's *Hero Tales and Legends of the Serbians*.

in Europe in their quality, they are unique in their survival to modern times as a living possession of the people. They were indeed long since driven away from Kiev, the early centre of Russian primitives, where they arose, by successive invasions which have swept the south, but they were carried north and found at last an inaccessible home—protected even from the Church, which always pursued the manifestations of the joyous Russian spirit of early days—towards the White Sea. It was amid the impassable swamps and forests of Olonets, to the north of Petrograd, that the scientific investigators of the early nineteenth century at last traced the songs of Vladimir of Kiev and his heroes—counterpart of Arthur and his Round Table—still sung from the mouths of the peasant bards as a living reality. In this respect, as in so much else, several centuries lie between the culture of Russia and that of Western Europe.

There has been much dispute as to the origin of the *byliny*. For some they have been the actual songs of the days of Vladimir in ninth-century Kiev. For the disciples of Grimm they were still more ancient, and represent fragments of a primitive Slav mythology personifying the forces of Nature. Later Stasov, whose followers carried his doctrines to an extreme, argued and indeed clearly showed that the Russian epic songs embody familiar Eastern legends and present well-known Eastern heroes, like Rustam and Krishna. We must probably recognize that there is some truth in all these theories. The Russian epic songs are really moulded from the very diverse sources to which the Russian plains lay open. But they represent the plastic genius of the Russian himself, welding them into a distinctive, beautiful and unique whole, his own special temperament repressing alike the Scandinavian spirit of bloodshed and revenge, the oriental spirit of imaginative extravagance, and impressing on them his own special spirit of humanity, of poetry, and of drama.

Thus the *byliny* furnished fundamental evidence of the genius of the Russians for great literature and of the continued vitality of that genius. Yet until the seventeenth century nothing came of this fruitful soil, and what appeared during that and the succeeding centuries is of more interest to the historical student of origins than to the lovers of literature. So that the greatest of the Slav peoples was the last of all to evolve a true literature; Serbia, Bulgaria, Bohemia had on this path long preceded Russia, while Poland had contended in culture almost as an equal with the great nations of Europe. Even the Russian language itself had yet to be moulded, alike for the purposes of prose and verse, when towards the end of the seventeenth century Peter the Great became Tsar, and the process was continued during most of the eighteenth century. But it was a process which in Germany had been accomplished in the sixteenth century; in England, where the process was completed about the same time, Chaucer had arrived long before; and in Italy and in Spain and in France the origins lie still further back. But during the whole eighteenth century in Russia plodding pioneers were tentatively feeling their way in the language, and the literature they produced was for the most part merely the feeble imitation of foreign models, English or German or French.

English literature, it may be remarked, has always exerted special attraction and influence in Russia, and although on the surface English and Russian ideas and habits are widely unlike, the deeper intimate spirit of the English genius, as revealed not only in political institutions but in literature, seems to appeal more strongly to the Russian than that of any other nation. That still remains true of recent times; in 1889 a special investigation made in Kharkov showed that of foreign authors the most popular were Dickens, H. B. Stowe and Shakespeare.[1] Lomonosov, however, the huge, rough peasant from Archangel who early in the eighteenth century effected so much in moulding the language into a medium for literature and also in extolling Russian science ("a university in himself", he was called), may be said to have derived his chief early inspiration from Germany into which land he had in youth wandered. His contemporary, Sumarokov, the first professional literary man in Russia, derived all his training and methods from France, because he belonged to the nobility which has in Russia for two centuries always favoured a French education, although French influence has exerted no permeating effect in the Russian soil; he was a copious, versatile

[1] L. Wiener, *An Interpretation of the Russian People*, p. 185.

and conceited author of little value, but highly esteemed until Karamzin arose and undermined his reputation. Karamzin, with whom at last we reach the threshold of true Russian literature, was mainly English in his enthusiasms. He had visited England and written of it with appreciation in his *Letters of a Russian Traveller* in 1791. To him the English were, as he wrote later in one of his novels, "the most celebrated nation in Europe". Influenced by the English, Karamzin first introduced a direct·simplicity into the conventional and artificial efforts of Russian writers to attain style, although his simplicity sometimes took on the form of sentimental and feminine sensibility which for a time prevailed in England and had been inspired by Rousseau. At the same time he was the first notable historian of Russia. He it was, someone has said, who created the Russian reading public. The way was at last prepared for the genius of Russian literature.

It would seem that the soil of the Russian spirit had so long laid fallow for literature, it had become so rigid and unyielding, its growth had been so superficial and so trivial, that it required not only men of potent genius but men who possessed the fresh originality of partly alien ancestry to drive the ploughshare deep into the apparently barren soil and to bring to fruition a splendid and genuine growth of true Russian literature. Certainly these conditions were fulfilled by the great initiator of Russian literature, Pushkin, who was the son of an aristocratic Russian father (with remote Prussian and Italian ancestral elements) and a beautiful mother whose grandfather had been a full-blooded Negro in the service of Peter the Great; while Lermontov, who shares with Pushkin some of the initiator's glory, was the scion of Scotch Learmonths who came to Russia through Poland in the seventeenth century. The same phenomenon has been witnessed in the previous century, for Prince Kantemir, the first Russian satirist and a writer of remarkable freedom, was the son of a Moldavian king and a Greek woman. Radishchev, another satirist and political writer, who occupies a distinguished and honourable place in the eighteenth century, and through his opposition to serfdom and his advanced opinions came to a tragic end, was of Tartar descent; and Denis Fonvizin, whose comedies were such a revelation to his eighteenth-century contemporaries that he may fairly be called the creator of the Russian drama, while he also initiated the realistic impulse in Russian literature, was of German extraction.

Yet with Pushkin, for the first time, the free spirit of genius certainly entered Russian literature, liberated from the fetters of tradition, moulding speech in accordance with the inspiration of its own originating will. This by no means meant that Pushkin disdained the pioneering work of his predecessors; on the contrary, it was only through their efforts that he became possible, and his verse is the medium forged by Lomonosov, now for the first time quickened by genius. Nor was Pushkin impermeable to foreign influence; he was profoundly influenced by Byron, whose romantic influence was indeed considerable in Russia because, as Wiener remarks, Russian literature is "essentially a literature of *bogatyrs*". But then Pushkin, with all his enthusiasm for Byron, had little affinity with the English poets; he remained Russian and himself. No great or profound thinker, though a keen and independent critic and a brilliant and fascinating personality, he created and carried to its finest heights the Russian lyric, which in his hands recalls the earlier lyrics of Heine,[1] and he was in the modern sense the first Russian novelist. In Pushkin the great artist for the first time appears in Russia; however superficial, however indifferent to the deeper problems of life, he was yet simple and spontaneous, at once a master of form and a master of the heart. He possessed also all the versatility of the artist as well as the artist's licentiousness in life and work. Like the wise cat in his own *Ruslan and Lyudmila*, chained by a chain of gold to the green oak, singing songs when it goes to the right and telling tales when it goes to the left, he was not only the first of Russian poets, but the first of Russian novelists, even by the introduction of the element of realism, so that it has been possible to say that Turgenyev and Tolstoy descend in a much more direct line from Pushkin than from Gogol. This latter statement it is,

[1] The little book of *Poems* by Pushkin, literally translated by Ivan Panin, may assist the English reader to reconstruct for himself in imagination the lyrical spontaneity of the original.

however, difficult to accept, for Pushkin's stories with their dash of romanticism, their high spirits, their Western air, seem nearer in tone to Stendhal or even Balzac than to Turgenyev and Tolstoy, though it must be noted that Tolstoy regarded Pushkin's prose works as his best.

Lermontov, who was more of the school of Shelley than of Byron, by his *Hero of Our Own Time*, also wrote what has been called "the first Russian psychological novel". It is significant of the tendency of the Russian creative imagination that its first poets should also be its first novelists. Gogol was not a poet, and that perhaps was why he was able to fling away for ever those last shreds of romanticism, to which Pushkin and Lermontov alike clung; the latent poet in every Russian in him remained defused in emotion or etherealized in atmosphere. "The splendid Pushkin," as Turgenyev termed him, brilliant, versatile, rather superficial, and the serious and intense Lermontov, unlike as they were to each other with all their Russianism, were still also rather exotic, so producing an ambiguous effect; and with all their licence they wear the pose of an antiquated fashion which has limited their continuous popularity in Russia and made them little more than great names in the world of international literature. With Gogol, who was more exclusively and intensely Russian than either, Russian literature enters that higher sphere of art which is independent of accidents of time and space. Gogol's masterpiece, *Dead Souls*, remains the central novel of Russia, the Russian *Don Quixote* or *Robinson Crusoe*, and it is characteristic that its hero is a simple-minded rascal, and a failure even at that. *The Cloak*, which is perhaps his most typical story, is merely the simple record of the trivial tragedy of a poor government official whose coat was worn out and who was scarcely rich enough to afford a new one, yet written with such immortal art that it was possible for Dostoyevsky to say that all Russian fiction has its origin in *The Cloak*. Himself, like his poor threadbare functionary, a sensitive, suffering, morbid creature, in the end almost or quite insane, alternately fleeing from life and boldly facing it.[1] Gogol

---

[1] I may refer to a suggestive and helpful, if not perhaps always convincing, study written from the standpoint of Adlerian psycho-analysis, Otto Kaus, *Der Fall Gogol*. Munich, 1912.

founded an art of delicate and penetrating realism which fastened on to the humble things and the humble people in life, revealing them for the first time in a true and clear light which had in it no vestige of sentimentality. So Gogol leads straight to the heart of Dostoyevsky and is part of the Russian spirit, as it seems to us, which may be traced in all the leading Russian novelists of the nineteenth century who came after him. With Gogol the Russian novel was in form and spirit established. Nothing remained but to give it perfection, and depth, and greatness.

This was the task performed by the three European figures of Russian literature, Turgenyev, Dostoyevsky and Tolstoy, with whom we may name, if on a slightly lower level, Goncharov and Chekhov. In Turgenyev—though he bore a name that is of Tartar origin—the Russian genius attained the finest climax of art it has ever reached; no Russian, it is generally agreed, has possessed a more exquisite mastery of the language, none a more sensitive penetration of character or a more refined strength in presenting it. He has been termed the "Russian prose Pushkin". All the haunting fragrance of the Russian spirit was expressed in purest essence by that delicate giant of whom Goncourt in his *Journal* has given so many fascinating glimpses, and we may return again with undiminished joy to the beautiful series of his books, from the first revelation of natural life and of unnatural serfdom in the *Sportsman's Note-Book*, to the last exquisite prose poems of *Senilia*.

Dostoyevsky plunges us into an altogether different world: Turgenyev had absorbed all the culture of the West while yet remaining himself. Dostoyevsky was a Russian of Russians, so Russian that for many of his own countrymen, eagerly seeking to enlarge the national outlook—as, for example, Kropotkin—his best and most characteristic books are unreadable, while for many outside Russia, untouched by this prejudice, he seems not only the deepest and most significant spirit in the entire range of Russian genius, but the greatest novelist of the whole world. The genius of Dostoyevsky is so naked and extraordinary, so entrenched in the sphere of instinct and emotion, that it has sometimes aroused critics to extravagant utterances. It is perhaps enough here to say that in certain aspects it recalls Shakespeare. It is true that Shakespeare was a supreme and deliberate artist, while the epileptic Dostoyevsky, battered by poverty and disease, was only an artist by fits and starts. It is also true that Shakespeare was a fundamental and inevitable poet, while Dostoyevsky was scarcely a poet at all, such poetry as lay in his temperament being transformed into religious mysticism. But, in addition, Shakespeare evoked the incomparable dramatic vision of elemental, barbaric, incalculably impulsive souls—Lear and Macbeth and Othello and Falstaff and Hamlet—and he moved instinctively and familiarly among those violent and subtle souls, manipulating them at a touch, so that they were never too huge, never too delicate for his mastery. We do not see the vision of such souls in England to-day. But we see them in the pages of this Russian, and we see, with a thrill of wonderment, that Dostoyevsky moves as intimately and familiarly among elemental, barbaric, emotional souls as Shakespeare, manipulating them perhaps with an even greater sureness and precision of touch. That is enough to ensure Dostoyevsky's immortality.

It is, however, in Tolstoy, that the Russian genius for the novel attains its complete expansion. Dostoyevsky had never known by experience the normal life of humanity. Notwithstanding his profound insight into the soul, above all his own soul, he looked at the world from the outside, he was the spectator of life. He knew the soul so well because it was only in the soul that he lived. Tolstoy comes before us as a great artist who was a normal man—in so far as an artist can be normal—and who had lived the full life of a normal man in its whole gamut, from the life of war and pleasure to the life of meditation and devotion. He had lived as a noble and as a peasant, he had mixed intimately alike with society and with nature. So that at all points he faced life as an equal, who knew it by experience, who had learned its secrets, and could with equal ease alike either disengage its most delicate aroma or penetrate with calm and lucid cruelty to its utmost heart; his vision penetrated to the core of life with the same admirable precision with which it rested on the surface of life. Thus he was so great an artist because he was so great a master of the secrets of life and for the same reason so great a teacher. He stood before the world as the supreme representative of Russian genius and the chief exponent of the moral message implicit in the Russian soul. Both as artist and prophet, by force of being Russian to the largest and fullest extent, he was not only the most popular author of his time in Russia, he transcended Russia and became universal. He was the most towering figure in the spiritual world of his time; no other voice reached so far, no other man was regarded with such reverence. The influence of Tolstoy cannot be compared with the influence of Rousseau in revolutionary magnitude and originality, but it may be doubted whether there has been any spiritual force in the world since Rousseau so powerful as that of Tolstoy. It is significant that Tolstoy was inspired by Rousseau whom he adored. It is indeed this very fact that Tolstoy was not so original as thinker and teacher as he was as artist that makes him a less significant figure in the world's history than he would otherwise have been; as is the case with so many other leading Russians his greatness is less in the sphere of intellect than in that of instinct and emotion; as to ideas he took those of other people wherever he might find what suited him, from Proudhon, from Henry George, from Edward Carpenter, from a poor Russian sectary, Syutayev. What he imported was the immense emotional force of a great personality and the genius of a great artist, the ever fresh vitality and simplicity of a great child.

.   .   .   .   .

Russian arts, and especially the Russian novel, have an interest for us beyond the aesthetic quality, however high we may reckon that to be. They are, in a rare degree, the intimate revelation of the people which produced them. Among all the great Russian novelists, however they may differ in other respects, there is a certain convincing sincerity, an appealing sympathetic personal quality; we feel that at all events these books lay before us the souls of their writers. To the reader familiar with the great English novelists these characteristics of Russian novels are at once strange and attractive. Our English novelists have never been simply and frankly personal. They may have been individual, even eccentric; they may have written their books to discharge their exuberant energies, but certainly not from any over-mastering impulse to reveal the secrets of their own souls. Indeed the word "soul" never occurs to us when we think of the English novelists, of Fielding and Smollett, of Jane Austen and Scott, even of Richardson. If we turn to more recent writers, while it is true that the women novelists may often form an exception, the men still remain free from any directly personal contact with their readers. They possess personal qualities, even in high degree, it is true; they present revelations of energy, revelations of life, even of art, but scarcely revelations of personality, merely the awkward disguises under which very sensitive persons seek to hide their personality. Thus to turn to the Russian novelists is to enter a new world, for here we find writers of the most unquestionable power, who yet disclose themselves, under transparent disguises, with childlike simplicity and frankness, with no dread of false shame as to what we, the readers, may think of them. That profound difference, allied with real affinities of emotion and energy, may well be the reason why Russian novels appeal so intimately to English readers and English novels to the Russians.

Hence arises the Russian genius for writing memoirs. They are not indeed memoirs of the kind in which the French, the greatest writers of this kind of literature and the most prolific, have excelled. The French memoirs may be skilful, brilliant, sincere, but one feels that they arise from a soil of complacent egoism: "See what a large part I played in the world," the writer seems generally to say, "and how well I played it." But the memoirs of the Russians are unaffected and almost impersonal narratives written by instinctive artists, and often of the nature of confessions. They are not the records of achievement but of experience, and often of sad and even humiliating experience. Waliszesky, referring to Russian literature generally and especially to Tolstoy, remarks that the whole Russian school makes no attempt to idealize the self but rather the reverse, and that this constitutes what may be considered the truest element of Russian originality. It is this originality—associated with the Russian tendency to self-castigation—which comes out in a whole series of remarkable books having the beauty of objective art and yet the fascination of personal confession, books such as Tolstoy's *Child-hood* and *Boyhood*, Dostoyevsky's *The House of the Dead*, and Sergei Aksakov's *Family Chronicles*. A characteristic book of this class, scarcely to be paralleled outside Russia, is the *Memoirs of a Doctor* by Veresayev, the pseudonym of a Dr. Smidovich, who here sets forth the professional doubts and mistakes which have happened to him during his career. This book caused much indignation, even in Russia, among the author's medical colleagues who feared the results of his revelations. "It may sometimes be necessary," he wrote in justification of his book, "to deceive a man who is seriously ill. But society, taken as a whole, cannot be considered seriously ill, and it is harmful to adopt towards it the attitude of perpetual false-hood." The object of the book is not, as it would almost certainly be if written outside Russia, either to belittle the practice of medicine or to castigate rival practitioners. In the true Russian spirit of humanity and humility he sets forth, in a manner that sometimes recalls Tolstoy, the errors and weaknesses which are alike his own and those of others, the shame and the pitifulness which are in part inherent to human nature, in part the result of the social system, and the outcome of the sad record of his experiences still ends on a note not to be mistaken, however tremulously it may be sounded, of work and hope.

Anyone who has traversed Russia and come into social contact with the various classes of the population soon begins to realize that the writers of Russia are not only laying bare their own souls; they may dare to be sincere because they are laying bare some aspect of the soul of the race they belong to. After a visit to Russia we realize how closely the great Russian novelists have reflected the national soul; we also realize—perhaps more vividly than is possible to a Russian—how really coherent their varying utterances are. If we wish to take up and place together a handful of the most impres-sive and significant Russian novels—it matters little which we select —we seem to find the most various tendencies and attitudes, the views of nobles and criminals and madmen, of those who strive to build up society anew by force, or who oppose such methods, or who smile at them, of those who face the East and those who face the West, and those who fix their gaze on their own land. Yet one and all they express that complicated amalgam of East and West, of energy and passive mysticism, of daring sincerity and morbid sensitiveness, which go to make up the weakness and strength of Russia. We cannot, as Gorky would have us, divide Russian characteristics into two groups, Eastern and Western, and eliminate one group, even if we could be as sure as Gorky as to which group is Eastern, which Western, and which most worthy of preservation. Vereshchagin, the painter, who was, it has been said, "as savage as a *bogatyr* and as meek as a saint", was a typical Russian. The seemingly opposed characteristics are fused in the same individual. In every Russian, indeed, Baring has remarked, there is something of Peter the Great, something of Dostoyevsky's Prince Myshkin, something of Gogol's Hlestakov.[1] We may not agree that this remark holds true of the individual Russian, but it may certainly be admitted that one or other of these characters—the energetic and eagerly progressive barbarian not averse to violence, the gentle humanitarian mystic leading the life of the spirit, the ingenuous scamp of versatile imagination vainly seeking a short cut to temporal success—encounters us at every turn when we approach Russian life.

In referring to the contrast between Russian and English novelists I made a partial exception in the case of English women novelists. The exception is significant. In these Russian books we see on the emotional side—for there are superadded an intellectual force and instinct for art rarer in women—qualities which are in the finest sense feminine. The frank preoccupation with personal feeling, the audacious instinctive conviction that personal feeling must be translated at once into practical action, and the tendency to secret morbid reverie when action is impossible, these are at once essentially feminine traits and essentially Russian traits. That perhaps is why, as Laura Marholm has remarked in writing of Tolstoy, "no other literature had understood women and described them as vividly as the Russian", more especially, as she remarks, in its "instinctive grasp of the side of woman's nature which is not turned towards

[1] M. Baring, *The Russian People*, p. 56.

man". They are as conspicuous in Russian life as in Russian literature. I have had occasion to point out elsewhere, when analysing
the elements of British genius, that, for instance, so masculine a
race as the Scotch have produced few eminent women, while a
more feminine race, like the Irish, have produced many;[1] and
Taine also noticed how in proceeding from the north to the south
of France we find ourselves among a more and more feminine people,
among whom at the same time women tend to take a more and
more conspicuous place. It cannot be said that the qualities of
Russian women are quite the qualities of the women of Mediterranean race, but it is certainly true that women in Russia, as well as
in the other Slavonic countries, especially Poland, have always
played a very active part. It is this ardent, practical, emotional fibre,
expressing itself in the most diverse ways, and running through
the whole of Russian life as well as of Russian literature, that enables
women to play so large a part in Russian civilization.[2]

No doubt it is not merely the special condition of the Russian
temperament and Russian life which have given prominence to the
feminine element; we must take into consideration the special
character of Russian women, and the interaction of these two
factors, the women and their environment. The ancient Russian
tradition still embodied in custom usually placed women in a sub-
servient position in marriage, and ostentatiously permitted to the
husband the use of the whip. But, as has already been noted, the whip
has not always seemed offensive to the Russian mind and has even
created an appeal. Moreover, it has been noted of Russian women
that while by custom and habits they are submissive, they are apt
to turn the tables and become indomitable, even tyrannical, thus
revealing exactly the same twofold character which was noted of
Russians generally in the seventeenth century, women, as often
happens, retaining the primitive characters of the race longer than

[1] Havelock Ellis, *A Study of British Genius*, p. 28.

[2] "The Slav character," wrote Herzen who is always so illuminating when he writes
of Russia, "presents something feminine; intelligent, strong, full of varied aptitude,
it lacks initiative and energy. The Slav nature seems not to suffice to itself but to
need a shock to arouse it. Then it possesses an extraordinary power of development"
(Alexandre Herzen, *Du Développement des Idées Révolutionnaires en Russie*, 1853,
p. 11).

the men. Among intellectuals, people of this two-fold servile-tyrannical type mostly ceased to exist after Peter the Great's time.

There seems always to have been a tendency among Russian women to take a prominent part in life. The Arthurian Round Table and its knights, which is the European group of stories most nearly recalled by the early epic legends of Russia, contains no heroines. But in ancient Russian legends heroic deeds were performed equally by men and women; to the hero, the *bogatyr*, corresponded the equally courageous heroine, the *polyanitsa*.[1] Notwithstanding, also, the prevailing marriage customs and their ritual masculine superiority, in the south at all events, it was the woman, not the man, who chose the partner in marriage. Beauplan, in his *Description of Ukraine* (where he spent seventeen years), gives an interesting account of how, in his time, the latter half of the seventeenth century, the Ukrainian women chose their husbands and succeeded in courtship, he remarks, much better than men would.[2] Russian women have been prominent in every field. Thus in literature during the eighteenth century, when literature in Russia was still young, and women possessed no educational advantages fitting them to cultivate what might then be regarded as a rare exotic product, they yet yielded as many as seventy representatives to literature. During the nineteenth century women began to become actively attracted to science and medicine; by 1906 at the Imperial Institute of Medicine more than a third of the workers were women, while in the Pathological Laboratory the women far exceeded the men. Both in medicine and science generally they have distinguished themselves, and it is well known that the most

[1] Isabel Hapgood, *Epic Songs of Russia*, p. xxix.
[2] Casanova knew Russia a century and a half ago, as indeed he knew most parts of Europe. "Russia," he wrote, "is a land where the sexes are confused; women govern; women preside over learned societies; they take part in administration and diplomacy; they do not ride at the head of the troops, but that is the only privilege these Tartar beauties seem to lack." As regards this last point, however, it may be noted that, in the World War, Russian women succeeded in enlisting, and even in distinguishing themselves as soldiers. After the establishment of the Revolution this seems to have taken place on a larger and more recognized scale, and we hear of the women's contingent, in detachments consisting of over two hundred women and girls with hair cropped, in full men's uniforms with rifles, many of them decorated for bravery on the field; we also hear of a naval guard of six-foot women.

THE GENIUS OF RUSSIA

eminent woman of science of recent times, Madame Curie, while not Russian, was a Polish Slav. In the two most extreme manifestations of Russian life, again, women have payed a conspicuous part: they have been active in the mystical or communistic religious sectarian movements which have flourished among the peasants, and besides the heroic *bogatyrs* of the great Russian revolutionary movement of the nineteenth century, the *polyanitsa* has frequently been recognized as the equally heroic peer. If, indeed, we accept the evidence of Russian novelists we might say that the Russian women are throughout the superior of men in energy and character. "All you women of Russia are higher and more vigorous than we men," exclaims Solomin in Turgenyev's *Virgin Soil*. This is not the testimony of any single novelist, as we might perhaps say that it is in England more especially of George Meredith. All the great Russian writers, from Pushkin on, have presented this view of women. Their "heroes" may be, usually are, strong only in aspiration, for the rest, meek and irresolute, and endless series of variations on the theme of Hamlet. But in opposition to the men the women are firm and courageous, unshrinking in their devotion to the ideal when once they have seen it. Even Goncharov, who created the classical picture of this type of man, set against Oblomov the corresponding woman, Olga, perhaps the best representative of the ideal type of the Russian woman ever created.

"There are mornings in summer when the sunshine is radiant, and when the earth smiles so fresh and sweet that body and soul expand in exultant health and strength; and then, no matter where we are, the Russian world comes to our eyes, and the Russian woman, with her hearty laugh and motherly figure, rises before us as the living incarnation of such a morning, never French women or German or Scandinavian, but only Russian women, for it is only they who harmonize with Nature in an indefinable sense of unity and enjoyment." It is so that Laura Marholm begins an essay on Tolstoy in which she throws out some illuminating ideas on Russian women. She was herself born in Russia, though of German descent, but the impression she records must certainly often have been experienced by those who have ever moved among the robust, natural, spontaneous, and cheerful peasant women of Russia. And in the main the same impression is produced by the women of higher class we may meet in life and in literature. They seem rarely to reveal any of that tortured and self-torturing conscience which is so marked even in the very expression of the men.

The reason, Laura Marholm suggests, why the Russian woman is in advance in many respects of the women of other lands is that there has been in Russia no historic period of the cult of woman with all its visible and invisible offshoots, so that even in their religion it has not been a super-natural or non-natural "spotless Virgin" to which their adoration has been directed but woman in the exaltation of her supreme natural function, the "Mother of God".[1] There may here well be a clue to the special characteristics of the Russian woman and the atmosphere which surrounds her. The spirit of chivalry which dominated Western Europe and has left an influence traceable even to-day, artificial and unreal as it was, could not but be poisonous to women. From the point of view of chivalry, women existed as an excuse for the exercise of knightly virtues. Prowess, honour, gentleness, courtesy were all cultivated as the foundation of the feebleness and nullity of woman. She was only called upon to be— or to pretend to be—weak and pure and lovely. Thus she was a worthy stimulus to the knightly virtues of man. But no one dreamed of demanding the exercise of corresponding chivalrous virtues in her. She had indeed a more than sufficient task in winding herself up to the adequate affectation of the extravagant artificialities she was called upon to assume. Our Western literature to-day, and even much of our life, is still full of the echoes of this mediæval fantasy. But Russia has been free from it, the Russian woman has only had to contend with the more ancient oriental seclusion which oppressed even classic Greece. That is why we breathe so unfamiliar and de-lightful an air of freedom in Russian novels.

[1] Laura Marholm Hansson, *We Women and Our Authors*, translated by Hermione Ramsden, 1889, p. 139. Wiener has more recently suggested (*Interpretation of the Russian People*, p. 205) that "the vigour and enthusiasm of Russian women is due to isolation from the world". But this no longer applies and has, of course, never applied to the bulk of the population, either in Russia or anywhere else; and, more-over, it may be doubted whether relegation to the Russian home is itself a pre-servative from disillusion.

We have to bear these considerations in mind when we are faced by that "laxity", as it seems to the Western mind, which marks Russian sexual morality. When Malthus visited St. Petersburg more than a century ago he was surprised to find that to "have a child was considered one of the most trifling faults a girl could commit".[1] Such laxity abounds in the West also, but in the West it is associated with the masculine attitude, not with the feminine attitude, towards sex. We have inherited a conception of feminine virtue, which springs from the union between mediæval asceticism and mediæval chivalry, which regards honour in women as consisting—altogether unlike honour in men—exclusively in chastity. Purity, thus understood as chastity alone, has become idealized, as the one essential characteristic of conventionally respectable womanhood. This is not the case in Russia.[2] This by no means necessarily implies

[1] Malthus, *Principle of Population*, 2nd ed., bk. ii, ch. 3.

[2] See Rothay Reynolds, *My Slav Friends*, p. 159. I have already quoted from a Russian correspondent some remarks concerning the middle and upper classes. The same correspondent writes regarding the peasants of Little Russia in his boyhood: "We passed holidays in my uncle's village. In the midst of numerous women servants and farm girls I was plunged in a Cytherian atmosphere. I soon made acquaintances among the girls around me, guided, indeed, by a cousin who explained that these robust viragos were willing to yield everything for a trifling present, a packet of hair-pins, or a cheap ribbon, a cake, or even a piece of sugar. And, in fact, I found that in consideration of such ridiculous offerings the 'vierges fortes' of Ukrainia would allow me various intimacies, wherever we might be, in a room, a shed, behind a haystack, or in the bushes. With my cousin and other youths I would, too, see them bathe in the stream. We would exchange remarks of double meaning with them and they would burst out laughing when they understood the allusions. The village girls were used to every audacity and nowise offended. In the large kitchens of country nobles, where dozens of servant girls, coachmen, field-workers, etc., dined and took tea together the most daring familiarities were permitted. I was often impelled to enter the kitchen at such times. The general conversation was a constant play of obscenities and gestures kept pace with words. I have been told that sometimes in the banquets of the 'black kitchen' (where the meals of the servants and workpeople are prepared) still more outrageous tricks would be played on feast days under the influence of copious libations graciously distributed by the master or overseers. Men would suddenly seize some pretty girl from behind, raise her from the bench she was seated on, and hold her for a few moments upside down with uncovered legs in the air. And the victim would cherish no long enduring grudge against her persecutors. I know, too, that the village 'vespers' or wakes (vechernitsy) of Little Russia—jovial nocturnal recessions of unmarried men and girls, where the girls sewed or embroidered and the men played, sang, or told stories—often ended in a peculiar way: lights would be extinguished and each youth placing a girl on his knees, the couple would masturbate each other, after which they returned contentedly home. One could often see girls and young men idling in ditches, barns, or hay-cocks. If they became pregnant they had recourse to abortifacients; every young girl knew the use of ergot, and old

that there is much more actual unchastity among Russian women than among Western women, but it is certainly favourable to openness, for concealment becomes unnecessary for the end of retaining social dignity and self-respect. It has taken the Russian long to achieve political freedom, but the Russian man, and even the Russian woman, has long possessed social freedom in a far higher degree than Western Europe. Kovalevsky considers that Russian "immorality" is a survival of easy forms of marriage.[1] That may be, but the survival could scarcely have taken place if the prolonged seclusion of Russia from the rest of Europe had not shut out those highly-strung mediæval ideals which, in a transformed shape, still flourish among ourselves. Hence that fresh natural spontaneity which we feel to be incarnated in the Russian woman alike of real life and of literature.

Allied to the feminine element in Russian literature is the marked humanity. To the Russian novelists human beings seem to be so sacred, so fascinatingly interesting, that any crime may be committed in the name of the ethical fervour they inspire, and nothing wearing the garment of humanity is too mean to worship. Here, again, the contrast with Western novelists, French and even English, is notable. Richardson, indeed, had something of the absorbed reverence for the detail of emotional life which is habitual among the Russians, but for the main part the Western novelist is mainly occupied with his story; his creations are puppets, over whom, indeed, he may sometimes shed a few sentimental tears. So it is with Sterne and Scott and Balzac and Zola. Even the humanitarian zeal, so common among English novelists, and typically displayed in Dickens, is wholly alien. It is humanity, not humanitarianism, that inspires the Russian; philanthropy, that characteristically English product, has

women were skilled in mechanical methods. Public opinion, however, was not severe towards the weaknesses of the flesh. Everyone knew that a certain widower had had children by both his daughters, one of them a minor, yet this interfered in no way with the consideration he enjoyed." When my informant subsequently went to live in Italy he was impressed by the contrast in this matter between the two countries, the young Italian woman who had an illegitimate child being treated with contempt instead of indulgence, so becoming really "ruined".

[1] M. Kovalevsky, *Modern Customs and Ancient Laws of Russia*, p. 13.

little attraction for him. He may gaze at men with the same concentrated minute gaze as Huysmans, but instead of being fascinated
by the horror of the vision, or only by a supreme effort melting
into tenderness, it never even seems to occur to him that there is
anything anywhere not to love.[1] The two central works of Russian
imagination, as they are sometimes considered, Dostoyevsky's
Idiot and Tolstoy's *Resurrection*—the work of men in most respects
looking very differently at life—are absolutely alike in the minute-
ness of their gaze at everything in men and women that physically
or spiritually is weak and mean and perverse and unlovely, and
alike also in finding here the reasons rather for love than for contempt. Tolstoy brings his insistent physical realism and his calm, keen
analysis of human nature to illustrate the Sermon on the Mount,
and Dostoyevsky devotes two large volumes to the delineation of a
man whose simplicity is the laughing-stock of all, an epileptic
imbecile who is yet a saint. This perpetual minute and sympathetic
contemplation of the poor and humble, the suffering and the diseased,
the peasant, the prostitute, the criminal, the madman, we find
throughout the work of the chief Russian novelists. Sometimes it is
associated with a ferocious desire to overturn the bases of society
where so much evil is possible, more often it is a resigned but impassioned fervour of love for piteous human things; but always in
extremes, so reflecting the two racial elements, Eastern and Western,
of which Russia is composed. These two extremes make up the
temper of the Russian people.

Besides these great masters of the Russian novel, there are others
of scarcely secondary and, in some respects indeed, equal importance.
There is especially Goncharov. Born of good and purely Russian
family on the banks of the Volga in the early nineteenth century,
in an entirely Russian environment, he lived a long and peaceful
life as a government official. While sympathetic and sensitive to

[1] This is true even of the Russian soldier; R. Scotland Liddell, writing from intimate acquaintance with the Russian army during the World War (*On the Russian
Front*, 1916, p. 28) says that the Russian soldier goes into battle vowing that he will
flay the Germans and chop them into mincemeat. "But if a fortunate German soldier
should drift into the arms of the fierce Russian, he finds himself treated as an honoured
guest." The Russian becomes the German's slave and stints himself of his little luxuries
for the German's sake.

Western and especially English literature, he remained strictly within the Russian tradition, the disciple of Pushkin and Gogol. He wrote only three novels, but one of these, *Oblomov*, published in 1859, is immortal because it is universally recognized to be the best portrait of the most characteristic of Russian intellectual types, the type more or less admirably presented by Pushkin in *Onegin*, by Lermontov in *Pechorin*, by Tolstoy in *Pierre Bezukhov*. *Oblomov*—as it has been necessary to point out on a previous page—is the complete Russian Hamlet, without even that fitful energy which worked Shakespeare's Hamlet. It was a type that Goncharov might see around him, as well as find in his own family and in his own heart, for his novels are considered to be largely autobiographical. He has drawn it, in that sympathetic yet gently critical manner which marks his work with its heart of gold, its fine tastes, its noble aspirations, its defective will-power, its indolence, its fatigue, its boredom, its final renunciation of the tasks of life.[1]

Another great writer must also be mentioned, Sergei Aksakov, who died of old age in 1859, the year in which *Oblomov* was published, publishing his own most important books, the *Family Chronicles*, only a few years before. It is perhaps due to the fact that he developed late and belongs in spirit to a rather earlier generation that Aksakov is regarded by many as a reactionary whose thoughts dwelt complacently on the old serfdom which was finally to be extinguished immediately after his death. As a writer, moreover, his earlier books were written in the pseudo-classical style which was already becoming extinct. But when at last he fell under the liberating influence of Gogol he found his true self and became a great artist. He was a realist in whom there was, as in all typical Russian novelists, a latent poet and a true lover of Nature. It is characteristic alike of his realism and of the dominance of the novel in nineteenth-century Russia, that his *Family Chronicles* are in reality the thinly disguised history of his own family and his own childhood. In his hands they became masterpieces of fiction, models for

---

[1] An admirably full and scholarly account of Goncharov's life and works, largely based on original material gathered in Russia, has been written in French by André Mazon, *Ivan Goncharov*, Paris, 1914.

writers who have followed, and Aksakov has sometimes been termed by enthusiastic Slavophils, the Russian Homer. It may at least be said that the *Family Chronicles* challenge comparison even with the early work of Tolstoy.

There is yet another Russian master of fiction, who belongs to the great tradition and ranks little below the highest, even though he never wrote a single long novel. Chekhov, born in 1860, and dying in 1904, continued and developed the spirit and art of Gogol and of Turgenyev through some of the darkest and most despairing days of Russia's history. He was born in southern Russia, in the land of the Don Cossacks, on the shores of the Sea of Azov, the son of a serf who had freed himself by his own abilities and was able to send his son to Moscow University to become a doctor. But he soon abandoned medicine for literature, having indeed begun to write stories before he was twenty. Henceforth he continued to write short stories copiously, though with deep and delicate art, to the end, as well as numerous and equally remarkable plays. Before his death he became the most popular writer in Russia after Tolstoy. The ever recurring note of Chekhov, expressed in ever varying forms, is hopelessness and the futility of life. It seems an awe-inspiring theme, however Russian we may recognize it to be, and we seem to divine the presence of some underlying conscious-ness of failure in life on the part of this retiring man who died of consumption in early middle life. Yet Chekhov writes with such fine art and with so much restraint; he presents such varied pictures of life; his realism and his melancholy are so pervaded by human tenderness and poetic vision, that in Russia his popularity has been only second to that of Tolstoy, while outside Russia his high position is firmly established. We may say, indeed, that with Chekhov the line of the great Russian masters of fiction in the nineteenth century comes to an end.

Many admirable writers remain. However unlike they may be in rank and in character, there is no failure of quantity or of accom-plishment in the Russian novelists of to-day. Of them all Maxim Gorky (whose real name is Pyeshkov), doubtless the most potent and the most revolutionary, seems to have most in common with the great writers of the past.[1] There is the same firm and incisive touch, the same breadth, the same artistry—limited by that peculiar inability to achieve success in full-length novels which seems to mark all Russian writers of fiction since Chekhov—and the same sympathy. Yet with a deep difference. Gogol and Turgenyev and Dostoyevsky and Tolstoy and Chekhov were all men of upper or middle class. They were not of the people; they brooded over the spectacle of suffering with tender love, they more or less believed in its future alleviation, but they were not actively rebellious against it and for the most part even idealized it. Their sympathy was of the heart. But Gorky's sympathy is of the blood. He sprang from the suffering Russian masses; born on the banks of the Volga, the son of an artisan and a remarkable peasant woman, he lived the hard life of the people in youth, and it is his personal suffering, too real and bitter to idealize, which is in question. So he has become not only an artist, but for the first time in Russian literature an artist who is also a rebel. That is the secret of his attack on Dostoyevsky, of the ferocious vigour with which he turns against nearly everything we have been accustomed to regard as most essentially Russian, asserting, with dubious justice, that it is "Mongol", while the "Slav" Russia for which he strikes is, it has been said, a "Russia optimistic, cocksure, business-like, well-dressed, smart and Western". But, however that may be, Gorky is a great initiator. His ideals, in the form in which he himself presents them, may not prove permanent, but he has introduced a new spirit of virility into Russian literature. His heroes are rebels, for the most part rebels who have failed. But they disdain to take refuge in the old Russian fortress of melancholy quietism and passive resignation to circumstances; they retain their strength, their confidence, their optimism. The old refuges can never be set up again with the same unquestioning faith. Gorky has killed Dostoyevsky.

Andreyev approaches life in something of the same rebel's spirit

[1] As Gorky deals largely with the lowest social classes whose lives he is intimately acquainted with, he is sometimes classed with the folk-novelists, though as an artist he far transcends any of them. They form, however, a significant and important group in Russian literature. Kropotkin has a sympathetic and interesting chapter on them, from Grigorovich to Gorky, in his *Russian Literature*, ch. 7.

as Gorky, and in even more savage ferocity; for, though not strictly of the people but of humble middle-class family, he suffered in early life from misery and starvation and once attempted suicide. But he lacks alike the realistic force of Gorky and the gentle humanity of Chekhov who is considered his master; his imaginative ambition seems often to go beyond his artistic means, and his real power tends to be dissipated in violence and extravagance. His plays, as the reader of them may well believe, have not proved successful on the stage, even with all the serious care of the Moscow Arts Theatre.

It is Sologub who is commonly regarded as the legitimate heir of Chekhov. Yet Sologub—the pseudonym of a retired school-teacher whose real name is Teternikov, the son of a peasant who became shoemaker—seems as remote from Chekhov as, on the other side, from Gorky and Andreyev. He is a consummate artist, with an exquisite sense of the physical beauty of the world, and so far as can be judged from translations the finest mastery of words of any writer in Russia to-day.[1] But though he is always concerned with life, he holds himself as aloof from life as, it seems, he holds himself from his literary public. His stories are fables and fairy-tales of mankind, sinister fables for the most part and macabre fairy-tales. There is beauty on the surface of them and the semblance of pathos. But beneath the surface one often seems to feel the hard and cruel touch of an artist for whom mankind only exists as the crude material of art. "I take a piece of life, coarse and poor," Sologub has himself written in a preface, "and make of it a delightful legend." It is a method far from that of Dostoyevsky, and even of Chekhov, far indeed, one may add, from that which we had come to consider the method of all the great Russian novelists. Perhaps that is why Sologub, though he may well be the finest artist in Russian fiction to-day, is far from being the most popular living author.

Kuprin may in this respect have a better claim. While he definitely belongs to the twentieth century and not to the past, he moves in a sphere where all may follow him, always close to life—though more

---

[1] Sologub had indeed been peculiarly fortunate in his translator, Mr. John Cournos, to whom we owe admirable versions of *The Old House* (a volume of short stories) and *The Created Legend* (more correctly *Drops of Blood*).

to the romance than the realism of life—so that he appeals to all classes (he is said to have been the only modern novelist whom Tolstoy liked), and is to-day the most popular novelist in Russia after Chekhov, while outside his Russia he is gaining, and is easily fitted to gain, the same popularity. For there is little about him that we are accustomed to regard as distinctly Russian. He has the universal instincts of the good story-teller; he is full of copious and exuberant vitality, and without prejudice he takes his material where he can find it, humorous or tragic, bizarre or merely human. Without doubt he is an admirable story-teller, sometimes compared to Kipling and O. Henry, though we might perhaps better regard him as a sort of second-rate Maupassant. When we read him we forget that Dostoyevsky and Tolstoy ever existed; for there is nothing here to remind us either of the exquisite art or the tender melancholy of the great Russians of old. Kuprin is much too coarse and wholesome for either. It is remarkable that Kuprin's affinities in Russian literature seem, so far as a foreigner may judge, rather with the prose of Pushkin than of any post-Gogol novelist. On the whole, however, he seems to represent a movement towards that Russia which Gorky has proclaimed as the Russia of the future; we cannot fail to read him with pleasure, and whether our pleasure will be alloyed depends on the ideal we cherish of the Russia of the future.

* * * * *

A passionate absorption in human suffering easily becomes morbid. We see this in the representative writers of Russia. Garshin, who has written the most perfect stories of madness, himself became mad. Dostoyevsky, who of all writers has profoundly penetrated the secrets of morbid mental action, was himself a degenerate epileptic. There has always been a tendency to a certain unbalance and extravagance among Russian men of genius; it is a usual tendency of genius which they exhibit to an unusual degree.

Yet here again we are not concerned with merely individual manifestations. The neurotic and abnormal element in Russian men of genius reveals and exaggerates the element of unbalance and extravagance in the Russian people. They also tend in a higher degree than the people of the West to be morbid, sensitive, melancholy, doubting. It is that fact—and no vice of character or defect of attractive personality—which has so often rendered difficult the relations of people of the West with a Russian wife or a Russian husband. The pathological element is even yet more widely diffused. Every foreign writer eager to pour contempt on Russia has found a rich field to work here.

The pathological element in Russian life is well illustrated by two notorious cases in recent years, both peculiarly Russian in character: the trial of the Countess Maria Tarnowska for instigating the murder of her lover, and the career of the monk Rasputin. In the first case we see how an element of hereditary degeneration in a woman not without noble aspirations may lead to the evolution of a tragic romance of crime; the story, as based on her own confessions, has been published by Vivanti Chartres, with a preface by the distinguished Italian gynaecologist, Professor Bossi. The story of Rasputin (of which an accurate narrative was given in *The New Europe* for 1916) is still more instructive, and nothing could be more demonstrative of the pathological elements in Russian life since so many elements are here woven together. We see an ignorant, sensual and cunning monk, of the lowest birth, but, by a peculiar magnetic power over women and by the prevalence of superstition and credulity, exercising a supreme power in the land even in court circles, and able to control public policy with so much security that it was considered that the only way to remove him was by murder, and this removal was effected, with general public approval and complete immunity, by persons of the highest birth.

It would be a serious mistake to see in such manifestations as these, even if they could be shown to be very common in modern Russia, the signs of national degeneration and decadence. They are, on the contrary, the signs of incomplete civilization and of a barbaric extravagance. In Western Europe during a few centuries, at the Renaissance and later during periods of the highest evolving civilization, similar manifestations have abounded. The plays of Shakespeare, of all the tragic dramatists of the greatest period of English history, are the magnificent representation of such episodes which were then only beginning to recede into the background of Western European life. Yet we are not tempted to regard Shakespeare as the poet of degeneration and decadence.

Not only is the birth-rate enormously high in Russia, but the death-rate is also enormously high. In statistical summaries taken of the birth-rates and death-rates of the different European countries, the Russian birth-rate and the Russian death-rate nearly always come out higher than those of any other country, the infantile death-rate, especially, to an enormously higher degree. Such high birth-rates and high death-rates mean, and must always mean, a very low social level, a deep stage of ignorance and superstition, and a vast amount of disease and misery. Among the poor in some districts half the children die before they are a year old. Cholera, diphtheria, typhoid, even typhus, and all infectious diseases flourish. The habits of the people as well as their fatalistic beliefs lend themselves to these results. No doubt the supposed uncleanliness of the Russian population is a myth; the Russian peasant is scrupulously clean. The Russian delights in bathing, not only in his own peculiar institution, the hot-air bath which everywhere abounds and is open to the lowest classes (for the poorest Russian insists on his Saturday bath), but during summer in open-air bathing which is sometimes carried on with almost Japanese frankness.[1] Only just outside Moscow I have seen a full-grown girl bathing unabashed in a way-side stream; and on a popular summer feast-day, when a merry troup of peasants crowded into the train, regardless of class, they were radiantly clean, as inoffensive to sight and smell as could well be desired. No doubt the conditions of Russian life foster dirt. Poverty, ignorance, cold, the necessity for close rooms and much clothing, are conditions that easily produce filth, even among a people of less resigned temperament than the Russians. Those, however, who point to the stores of facts which have been accumulated

[1] "In the country in Russia," writes a Russian correspondent, "people of every age and both sexes are accustomed to bathe, absolutely naked, in the rivers or the sea; the bathing is not, however, promiscuous, the sexes form separate groups, but near to each other, and among village youths and girls of fourteen to eighteen, the two groups, absolutely naked, will stand in the water to their knees facing each other, making jokes, and aiming lumps of mud at each other amid shouts of laughter."

concerning the insanitary conditions of Russia forget, if they have ever been aware, that it is but a little while since similar conditions prevailed in Western Europe, and that even to-day we are in no country very far removed from them. Russia is only now emerging from mediæval conditions, yet it is little more than half a century since Chadwick, in a report written for the British Government, showed the existence, even in London, of insanitary conditions and filthy habits of life at nearly every point exactly paralleling the facts which in Russia are now held up for our scorn. A century ago it was the same in France, as M. Alfred Franklin has shown in the volume on *Hygiène* in the interesting series of his *Vie Privée d'Autrefois*. It is to the scientific zeal of the Russians themselves that we owe our minute knowledge of the conditions under which the Russian masses live. Russia herself holds the mirror up to Russia, and Russian life as well as Russian character have never been more keenly analysed than by Russians.[1]

Unfortunately the Russian peasant in emerging from the old evils of mediævalism has fallen into the new evils of industrialism. In Western Europe there was an interval between these two sets of evils. When the Industrial Revolution took place in England at the end of the eighteenth century the Middle Ages had already been left behind. But in Russia, where social development has lagged far behind Western Europe, there has been no interval and the evils of industrialism have worked even the more virulently since they have been directly superimposed on the evils of mediævalism. The causes are different but the results are the same, though manifested in a still more exaggerated form, and therefore they are accepted without protest by the victims, and there is no adequate protective mechanism against them.

More than sixty years ago the pernicious influence of the early industrial factory movement on the simple village life of the Russian peasantry near Moscow was represented by the novelist Grigorovich in his book *The Fishermen*. Since then the industrial movement has immensely accelerated and the conditions have become

---

[1] In 1892, in *The Nationalization of Health* (pp. 207–23), I brought together many facts bearing on these points from reliable sources.

correspondingly worse. The introduction of industrialism always at the outset involves a rise in the birth-rate. Russian industrialism dates from Alexander I, and the accelerated rise in the Russian population began in the first quarter of the nineteenth century. At the same time the population began to become increasingly urban, although this movement is still far behind the West. In England more than half the population now live in towns. In Russia, while in Peter the Great's time only 3 per cent were urban, even by 1860 it was still below 10 per cent, and at the end of the century had only risen to 13 per cent. In 1905 it remained still 13 per cent and was even rising rather than falling. Sweden alone resembles Russia in this small proportion of urban population. It is in the south, among the Little Russians, that we find alike the chief growth of urban industrial life and the chief increase in the population. The population of Russia at its recent rate of growth is tripled every century, Milyukov states, and though that is slow compared to the rate of growth of the United States during the past century, it is faster than elsewhere in Europe, Russia adding to its number every year nearly three million new individuals, or as much as the whole population of a small European country. But the increase is far from corresponding to the high birth-rate on account of the enormous infantile mortality which, while everywhere high, is much higher among factory workers than among peasants. This indeed is a normal difference even in the most civilized countries, and, speaking on the whole, the more extensive the employment of women the higher the infantile mortality.[1] In Russia both rates of mortality are on an enormous high scale. Thus Dementyev, in a study of industrial work among Russian women published in 1903, states that while among the children of women in the country the infantile birth-rate is 343, among women engaged in industrial work it is 533; that is to say that more than half of the children born die before they are

[1] Thus in Massachusetts, while the infantile death-rate for the States generally was 160, the six cities with high infantile death-rate (209) were very large and employed a large proportion of women, while the six cities with low infantile death-rate (138) were much smaller and employed a smaller proportion of women ("Infant Mortality and its Relation to the Employment of Mothers," *Report on Condition of Women and Child Wage-Earners in the United States*, vol. xiii, Washington, 1921, p. 39).

one year old. It is not surprising that in many cities the total deaths exceed the births. In this first stage of industrialism intervening on a primitive ruralism not yet delivered from its primitive evils we see a great source of the unwholesome physical aspects of Russian life. To some extent, indeed, though far from completely, the evil effects its own remedy, for the feeble and diseased elements thus generated are largely destroyed. To some extent we may attribute to this circumstance the large proportion of robust and healthy individuals in the Russian population, and to a still larger extent we may attribute it to the still dominant country life which with all its evils is so far more beneficial than a town life. Even the ravages of syphilis and alcohol (perhaps on account of its orgiastic rather than habitual exercise) have not had all the evil results we might have expected.[1]

Nothing is likely to contribute so much to improvement in these elementary hygienic aspects of Russian life as the growth of education, a growth which cannot fail to be mightily stimulated by the Revolution. Tsardom found such dangerous enemies in the intellectual classes that its government could scarcely be expected to show great enthusiasm in the cause of popular education, notwithstanding the help which such education could not fail to give to national development and wealth. Yet this education, backward as it still is, has all the time been progressing. According to the Census of 1897 over 76 per cent of the mass of the rural population of working age were illiterate, and even among members of the local agricultural societies, the cream of the rural population, the proportion was about 20 per cent. In 1903, it is stated, the proportion of illiterates had fallen to 60 per cent, and in 1911 to 31 per cent. So that if—as is not certain—these figures may be regarded as

[1] It may be largely owing to this absence of habitual drunkenness and perhaps also, as Stephen Graham suggests, to an absence of drinking among women, that the criminal anthropologist in Russia fails to find striking examples of physical degeneracy so often the result of chronic alcoholism, and that the race is, on the whole, so robust. Hereditary nervous disturbance is shown with special frequency by mal-development of the jaws and teeth and palate. On visiting the Asile Rukavichnikov at Moscow, an industrial school for young criminals, with Dr. Talbot, who was investigating this point among similar classes of the population in nearly every country in Europe, it was found that the proportion of such deformities was singularly small.

reliable, the growth of education, even under the most unfavourable social and political conditions, has been extremely rapid.

Russia at the present time is a vast laboratory for the experimental manufacture of the greatest of European nations, fated to mould, as much probably as any nation, the future of the world. Such a process is always going on everywhere at some stage of acuteness, but in the rest of Europe the formative stage in the growth of peoples has long gone by, and while it lasted there were few or none able and competent to observe it. In Russia we see the process in its most acute form. This enormous birth-rate, this death-rate so enormous as sometimes to equal the births, this creation of human beings on so vast a scale, and the testing and proving of them in the most trying of climates—in this great experimental operation Nature is, on the whole, still left to attain her own results in her own way. In such an acute and destructive process of natural selection not only are the weakest lost, but a certain number of human failures are necessarily left. Thus there are neurotic and degenerate elements in all classes of society, though, as the comparative harmlessness of Russian criminality and the absence of the physical signs of degeneracy clearly indicate, the process of selection on the whole works truly. The Russian pessimist and the hostile foreigner see nothing but decadence. The thoughtful observer knows that such decadence is but an inevitable by-product in the formative process of a great nation.

·　　·　　·　　·　　·

Vast as is Russia, and alien in many ways to the Western mind, yet, when we have surveyed the great lines of its activities, and seek to grasp them as a whole, at a distance from which details are lost, the total picture, however impressive, is yet wonderfully simple.

Primarily and fundamentally European, Russia by geographical position and to some extent by racial affinities yet blends together harmoniously the East and the West and forms the great bridge between Europe and Asia. Isolated, moreover, during many centuries, through natural and cultural influences, from the Europe to which it fundamentally belongs, Russia was able to develop independently and to fuse into one whole the blend of East and West which to-day it presents to us, a kind of oriental-occidental culture, which in its mingling tends to transcend alike the narrow self-conceited materialism of the West and the misty metaphysical idealism of the East in a human and yet aspiring naturalistic humanism.

We see that the flat and open nature of much of the configuration of Russia, so favourable to nomadism, has rendered the people remarkably homogeneous in physical texture, considering the vast area they cover, as well as in language. The fundamental temper of this population is peaceable, kindly, rather passive, even melancholic.[1] But this very temper has permitted the invasion, and the eventual assimilation of more violent or more vigorous racial elements.

The first of these intruding elements is represented by the Norsemen or Varangians, Rurik and his successors, who formed small settlements in the north and a little later constituted the nucleus of the great Russian State at Kiev. They are said to have been invited to restore and maintain order much as Hengist and Horsa were, according to the story, invited over to Britain. However that may be, the Norsemen of Russia possessed in full measure that Norse genius for strong and daring conceptions, for military and political organization, of which their kinsmen scattered the seeds in England, and through the Normans spread abroad in Europe. Russian political organization is attributed to the Scandinavians, just as

---

[1] The possible influence of climate in helping to mould these characteristics has already been mentioned, and the more cheerful temperament of the Little Russian of the south as against the Great Russian of the north tends to support such an assumption. Various writers have attributed importance to climate in its bearing on Russian character. Novikov, for instance, says the Russian seems to have modelled himself on his climate with its extremes of cold and heat; Baring attributes his tough strength to the tempering influence of climate; Fouillée observes that the melancholy of the Russian, like that of the Briton, is the result of climate, and only found in northern Russia. Koltsov, the folk-poet of the south, cannot be said to be free from sadness, though his songs express the cheerful optimism and love of life, the strength and resigned fortitude of a people with much to battle with, even in the matter of climate. Klyuchevsky (*History of Russia*, vol. i, p. 218) considers that it is not so much the climate as the physical features of northern Russia, with its swamps and forests which have impressed on the Great Russian his keen observation of Nature, his resourcefulness, his patience under hardship and misfortune, his long-suffering.

Russian religious organization was contributed by the Byzantines, and administrative organization, it is held, largely by the Tartars. To the Tartars, also, we may doubtless attribute a contribution of energy which, if at first destructive and solvent, worked more harmoniously. For the Tartar element is not to be underestimated when we recall the heights of perilous adventure and the depths of tortuous skill possible to a race which produced Timur, the Tamerlane of Marlowe, and Jenghiz Khan, the "Scourge of Asia", and Akbar, the Great Mogul, "Guardian of Mankind". A highly important element later, and almost up to the present, was contributed by the German neighbours of the Russians. Many prominent Russians at the present day bear names which indicate a German origin. The Romanov dynasty was often closely related to Germany, and has been described as a half-Asiatic, half-German institution; it was the presence of the Asiatic Tartar which made it necessary and the presence of the Teuton which made it possible. Even to the end Tsardom was charged with undue subservience to German aims. Catherine II, one of the chief of Russian monarchs, was a German, and she introduced a vast number of German colonists who were of great benefit to the country. Of recent times the Germans have been chiefly conspicuous in the industrial and commercial life of Russia. This is inevitable on account not only of the energy and ability of the Germans in these fields but also of the common frontier and of the need each country has of the other's products. Germany is the chief importer to Russia and the chief exporter, England coming next, but Germany enjoying from every point of view the advantage not only of proximity but of the German's greater familiarity with Russian conditions and his better ability to adapt himself and his manufactures to these conditions. "The German can feel at home on Russian soil", Professor von Schulze-Gävernitz remarks, "since some very unpleasant phenomena of Russian life are not unknown to him at home."[1] It is not surprising that the German has often settled down in Russia to develop

[1] *Volkswirtschaftliche Studien aus Russland*, 1899, p. 612. He points out that the English manufactures are "too good" for Russia, and too complicated for the Russian to understand.

the fruitful possibilities offered to his commercial skill and patience, or that the element of German origin in Russia has become an energetic and capable factor in the nation. When Goncharov desired to place besides his indolent Russian hero, Oblomov, a model of practical energy he made him a man of German descent. There is, none the less, another side. However profitable a field of exploitation Russia might be to the German, and however helpful he might prove to Tsardom and even to the country generally, the Russian people hated him. There are vigorous expressions of this feeling even before the eighteenth century when the Germans first became powerful in Russia. "No people under the sun since the beginning of the world has been so abused and disgraced by foreigners as we Slavs by the Germans," wrote Yuri Kryzhanich even before the days of Peter the Great. The part the Germans have played in Russian life and the Russian view of it have been admirably described by Herzen, who was himself on one side German. The Russian Government, he points out, found in its German officials just what it needed: the regularity and impassivity of a machine, stoical obedience to any command, assiduous powers of work, a certain probity that the Russians lack, sufficient but not too much intelligence, complete contempt and ignorance of the Russian people. On the one hand they were pedantically bureaucratic and disciplinarian, completely servile to Tsardom, on the other hand arrogantly insolent towards the Tsar's subjects whom they regarded as barbarians.[1] It is not difficult to understand the resentment the Germans aroused in Russia notwithstanding their real services to the development of the country.

In modern times there had been no other notable invasion of an outside population into Russia. Such new elements of energy as have come to the front are mostly outlying peoples within the Russian borders who have only lately been developed and trained to take part in the national life. Putting aside the Jews, who have long been active in economic life, the Georgians of the Caucasus seem of late

---

[1] Alexander Herzen, *Du Développement des Idées Révolutionnaires en Russie*, 1853, p. 40. It is remarkable how closely the characteristics correspond to those ascribed to the Germans in more recent days.

to have begun to play a notable part in Russian life, and it may be remarked that Chkheidze, who at one moment in the Revolution seemed the most influential figure in Russia, is a Georgian.

The main direction of Russian history in the past has, however, been due to the indirect more than to the direct influence of racial factors.

These influences have specially worked together during many centuries for the isolation of Russia. Even the conversion of the Russians to Christianity, which in the West had a beneficial inter-nationalizing effect, in Russia only served to cut off the country from the West. For the Eastern Church had no communion with the Western Church, while the fall, later on, of Constantinople to Islam and the advance of the Turks in the Balkans destroyed the spiritual source of the Russian Church, which sank to the lowest depths of ignorance and superstition. Tartar devastation and oppression not only contributed greatly to the same isolation, but it was the direct stimulus to the growth of Tsardom and the reason for the special qualities Tsardom developed, qualities that were scarcely in the primitive Slav character. So it was that the Tartars of the thirteenth century, and the Tsardom which arose under their pressure, set back Russia for centuries, and indeed impeded its natural development until our own day. It is possible indeed that, in the long run, the isolation of Russia was not an unmitigated evil but even a great benefit. It contributed to making that people into a homogeneous whole and in giving them that independent force and vitality, full of promise for the future, which no other Slav people has possessed. There are, it must be remembered, many other Slav peoples in Europe, the Poles, the Serbs, the Czechs, together with various other peoples in Austria and the Balkans, as well as a large proportion of the whole population of Germany. Yet all these Slav peoples, however brilliant the history of some of them for brief periods has been, have never succeeded in permanently maintaining their independence; they have all possessed an element of weakness which has caused them to succumb to their neighbours. Russia alone stands not only in magnitude, but through a spirit of enduring strength which overcomes weakness.

During the eleventh and twelfth centuries, before the arrival of the Tartars, Russia was not isolated to any extreme degree; it excelled in trade and was not far behind in culture. The Russians of those days were naturally inclined to form comparatively small free and independent communities, of a more or less republican character. The Byzantine chronicles, the earliest authorities on the matter, are unanimous, Kovalevsky states, in saying that the Slav peoples knew nothing of a strongly centralized autocratic power. Only two Russian tribes had princes, the others lived as free clans, often at war with one another. Procopius, in the sixth century, stated that the Slav tribes were democracies; a Byzantine emperor said that the Slavs loved liberty and could not bear unlimited rulers. "The Slavs are a free people, strongly opposed to any subjection," said again the Emperor Leo.[1] It was not indeed until the fall of Pskov in 1510 that old Russian freedom was finally destroyed.[2] The same century saw the beginnings of serfdom; up to that time the peasant had been freer in Russia, though his material conditions were more primitive, than in France, Germany or Spain. It was not until this time that the legal process of tying the peasant to the field, which in other countries had taken place several hundred years earlier, was effected in Russia. Serfdom was consecrated by law in 1609, and still further extended by Peter the Great and other Tsars, who liberally endowed officials, at no cost to themselves, with lands occupied by free village communities the members of which were forced to become serfs.[3] Serfdom was not abolished until 1861. The general result was that, however important that secret and painful process of internal development may have been, from the Crusades to the French Revolution, as it has been said, Russia took no part in any of the manifestations of European life. It must not, however, be forgotten that during this period, and especially up to the close of the nineteenth century, Russia had still been performing an immense service for Europe. At moments

[1] M. Kovalevsky, *Modern Customs and Ancient Laws of Russia*, pp. 121, 131.
[2] There was a notably high level of political organization and of individual character and morality at Pskov, in many respects higher than in the rival independent city of Novgorod (Klyuchevsky, *History of Russia*, vol. i, pp. 356 et seq.).
[3] M. Kovalevsky, *Modern Customs and Ancient Laws of Russia*, p. 218.

of the greatest danger, Russia, however stolid, however undeveloped, yet stood as the guardian against the last warding off of
the Asiatic—the advance guard and the rearguard of European
civilization, it has been called—and without Russia the Europe we
know to-day might have had no existence at all.

The swift and easy Revolution of 1917 by which Russia finally
liberated herself, so completely and yet so peacefully, from
Tsardom, which had enclosed and cramped her energies for four
centuries, caused surprise to many. Yet it was merely the emancipation of the Russian's natural instincts and a return to his primitive
ways of thinking and feeling. The advanced thinkers of Russia
had for so many years been repeating the fundamental truth about
Russia that for many ears the repetition had grown stale and meaningless, and the revelation of the fact came as a surprise. Obedience
to an autocracy ruling despotically from above is not in the Russian
temperament. "Centralization is contrary to the Slav genius," said
Herzen; "federalism is its offspring." Tsardom acted as an en-
sheathing capsule painfully compressing the nation it enclosed and
seeming to delay the expansion of its energies. Yet, as we see
throughout nature, such hard resistant capsules are the conditions of
vital birth. They are made to decay and fall away in obscurity at
last, and not till then can we realize the function they have fulfilled.

It may well have been through this long seclusion, this out-
wardly arrested development which has yet been so favourable to
inner development, that the Russian has preserved so much of the
child, alike of the child's simplicity and sincerity and of the child's
radical and clear-sighted impulse.[1] We may still, like the old
Slavophile historian Zabyelin, typify the Russian of Tsardom as the
epic *bogatyr*, who, growing tired at last of being restrained in the
position of a minor for thirty years and playing with the children,
when at last he breaks loose is terrible in his untried strength,

---

[1] R. Scotland Liddell, an English journalist at the Russian front during the World
War and also a member of the Polish Red Cross Volunteers, after remarking that the
Russian soldier is "the finest soldier in the world" (*At the Russian Front*, 1916, p. 24),
says that the Russian soldier is really like a big child, and that Russian officers agreed
with him in this opinion, though one (General Zakharov) added: "But it is also the
worst point of Russian men."

though always tender to the widow and the orphan. He has remained a child so long that though he performs the valiant deeds of the hero he remains still a child in spirit. It is so that we have seen the Russian in the magnificent outbreak of his Revolution.

Yet undoubtedly there was development, social and economic beneath the shell of Tsardom, even when we disregard the superb expansion of Russian art. The Russian peasantry and industrial classes have, for instance, acquired great capacity for organization, self-help, and practical action. This is conspicuously shown by the Zemstovs (established in 1864) and agricultural societies and especially manifested by the extraordinary co-operative developments which took place during the World War and mainly in the villages. In the course of a feud the Russians thus spontaneously developed the most immediately practical aspect of the Labour movement, in response to definite economic difficulties, to a greater extent than any other people have carried it.[1]

A great deal has been said concerning the enormous industrial expansion of Russia during the past century, and concerning the great Trans-Siberian railway which will certainly have a tremendous influence in stimulating the development of new trade-routes and readjusting the trade balance throughout the world. Many writers have laboured this point, and have pointed out at the same time how a large part of the south of European Russia, formerly almost a desert, is now dotted with populous manufacturing towns and factory chimneys, while the enormous natural wealth of Asiatic Russia, both above the soil and beneath, is rapidly beginning to be exploited by the energetic population of Siberia. Certainly this industrial extension has been very great. But perhaps something too much has been made of it. Her position as the natural land-carrier between Europe and Asia gives Russia an inevitably important commercial position; her great natural wealth gives her an inevitably important industrial position. One may doubt, however, whether industry and commerce are the main lines along which the special

[1] See, J. V. Bubnov, *The Co-operative Movement in Russia*, 1917. It is here stated that in 1915 the Moscow Co-operative Union embraced nearly two thousand societies with a turnover of twenty-two million roubles.

and peculiar characters of the Russian people will be developed. This is indicated by the fact that the industries of Russia have hitherto been to a considerable extent in other than Russian hands, and, though we may certainly expect this state of things to be altered in the near future, it serves to show that the Russians are not pre-eminently a commercial and industrial people. During the nineteenth century this was a fatal defect. The peculiar conditions of that century, however—the rise of machinery and consequent enormous increase in industrial production which marked its early years, together with the vast new markets which still remained to be fought for, by business methods or more warlike methods—can never occur again. While industry and commerce must remain factors of importance in the world's life, they will henceforth tend to run on lines of more ordered routine; they can never again be supreme factors in the destiny of nations. They are not the whole, nor even the largest part, of civilization.

Thus it is that in the future those special qualities of the Russian people which in the previous pages I have briefly sketched, and those special conditions under which those qualities have to be exercised, must inevitably play a part of the first magnitude in the history of the world. Russia already occupies over a sixth part of the terrestrial globe; its position makes it the chief power in the old world. England's empire, it is true, is large also, but England's empire is made up of small portions in many parts of the world; it was formed by a race of bold sailors, who planted a flag here, or clung to a rock there; the interests of all these separate fractions are opposed; it is an unstable empire, of which the largest portions are already republics in all but name, and could by no possibility be consolidated into a single unit. The Germans, again, are as strong and capable a race as any, but, even apart from the fact that they lack initiative and possess no aboriginal civilization, they are at present hemmed in on every side. France cannot be brought into competition here, for the virtues of France are those of quality rather than of quantity. The only rival of Russia as a great world-power is the United States.

The Russians possess, more distinctly than any other people, a special mission of civilization. In Europe, it is true, they can mistake

THE GENIUS OF RUSSIA

their mission; in Poland and in Finland they have not been more successful than England in somewhat similar attempts to rule peoples of alien civilization. For the peculiar task of dominating those barbaric Eastern peoples which have not already shown some power of civilizing themselves, Russia is eminently fitted. She has herself, it is true, not yet perfectly attained either the civilization of the East or of the West; she has never reached the level of either China or of France. But even the elements of barbarism in her own life and ways, as well as the powerful Asiatic strain in her blood, mark her out for the task which naturally falls to her, and enables her to blend harmoniously with subjugated peoples, from whom British conquerors, for instance, would have been held permanently aloof by lofty disdain. But there is more than that. Beyond any other European people the Russians possess a degree of receptivity, a racial humanity of feeling, a fund of high idealism, and a sense of the relationship of ideals to practical life, which cannot fail to carry them very far. These things, far more than either an outrageous militarism or the capacity for frantic industrial production, in the end make up civilization.

Even in the past, as Leroy Beaulieu pointed out, the Slavs were the pioneers of the two chief movements of the European world before the French Revolution, the Renaissance and the Reformation, sending forth Copernicus before Galileo and Huss before Luther.[1] To-day we see that they are sending the pioneers of that politico-social revolution which is the great movement of our modern world. We feel, moreover, that for fruitful action in that field they are peculiarly fitted by the special racial qualities and the special historical condition which have enabled them to combine in so rare a degree a high idealism with humane naturalistic realism.

[1] These were Slavs of Western Europe, as was Struthius of Posen, a physiological precursor of Harvey and the first modern writer on the pulse. In more recent times the Slavs of Russia have produced many pioneers and initiators of the first rank even in the strictest paths of science. Such as Mendeleyev the chemist, Lobachevsky the mathematician, Lebedev the physicist, Kovalevsky the zoologist, Pavlov the physiologist, Mechnikov the pathologist (who on one side was Jewish). It would be easy to add many names of brilliant Russian workers in every branch of exact and applied science.

Never before to-day in the history of Europe has there been the same need for subtlety and daring and sincerity in facing great problems. Never before in the history of the world has there been the same urgent necessity for charity and humanity in human affairs, for the arts of binding people together in co-operation and spontaneous organization. Our traditions and our conventions and our pruderies have fallen away. Our old-fashioned ultimate resort to war and imperialism has been reduced to absurdity. We realize that we have to set up our ruined world on a new foundation. At such a time not only is Russia fortunately able to attempt the realization of her own intimate ideals, but the whole world is enabled to understand that in attempting this realization the genius of Russia is at the same time inspiring mankind in the great task which now lies immediately ahead. It would indeed be idle to forecast the development of Russia. We have nothing to measure it by. The world has never before seen a nation which was at once so colossal and so youthful. Everything in Russia, indeed, strikes the traveller as large, youthful, virginal. It is this sense of largeness, the immensity of the fate which lies before them, which seems to emphasize unconsciously these people's gravity and sense of responsibility. When I think of Russia and try to represent her to myself in some single image, there comes into my memory the figure of the youthful giantess, still not full grown, who was led from her Russian home on the Don some years ago to be stared at in the countries of the West.[1] Unlike most of her kind, Elizabeth Lyska was healthy and well-formed, of remarkable beauty, very gentle, with a sense about her of yet undeveloped force. A company of anthropologists had been invited to meet her, and she gazed down at the pigmy men of science examining her, with a smile on her grave sweet face, half tender, half amused. That colossal child, with the mystery of her undeveloped force, has always seemed to me since to be the symbol of her people.

The Russian Revolution, by eliminating the ruling caste with its

[1] It may be noted that a somewhat similar image had already independently commended itself to one of the most typical and distinguished of Russians. In 1858 Alexander Herzen symbolized Russia as "a young and robust peasant girl".

often Germanic affinities and the bureaucracy which was merely the repressive instrument of that caste's policy, has brought to the surface the vast mass of the Russian people and revealed in them an intelligence and a degree of ideal aspiration which may seem surprising. Yet it can scarcely be termed a revelation, for throughout the great intellectual representations of Russia in the past have been, to a degree unparalleled in any other country, not the creatures of the ruling caste but their victims, martyrs in the cause of democratic Russian ideals. These ideals may seem confusing in their shifting varieties, yet they are but variations on the same themes. The Russian is revealed afresh as pacific, as humanitarian, as, in the primary and elemental sense, religious.[1]

The Russians have no aptitude for philosophy. They are too versatile and impulsive, too eager to reach practical applications—a characteristic often regarded as feminine—to be content to abandon the world and find contentment in the creation of metaphysical systems, as has often been easy for their German neighbours on the West and to the Chinese to the East. The Russian, says Waliszewsky, has a horror of abstractions, and Wiener remarks that "Russia has not produced a single philosopher worthy of the name". Many Russian names are indeed mentioned by those who seek to show that Russian is not behindhand in this exalted intellectual accomplishment. But they are not convincing. There is indeed de Roberty, but he was of French, German and Belgian stock as well as Russian, and he found his natural home in Paris. There is also Solovyev, but he was critic and poet, as well as philosopher, and in all these departments he seems to have been, more than anything else, a brilliant amateur. Even as philosopher Solovyev bears the Russian mark, for his philosophy is in reality a variety of religious mysticism with a distinctly social and practical tendency. It is here that the Russian is at home, even the Russian peasant, however illiterate. For centuries Russia has been an inexhaustible soil for the spontaneous growth of

---

[1] Dr. Harold Williams, describing a demonstration of extremists against the Provisional Government, in Petrograd during July 1917, remarks: "Most of the inscriptions on the banners were violently revolutionary, but the people who carried these flags, and those who followed them, looked as placid and cheerful as children marching to a Sunday-school treat."

unorthodox more or less mystical religious sects, often communistic, sometimes nihilistic in belief, occasionally fantastic or pagan, in character, and in devotion to these faiths thousands, millions rather, of Russians have suffered or even died. There is little specifically Christian or even theistic in these popular sects, which in this respect resemble many of the sects of early Christian centuries. Although Christianity was introduced into Russia in the tenth century, it may be maintained that it has never penetrated Russia, and Russia has played no brilliant part in Christianity, never having produced any great Christian saint, theologian, missionary or preacher.[1] The spontaneous religious impulse of the Russian peoples is almost as closely related to Shamanism as to Christianity. But its specific Russian character lies in its humanitarianism, in the Russian's instinctive tenderness and reverence for his fellows. The origin of this Russian characteristic may not be clear. To me it has always seemed that it is largely to be ascribed to the rigour of the climate which has cemented men together in the struggle against a common enemy, and made mutual helpfulness instinctive. Casanova tells how a Russian, perceiving that his ears were in danger of frost-bite, began vigorously rubbing the traveller with snow, and the same story has often been told by others. The humanizing rigour of the climate—which in Russia may have been fortified by the rigour of autocratic despotism—may be traced elsewhere, as among the Eskimo, while,

[1] As already remarked in discussing Russian art, the religion of the Greek Church is mainly external and spectacular, little attention being directed to the inner life. A Russian correspondent writes: "In our family and the families we knew no one spoke to the children on religious topics. This grieved the housemaid who wished to convert the little pagans, and taught us religion. She finally decided to take me to church to communion, to which the Greek Church admits even children. But first, she explained, I must confess to the priest. I prepared myself, therefore, with much trembling over my small sins, but also determined to be quite honest about my small faults. Great was my surprise when the priest, instead of inquiring into my sins, merely asked if I knew the prayers, and the Creed, which I accordingly recited, more or less badly, as the housemaid had taught me, for the liturgical language in Russia is Old-Slav, which is as remote from modern Russian as the language of Beowulf and Caedmon from modern English. Then I communicated, without any emotion, only wondering how it was that the bread and the wine had not the slightest taste of flesh and blood. I may remark that the priests of the Greek Church, unlike Catholic priests, never ask questions concerning the sexual life. I remember a lady, converted from Catholicism to Greek Orthodoxy, who was indignant—even disappointed—at the summary and superficial questions put to her by her new confessors."

in Spain also the rigour of climatic extremes has probably contributed to make it a land of mutual helpfulness and kindness. Whatever its origin, there can be little doubt about the fact, which is sufficiently attested alike by the experience of the visitor, and by the evidence of Russians, indeed by the manifestations of the Russian spirit in every field. It is even indicated in the structure of the language, and Kropotkin and others have remarked on the richness of Russian for rendering the various shades of human tenderness and love. "You perceive a divine spark in everyone," said a friend ironically to Korolenko, the novelist and publicist, on finding him in conversation with a tramp by the wayside. The friend's attitude was Russian, since, as Herzen has said, irony and scepticism are Russian traits, but Korolenko's was yet more essentially Russian.

It is this attitude, and not dishonesty, which underlies the Russian's feeling about loans, and his tendency to confuse theft with charity. The seizure of General Durnovo's house at the time of the Revolution by an unauthorized group of anarchists, the wide-spread sympathy which their action evoked (even though some of them seem to have been escaped criminals), and the serious political crisis thus brought about, here have their explanation. The attitude is deeply rooted and ancient. Herberstein, in the sixteenth century, found in Russia that when a man needs anything he might take it from another, and if, before the judge, he makes no denial of the deed but declares he needed the things he took, the judge admitted his rights and said to the complainant: "If you, in your turn, stand in need of anything, seize it from other people."[1] The same attitude still persists, and is still recognized, if not by law, at all events by a large element of the people.

We see that while this humanity is, on the one side, a practical realistic human kindliness, so radical as to be indifferent to what is usually counted morality, it still remains, on the other side, a religious faith. "Russian life presents itself as a continuous series of faiths," remarks a character in one of Chekhov's stories; "that a Russian does not believe in God is merely a way of saying that he

[1] *Tracts Upon Russia*, Hakluyt Society, vol. ii, p. 57.

believes in something else.[1] It is this permeating element of religious faith which has so often made the Russian a social fanatic and a political martyr. The political writer, Bulgakov, some years before the Revolution insisted that the political party of the future would be, in the broad sense, a religious party, including even atheism as a religious force, the aim of such a party being to inspire political and social life with the spirit of love, liberty, equality and fraternity. About the same time, Micheal Stahovitch, one of the most moderate members of the movement of social revolution, told Walling that the movement meant "a change of all institutions, of all relations, of all life, of everything".[2]

These Russian faiths, whither will they take Russia, and perhaps Europe, in her wake? Russia, colossal, youthful and barbaric, possesses qualities which, when we bear them in mind, make recent events in this land appear a promising dawn. Yet it is not untimely to ponder as to the day ahead.

[1] When we speak of the "religious" spirit of the Russian it must never be forgotten that we refer to something different from any devotion to the superstitions of his official Church. From these the Russian, as he grows intelligent and education progresses, completely emancipates himself; even the higher conceptions of religion have less meaning for the intellectual Russian than for the Western European. Scepticism, said Herzen, is a Russian trait. "With my sister," writes a Russian correspondent, "I had been brought up outside religious influences, as is usual with the children of 'intellectuals' in Russia, for the mysticism of Tolstoy and Dostoyevsky is completely foreign to enlightened society in Russia, and women among us have as little religious belief as men. We Russians cannot, indeed, understand how it is that educated people in the West, and especially in England, take such interest in religious questions, listen to the moral commonplaces uttered in pulpits and quote the Bible on every occasion. Nor can we conceal our surprise when we hear people in the West, even serious philosophers and thinkers, discussing whether morality can survive religious faith, for we ourselves live in a society from which religious faith has disappeared without leaving trace. The typical Russian, from this point of view, is not the eccentric Tolstoy but Kropotkin, who, during his long life, has meditated on many things, but never on God or the soul." This attitude of indifference by the intellectual Russian towards the Church—in contrast to the affection of the intellectual Englishman and the hatred of the intellectual Frenchman—is due, as Milyukov shows, to the historical position of the Greek Church in Russia.

[2] W. E. Walling, *Russia's Message*, 1908, pp. 438, 448.

THE GENIUS OF FRANCE

NOTHING has been more astonishing to those who know France than the astonishment of those who see in the France of to-day a new and unexpected revelation. There could not be a more convincing proof of the truth of Sir Thomas Browne's remark concerning him that travelleth in vain having learnt not in France. There is certainly no country where we have had more opportunities to show our ability to travel in vain. For there is no country in which we have more "travelled", if one may use Browne's word in this connection, for to travel is, literally, to labour painfully as in childbirth, to the bringing forth of a new vision of the world, a new conception of life. It is not so that the English have travelled in France. They have gone light-heartedly as though there were no need for "travail" here, carrying their own familiar stock of phrases—"the scornful insular way of calling the French light" which aroused Mrs. Browning's eloquent anger sixty years ago—and their own little personal manias, through the rippling and smiling champagne lands of France to the hospitable city of Paris, and they have found there what they brought and been pleased or horrified accordingly. So it has become possible for the English to cry aloud unrebuked, in the words of Matthew Arnold: "French lubricity—Shocking!" while the sympathetic Germans from across the North Sea, infatuated with their delusion of racial suicide, shouted back gleefully: "French decadence—Pfui!"

When Karamzin, the pioneer of Russian literature, went to Paris in 1790 he was reminded of Sterne's saying that the French are "too serious". "Sterne was not quite in the wrong," he observed, adding that he noted a tendency to deal playfully with grave things and gravely with playful things; that sign of intellectual distinction, it may be noted, was thus visible even in the midst of the turbulent fury of the Revolution. A century earlier Muralt had remarked that the French even regard love seriously, and we see to-day, as the austere patrician of Berne was unable to see, that they were therein, as in so much else, the fore-runners of the modern world. To the average English mind, indeed, Sterne's remark seems a "paradox".

With our northern traditions of physical and spiritual gloom, we have confused seriousness with melancholy. That intellectual confusion has had unfortunate results on our philosophy and our morals, and nowhere has it more vitiated our outlook than in relation to France. That we English tend to be melancholic has been noted too often, and through too many centuries, to admit of dispute. It lies indeed in our Scandinavian affinities and in our northern atmosphere. But do not let us suppose that the tendency to gloom is necessarily more than an exterior quality, a quality of mist and iridescence and elusiveness, not indeed incompatible with a certain kind of sad playfulness, alien to the French spirit, which we call humour. It was of the English, not of the French, that the Venetian Ambassador, who could speak from observation, reported in 1557: "They go to the stake laughing." Seriousness, on the other hand, is not necessarily an exterior quality at all, but rather an interior quality; it is a sense of the gravity of things—for it was to things rather than to people that the word was originally applied—and an intentness and precision in piercing, pungently or poignantly, to the core of life. If it lacks the emotional aptitude for humour, the French spirit possesses the intellectual aptitude for wit. It moves in a clear air, such as habitually surrounds the Latin mind, and such an air may be sunny, even when it is sharp. There is no opposition between seriousness and gaiety. It may not be possible to be at once melancholy and gay, but it is quite possible to be at once serious and gay.

This may seem an elementary distinction to dwell on. Yet it is so fundamental, and has been so often overlooked by English critics of the French national character—unable to see that English melancholy is not necessarily serious and French seriousness not necessarily melancholy—that we cannot too carefully bear it in mind. The distinction is really plain to see, even in the most familiar comic journals of the two countries. We have but to compare *Punch* with *Le Rire* at any time during the last thirty years. It is the method of *Punch* always to avoid vital spots, to go round, searching for humour and whimsicalities, provided they are safely to be found in the sphere of triviality; when *Punch* desires to be serious it is merely solemn and dull. These characteristics are expressed in the qualities

of English design, in the niggling methods, the profusion of petty
and meaningless touches, the failure to reach bold and beautiful
and significant line. One seems to see, indeed, as one looks at a
typical English drawing in *Punch*, that prudery is really a technical
quality, or rather the absence of a technical quality. *Punch* represents
the search for amusement of those whose main anxiety it is to avoid
penetrating to the real facts of life, the recreations of a melancholy
man who refuses to be serious. But the French artists are always
serious. So far from wishing to avoid vital spots, it is at such points
that they directly aim. All their skill is here; all their comic effect
lies precisely in the surprise of audacity with which they succeed in
penetrating to some intimate fact of life. Nor is this only in the sphere
of sex, as our English minds brooding secretly on that subject are
prone to think. It is so with all the vital facts, even with death, and
the French artist can play daringly with disease and mutilation and
death in a way impossible to the English artist. This seriousness—
this precision and courage in finding the sensitive spots of life and
penetrating deep—is reflected in the French artist's mastery of line
which in its precision and daring is the exact technical embodiment of
the French moral spirit. It is noteworthy that the power of line is
lacking in English artists save the greatest, and by no means always
there, perhaps never found at all in our comic artists except in
Rowlandson. To the French, however, power of line is so native, it
is so genuine a transformation of the essential French genius, that we
come on the significant fact that the evolution of the bayonet—
which is the form it naturally takes in warfare—is more closely
associated with France, as even the name indicates, than with any
other country, and a more favourite weapon of the French than of
any other people. That same quality—to return once more to art—
is in the French pen, and it has been peculiarly conspicuous in the
French literature of the war. France, it has often been remarked, has
produced no war poetry of any value worthy to compare with the
minor but brilliant and abundant crop of English verse. English
prose literature of the war, on the other hand, it is generally recognized, has been clumsy and helpless at the best, merely good as
journalism. There is indeed at least one recent book which comes to

mind as at all events a partial exception, Brett Young's *Marching on Tanga* which owes its beautiful combination of qualities to the fact that it is written by an artist who has had a doctor's training in facing precisely and courageously the actual facts of life and death. But to the French artist that condition for fine literature comes by no accident of professional training, but as it were instinctively and by nature, rather, let us say, by the whole discipline of French life, in whatever field life may be lived. We see it in exquisite beauty in Charles Tardieu's *Sous le Pluie de Fer*, which combines a breath of Laforgue's delicate fragrance with the incisive daring to face and to describe the unforgettable "descent into Hell". But that union of qualities is the mark of the French spirit everywhere, in life as in art the outcome of French seriousness manifested in the all-embracing tradition of discipline.

That word "discipline" recurs again and again when we contemplate French art and French life. It is the special French moral secret, equally apart from the English secret of self-reliance and the German secret of state-organization. It is, indeed, intermediate between those two ideas, for while it differs from the English idea in having a perpetual reference to the harmonious web of society, it differs from the German idea in rejecting any mere externally imposed order. It differs, moreover, to some extent from both by being in greater degree a conscious tradition, for the English tradition, however ancient, has only become conscious in recent centuries and the German has had no existence of any kind until still more recent years. It is this consciousness of a great and beautiful tradition which has done much to confer the seemingly magic influence which France exerts not only on foreigners but on her own children, even when she had treated them badly. Muralt, the acute Swiss observer, writing a century before the Revolution, remarked that the French peasant seemed altogether miserable—ill-housed, ill-dressed, ill-nourished—and yet was content, apparently finding his black bread more savoury when he heard of the triumphs of the prince beneath whom he seemed crushed. The same spirit, the same disciplined instinct which subordinates self to a larger whole, is there to-day, manifested even in the smallest matters of life. It is to the French we owe the *queue*, with its cheerful recognition of the rights of others who come before oneself, and the Parisian workman at the barricades of 1848, who, when asked what he was fighting for, replied: "Pour la solidarité humaine, monsieur!" bore witness that an idea, which to the people of most lands is a mere abstraction, is to the French mind a concrete and realized fact. It is also the essential tradition of high civilization, and thus has been so potent to attract and to hold all those various peoples who are bound together indissolubly in what we now know as France; for though Alsace-Lorraine is the latest witness of this fidelity to the French tradition, the same fidelity had been previously just as conspicuously shown by all the other provinces and principalities slowly fused into France.

It is this tradition of discipline, very little modified by all the political changes of recent centuries, which moulds the individual Frenchman and Frenchwoman, and stamps their peculiar and unchanging qualities. This education begins in childhood. The French preceded the Americans in the regard for children, but their method has always been totally different. The care lavished on the French child is not expressed in adoration but in careful guardianship, in a constant discipline for that elaborate social mechanism of which he will one day form part, and from contact with which he must meanwhile be preserved, a feeling symbolized in the old French tradition which allowed the child to wear no colours but white and blue. In France one cannot fail to notice the nervous timidity of the small boy—so unlike the attitude of the English boy —who has to ask a question of an adult, as though an adult were a possible ogre. The French adult is not an ogre, but the boy is not brought up to treat him on a footing of equality, whence the surprise Taine felt in England at the absence of any deep separation between the life of the child and the life of the man. In the girl this same shrinking timidity, again so unlike the attitude of the average English girl, is encouraged to persist until marriage. I recall the wife of a Paris hotel-keeper, newly married and just installed at the Bureau, so shy and pale and slender, that, the first time, I addressed her as "Mademoiselle". But as the years went by a continuous transformation could be observed; with heightening of colour and progressive physical expansion there developed also an ever greater confidence and energy, and the last time I saw Madame, shortly before the couple retired, she stood firmly planted in the middle of her Bureau with an air of robust self-assurance that was almost insolent. The developmental process, we see, in both sexes alike, is the reverse of that among ourselves: with them discipline comes at the beginning and self-confidence is developed on that foundation; with us self-confidence is implanted at the beginning, while discipline and regard for others only come in the end, when they come at all, for we almost elevate indiscipline to a moral principle. No doubt there is much to be said for both methods, and the defects of the French method are to us obvious. It has often made the French slaves of custom ("Cela se fait! Cela ne si fait pas!" are to them, as Muralt said, sound reasons for approval or condemnation), and sometimes violent rebels against custom. It is this school of discipline, moreover, the gradual initiative to a great tradition, which sometimes imparts a certain deliberate and ceremonious self-consciousness, a certain air of parade, to the heroic manifestations of the French spirit. But that self-consciousness brings also a sense of precision and a power of direction, a stress on the realization of a glorious traditional ideal, perhaps more reliable, though not more potent, than the impulses of that "hypertrophy of the self" which Taine admired in the Englishman. The French have thus acquired a moral courage which more than compensates a defect of physical resistance. Ten years before the present war a distinguished English surgeon, with a great experience of French hospital patients, remarked that he had never known a French patient, man, woman, or child, to fail in courage. This discipline ensures the maximum of high sustained effort, the full flight of heroic daring, in a people of peculiarly sensitive, nervous, and vehement temperament—unchanged in this respect since the Romans first observed them—specially amenable to discipline and specially in need of it. At the same time, a nation made up of more widely varied racial units than any other has by this discipline into a great tradition been to an unusual degree raised above the self-regarding aims, and enabled to cultivate, in a higher and more conscious degree than any other, a concretely realized ideal of humanity.

"They are perhaps of all nations the most humane," said Muralt, though personally he found them less congenial than the English, and it is the humanity of the French which arouses alike their own pride in their nation and conferred on it a magic power to enthral the world. Its potency lies in the fact that while it is an ideal it is also a concrete sense of reality. It realizes not only the immutable sacredness of the great things of life but the infinite importance of the little things which make life worth living. "After my own dear country I know no country I would prefer to France," exclaimed Karamzin, and in every land how many have made the same declaration!

THE GENIUS OF SPAIN

WHEN I attempt to define to myself the special note of
mark of the genius of Spain I am faced by contradictions.
All nations, like individuals, must have the defects of
their qualities, and the defects of the Spanish character
are so emphatic, so various, at first sight so unrelated, that it is
difficult indeed to fit them into any single formula, however simple,
however complex. Whatever can be done by sheer force of genius
or the impulse of some ardent passion, whether in the physical world
or in the spiritual world, that a Spaniard has done. But in the
aptitude or the inclination to organize practical life, or to furnish
that basis of efficient mediocrity on which alone man's progress is
possible, Spain has always been hopelessly wanting; despots and
monks have alone sometimes succeeded in obtaining a temporary
factitious unity. In this respect Spain lies at the farthest possible
remove from Germany, where plodding pliability, easily accepting
the organization of a strong arm, furnishes results which in the
individual are inconspicuous but in the social body overwhelming.

There is no end to the audacity or the variety of Spain's achievements in the world. Spaniards and Portuguese penetrated to the
farthest seas before any other nation; to Spain, through her recognition and patronage of a Genoese adventurer, belongs the most
stupendous discovery that Europe has ever made. Even in the sixteenth century, when England had no empire at all, Spain was in
possession of a colonial empire which remained vaster than that of
any other country even until the last century. In the spiritual
world, as in the physical world, Spain can show the names of a few
of the world's chief pioneers and conquistadors. There have been
no great groups of Spanish novelists or painters, yet a Cervantes
stands out as the author of the greatest and most popular novel that
Europe has produced, and Velasquez now appears as perhaps the
greatest painter in Europe. We are accustomed to say that the
Spaniard has no genius for government. And yet no country has
ever produced greater rulers, and at one period no country
possessed better laws. The Spanish Balbus was the first barbarian

who reached the Roman consulship; the Spaniard Trajan was the first barbarian elected emperor, while Hadrian was also a Spaniard, and Marcus Aurelius was accounted one. So that, as has often been pointed out, Spaniards ruled the world during nearly the greater part of the period—from the death of Domitian to the accession of Commodus—which Gibbon declared to be the happiest in human history. At a later period Aragon and Catalonia possessed extra-political and municipal freedom when England was still crushed beneath the mailed hand of the Normans. Against the English Alfred, Spain can place her Alfonso the Wise, and in the long roll of great queens Isabella must always be placed near the top.[1]

Thus a first glance at the history of Spain, and at the great figures Spain has given the world, reveals little but a perplexing series of glaring contrasts. On the one hand no country in Europe can produce such a series of magnificent achievements; on the other hand we can nowhere find so prolonged a history of misrule and in-effectiveness and failure. From the days of Diodorus down to the present Spaniards have impressed other nations by their courage and obstinate tenacity; yet of all the great countries of Europe Spain alone had allowed herself to be effaced from the map of the extra-European world.

There is only one assertion that at the outset we can safely make concerning the genius of Spain. Its first characteristic is individualism. Its successes are due to fine personalities; its failures to the lack of concerted and organized action. Its contributions to the world have been the gift of men who were mostly indifferent to the virtues of association and subordination, who were, above all, original persons, careless of their environment, daring to assert themselves. So that, it has been possible to say, "the mad greatness born of spiritual exaltation gave Spain a predominance far greater than did war". Spain, as one of her own children has said, is "the land of holiness and of chivalry"; of all the manifestations of the human

---

[1] It may be added, however, that neither Isabella nor Berengaria, the favourite heroine of Spain, was wholly Spanish; Isabella combined two English Plantagenet strains with her Spanish blood, Berengaria was half English.

spirit there are none in which the personal qualities of the individual count for so much as the knight and the saint.

Both the knight and the saint are really militant personages, and the Spaniard has been from the first a soldier. Even the Romans learnt lessons in the art of warfare from the most skilful and determined enemy they had ever encountered; the national hero of Spain, the Cid, was a soldier of fortune, and down to the middle of the seventeenth century Spanish infantry was unsurpassed in Europe. It is noteworthy that even so peaceful a profession as that of letters has in Spain been throughout associated either with the conduct of affairs or more usually with the profession of arms. Merobaudes, the Spanish Christian poet of the fifth century, was also a distinguished soldier; Jaime the Conqueror, the great king of Aragon, is also as famous for his picturesque chronicles as for his fighting qualities. Bishop Roderic of Toledo, the chief chronicler of the thirteenth century, wielded his sword in the fight with the same vigour as he afterwards wielded his pen in describing the fight. Fernán Pérez de Guzmán, in the fifteenth century, when he retired from battles and the world, drew in his *Generaciones* and *Semblanzas* a series of historical portraits which are scarcely surpassed for keen, concise vigour. Santillana, the Glory of Spanish literature in the following century, was equally great in camp, council, and court. Garcilasso de la Vega, one of the most typical of Spanish figures, describes himself as dividing his time between his sword and his pen, "Tormando ora la espada, ora la pluma". It would be tedious to enumerate the examples which Spain offers of this unusual association, found even in the greatest of her writers, for Lope de Vega, who in mere amount wrote more than any Grub Street drudge, was a man whose chief interests were in life, and who was always ready to fight when called upon, while Cervantes was essentially a soldier, a battered veteran who wrote his books in the intervals of life. It is this characteristic more than any other which has given the chief impress to Spanish literature, its special qualities of swift, pungent, picturesque life, of vivid movement and intrigue, as well as its absence of self-consciousness, its carelessness of artistic perfection. The phenomenon can scarcely be met with elsewhere.

All the great English poets, for instance, from Chaucer and Spenser onwards, have been dreamers, spectators of the world, vividly interested, indeed, but rarely—as in a slight degree Milton—themselves men of affairs, and never by preference soldiers. Sir Philip Sidney was a soldier, but he occupies only a small niche in English letters. Ben Jonson was once a soldier, but it was merely a youthful episode; it was possibly the same with Chapman, who in some respects recalls the characteristics of Spain. And even if we turn to a southern country like Italy we find that the same holds good, and that from Dante to Carducci there has been no special connection between the sword and the pen. The predominance in Spain of these special embodiments of independent originality, the knight and the saint—more precisely the soldier, the man of affairs, and the monk—is so complete that every distinguished Spanish writer, down to Valera, may fairly be included in one or the other category.

This disposition is, indeed, once more represented in our days, for instance, in Blasco Ibañez's turbulent and adventurous career. Blasco Ibañez has sometimes been called the Spanish Zola. It is certain that the French novelist has influenced the later development of the Spanish novelist and that in general methods of approaching their art there are points of resemblance between the two writers. Yet the differences are fundamental. Zola was a man of the study who made novel-writing his life-work from the outset; for every book he patiently accumulated immense masses of notes (in which, as he himself admitted, he sometimes lost himself), and in a business-like and methodical manner he wove these notes into books of uniform and often impressive pattern, which become the more impressive because it was inspired by a novel doctrine of scientific realism. Nothing of this in the Spanish writer. However revolutionary his social and political outlook may be, he is not revolutionary in methods of art; he has scarcely even mastered the traditional methods. The habits of journalism have taken strong hold of Blasco Ibañez, and his more severe Spanish critics deplore the frequent looseness and inaccuracy of his style. There are passages of splendid lyrical rhapsody, and there are often the marks of a fine and bold artist in the construction of a story or the presentation of a character; but in the accomplished use of the beautiful Castilian tongue Blasco Ibañez is surpassed by many a young writer of to-day. Nor has he any of Zola's methodical fervour of laborious documentation. In his early novels he adopted the happy method of drawing on his own vivid early memories of Valencian life and character. These constitute his best and most memorable work; they include *Arroz Y Tartana*, *Canas Y Barro*, *La Barraca*. More recently his method has been to soak himself, swiftly and completely but for the most part very briefly, in the life he proposes to depict. A week may suffice for this, and the novel itself may be written in a couple of months. Thus for writing *Sangre Y Arena* it sufficed him to visit Seville in the company of a famous matador, and the preparation for *Los Muertos Mandan* was a boating expedition round the Balearic coasts in the course of which he was overtaken by a storm and forced to shelter on an islet where he remained for fourteen hours without food and soaked to the skin. Nor are the notes for his books written down; he relies exclusively on his prodigious memory and his intense power of visualizing everything that impresses him. His robust and impatient temperament enables him to work at very high pressure, oblivious of every attempt to interrupt him, even for eighteen hours at a stretch, sometimes singing as he writes, for he is a passionate melomaniac whose idols are Beethoven and Wagner. It is clear that a worker with such methods has little need of sleep; he is, however, a great eater, and feels, indeed, Zamacois tells us, a great contempt for people who cannot eat well; but when he is approaching the end of a novel all such physical needs are disregarded; he writes on feverishly, almost in a state of somnambulism, even, if need be, for thirty hours, until the book is completed, when it is perhaps sent to the printers unread, to be corrected in proof.

The man behind these books is no ordinary man of letters. He is a personality, and that fact it is which imparts so much more interest to his work than its purely literary qualities—though these are not negligible—would warrant. The abounding vitality and energy of the books are, we feel, a reflection of the abounding vital and energetic person behind them.

Vicente Blasco Ibañez was born in Valencia in 1867. The family sprang from Aragon, and it is certainly the bold, obstinate, firm-fibred Celtiberian stock of that region which we feel predominantly in this man's work. His parents kept a modest provision shop, and in this connection one may note the prominence which food, hunger and eating occupy in the novelist's work, and the singular vividness with which they are described. If Hunger and Love are the pillars of the world, it is the first with which Blasco Ibañez has been mainly concerned. He has indeed shown himself able to deal frankly and decisively with the erotic side of life. But he is not an amatory novelist; he is far more concerned with the problems of hunger than of love; all his best novels are powerful concrete presentations of economic aspects of life. The young Vicente was a turbulent youth, intelligent but rebellious to discipline, and more fond of sport than of books. He began life as a law student and speedily acquired a profound distaste for law and lawyers, whom he regards as among the chief agents of social evil. At seventeen he finally abandoned the law, and ran away to Madrid, to become a journalist. A year later he wrote a revolutionary sonnet against the government and for this offence was sent to prison for six months. Such treatment was not calculated to exert a soothing influence on a youth of Vicente's temper. The next years were full of agitation, of republican propaganda, and of conflicts with law and authority. In 1890, having been condemned to prison for speeches and agitation against the Conservative Government of the day, Blasco thought it best to flee to Paris, about which he wrote a book. A few years later he again fled, hurriedly, in a fisherman's boat, to Italy, on account of a collision between the people and the police in the agitation over the Cuban war. On his too reckless return he was seized by the police, handcuffed, taken to Barcelona, then under martial law, and condemned by the Council of War to a convict prison. The tribunal neglected, however, to deprive him of civil rights, and in a few months—to the astonishment of all Spain—the city of Valencia, which he had done so much to transform into a great revolutionary centre, liberated him from prison by sending him to Parliament as their deputy. As a counterblast to this anti-clerical declaration, the

clergy resolved on a demonstration at Valencia by choosing this
port for the embarkation of a national pilgrimage to Rome. The
pilgrims duly arrived at the quays under the superintendence of
ten bishops, but Blasco Ibañez and a few faithful followers were
prepared, and to the horror of the faithful he ordered the ten prelates
to be flung into the sea, whence they were speedily rescued by small
boats which the revolutionary leader (this is a characteristically
Spanish trait) had humanely placed in readiness. Such at least is the
recorded story.

At this time Blasco Ibañez was approaching the age of thirty and
was yet scarcely known as a novelist. As a youth he had indeed
published a story of wild adventure, which he afterwards bought up
and destroyed. He reached the novel indirectly, through journalism.
As a deputy he desired to spread his ideas through Spain, and therefore founded a newspaper, *El Pueblo*, into which he threw such
energy that it rapidly acquired wide influence, and as there was no
capital wherewith to pay a novelist the editor resolved to write his
own *feuilleton*. It was in this way that all the earlier novels—the
group of vivid pictures of Valencian life based on early personal
impressions—first appeared, attracting little attention, even when
published separately, until the French discovered and translated
La Barraca under the title of *Terres Maudites*. Soon afterwards
Blasco Ibañez became a famous novelist whose reputation grew
world-wide. Henceforth he devoted his energy exclusively to
the work of novel-writing, though latterly he spent a long period
in South America, wrote a large book on Argentina, and during
the Great War settled in Paris to write in the spirit of the novelist
and journalist a most extensive and picturesque *Historia de la Guerra
Europa* in serial parts.

How immense this man's energies are may be sufficiently divined
even from this brief sketch of his early life. We may see him
characteristically in the full-length portrait (exhibited in London a
few years ago) by another famous Valencian, Sorolla, whose work
in a different medium has so much of the same quality as his friend
the novelist's. Here we see Blasco Ibañez in the full vigour of
maturity. He stands facing the spectator with a cigarette between his

fingers, a grizzled solid figure with high receding domed forehead, bearded and moustached, a strong sagacious man, assured of his power, who is taking your measure calmly, critically, self-confidently, with a jovial, humorous smile. He is, you perceive, a man planted firmly on the earth, with a close grip of the material things of life, a man with great appetites to match his great energies. We miss here any delicate sense of the refinements of life or the subtleties of the soul. But we are unmistakably aware of a man with a powerful aptitude for human adventure, human passion, human justice, even human idealism. That is Blasco Ibañez, a typical representative of the Spanish spirit which has sometimes shown itself more distinguished, but is ever of very firm fibre, of well-tempered individuality.

. . . . .

No doubt the fundamental independence and originality of Spanish genius are not wholly inexplicable. One naturally turns in the first place to examine the racial elements composing the Spanish people. But even here the path is far from clear, and though it is no longer necessary to adopt the hasty conclusion of one baffled investigator who decided that the people of Spain had been dropped directly down from Heaven, it is only recently that any definite conclusions as to their origin have been generally accepted.

In studying the genius of France we find that every province of that country has an intellectual character of its own, and that when we examine French history and apportion the great men of the country to their proper districts, a vast mass of complex phenomena falls into harmonious order. At the first glance we should expect to find the same spiritual diversity in the provinces of Spain as we find in those of France. The obvious differences in the ancient kingdoms of Spain are so marked, and their political histories so distinct, that we look for something radically different in the temperament of their peoples as manifested in their men of genius. For the most part, however, it seems to me that we shall look in vain. We find, speaking generally, that religious fervour is predominant in Castile, practical initiative and commercial aptitude in Aragon and Catalonia, that Galicia and the other northern provinces produce

manual workers, while Andalusia and the other southern provinces
are marked by a love of the arts. But the distinctions between
Norman and Provençal, Breton and Gascon, are far more radical.
And when we come to map out Spanish men of genius (as I have
before mapped out French men of genius) according to their places
of racial origin the discrepancies are everywhere conspicuous. It is
not obvious why the Cid should come from the north-east, the
Great Captain from the south-west, why Martial should come from
the south-east, and Campoamor—the chief Spanish poet of recent
days, with a method of art and an attitude towards art resembling
that of Martial after an interval of two thousand years—from the
north-west. Nor, so far as I can see, have the great men of any
Spanish province characters so distinct as in Great Britain mark off
the finest men of Wales from those of the Lowlands, or the Cornish
from the East Anglians.

The early population of the Iberian peninsula we speak of as
being, generally, Iberians. This is convenient, especially when we
are concerned with the migration of this population to the north and
west. It is also to some extent correct, for the various peoples of the
peninsula became more or less blended, even when they were not
related at the outset, and a large part of the population may thus be
regarded as in every sense Iberian. But when we attempt to be more
exact we have to look upon the Iberians proper as only one of the
elements in the primitive population.

The conclusions and the surmises reached today, in the attempt
to harmonize modern investigations with the statements of the classic
geographers, seem to carry us very far back. The lowest traceable
layer in the population we seem to detect is that represented by the
Euscarians or Basques, the mysterious people who have led to so
ingenious and baseless theories.[1] In cranial type they are peculiar
though definitely broad-head; their language is very primitive and
of non-Aryan agglutinative type. Wilhelm von Humboldt, who

[1]It is useless to mention any of these theories, for there are objections to all of
them. See an interesting chapter on the Basques in Ripley's *Races of Europe*; he presents
all the facts, but his conclusions are as tentative and uncertain as those of all other
inquirers. See also briefer statements in Phlipon, *Les Ibères*, 1909, preface, p. xiv, and
Bouchier, *Spain Under the Roman Empire*, p. 6.

devoted much attention to them, thought they were a remnant of the primitive Iberians. This view is now quite discredited. The Basques are not true Iberians, nor are they to be indentified with the Vascones.

Regarding the next element in the population to appear, it is possible to speak with rather more confidence. This is the Tartessian or Turditanean element (for the two names are often roughly though not quite accurately regarded as interchangeable) of which Stabo had much of interest to tell, and which is now identified with the people of the Mycenaean or Ægean culture. They especially occupied the Mediterranean coast of Spain—perhaps defeating and driving north the ancestors of the Basques—and especially the Betican or Andalusian region, though when the Phoenicians discovered Spain in the twelfth century B.C. the Tartessians appear to have spread over nearly the whole peninsula and have penetrated into France to Aquitaine and Languedoc, as places indicate, Bordeaux and Toulouse being both said to be Tartessian names. They were a highly cultured people, more so than the later or true Iberians with whom we must not identify them, for they were carefully distinguished by the Greek writers, and had a labializing language as shown by their place-names in which the Iberians introduced a K or QU sound. They practised inhumation also while the Iberians cremated their dead; they were also intrepid sailors to a greater extent than the pure Iberians. It is supposed that the Tartessians belonged to an Indo-European stream of migration which passed westwards through North Africa, before the Phoenician conquest and raised altars to Atlas, the great Pelasgian marine and sidereal deity, precursor of the Greek Poseidon.[1] It is held that they crossed over into Spain near Gibraltar, at some period earlier than the founding of Cadiz by Tyrian sailors about 1100 B.C., and so ultimately spread as far as the Rhône. While they brought with them the elements of Ægean culture they developed them along their own lines and at a very early period. Phlipon considers that

[1] Phlipon, Les Ibères pp. 37 et seq. He invokes in this connection the Jason legend as reflecting the earliest Indo-European maritime expeditions, as well as the Daedalus legend.

the cyclopean walls of Spanish primitive citadels are of older type than those of Tiryns and Mycenae.[1] Strabo reports that Tartessian or Turditanean literature was said to be six thousand years old and Bouchier remarks that if we suppose the Tartessian year to be, as among some early peoples, of only three months, this date will bring us to about 1400 B.C. and coincide with the Mycenaen age.[2] Strabo also declares that so wealthy were these people that gold, silver, copper and iron equal in amount and similar in quality have not yet been found in any other part of the world.[3] The artistic skill of these people has only been revealed in recent times. The character and originality of their art is now known. It is usual and convenient to speak of Iberian art, but we must probably regard the characteristics of Iberian art as mainly due to the Tartessians. Phlipon considers that it is not clear that, as Henzey and Perrot have argued, Iberian art could have been based on either Phoenician or archaic Greek. In any case it is not mainly imitative but genuinely individual and Iberian, alike in its forms, its techniques and its style. It is an art that is certainly rough, without great technical skill, but very personal and distinctly realistic, suggesting not so much Phoenicia or Cyprus or Magnesia as the Middle Ages. The acrobat of Osuna standing on his head with vivid realism recalls a mediaeval gargoyle. The Tartessian work of the greatest originality, the Lady of Elche[4] is aloof from the Semitic and the Greek types, and there is even a certain modernity about it. It may be remarked that the Turditanian seems to have had a predilection for sculpture which he has stamped on all later Spanish art.

The people who produced this culture, perhaps softened by wealth and luxury, were unwarlike. They yielded to the next great

[1] Phlipon, op. cit., p. 292.

[2] Bouchier, op. cit., p. 69. But we cannot, of course, take very seriously the large figure of ancient tradition.

[3] Strabo, bk iii, ch. 2. So also Herodotus, Aristotle, Pliny, etc. While the Greeks marvelled at the wealth of Turditania they also seem to have regarded it as a very remote region, and Strabo suggests Homer's Tartarus, the furthest place beneath the world, was derived from Tartessus.

[4] See Havelock Ellis, The Soul of Spain, p. 108 and frontispiece. Phlipon, op. cit., ch. vii, "La Culture Ibérique".

invasion, that of the Iberians in the strict and narrow term, who in their turn spread over Spain and south-western France, and ultimately up to the North Sea. Yet the population of Spain, it is believed, still remained fundamentally Turditanean. The Iberians were definitely Indo-Europeans, like the Ligurians, to whom they were closely related, and they entered Spain at the two ends of the Pyrenees. Although not so cultured as the Turditanians, they possessed high qualities of character, and Pliny[1] placed them above the Gauls for ardour in work and for resolution of mind, *vehementra cordis*, a quality of spiritual passion which has ever since marked the Spaniard.

There was yet another and later early invasion, that of the so-called Celts, which took place somewhere between 500 & 450 B.C.[2] Phlipon accepts the theory of Hirt that they came along by the coast from Gaul to Galicia where the River Deva seems to have a Celtic name. But Hirt was mistaken in thinking that they came from England, and d'Aubus Jubainville has argued that they were Celts of the Gallo-Breton stock which only reached England in the second century B.C. These Celtici, or Celts of Spain, seem to have arrived slowly and in small groups and played a very effaced part in history, so that Livy never so much as mentions them. They were quite unlike the vigorous and war-like Celtiberians of central Spain, so that it was evidently the Iberians which dominated that blend. This is also indicated by the fact that the place names of Celtiberia are regarded as clearly Iberian. Celtiberia, it may be said, corresponded to the modern provinces of Burgos, Soria, Guadalajara, Cuenca, and Albacete, with parts of Palencia, Segovia and Saragossa. The Celtic centre is in the north-west; that is to say, in Galicia and adjoining parts of Portugal. While these people are ambiguously termed "Celts" and "Gallo-Bretons" we have to recognize that they were largely, and even perhaps predominantly, of Alpine race and therefore related to the people of the highlands of central France. This is shown by the fact that even to-day Galicia and the neighbouring parts of Portugal reveal the most broad-headed population of Spain. It is also indicated by all that we hear, or may infer, of their early

---

[1] Pliny, Lib. xxxvii, cap. 203.   [2] Phlipon, op. cit., 139.

history and character, of their gradual penetration, of their unwar-like temper, of their tendency to dwell in the hills, of their patient and laborious habits, of their reserve sometimes, in the opinion of other Spaniards, amounting to moroseness. The Galicians even to-day are, like the Auvergnats in France, known far beyond their own home for their willingness to undertake servile occupations. It is perhaps noteworthy also that it is in Galicia we find the shrine of Saint Jaimes of Compostella, the chief religious shrine of Spain for centuries, indeed a place of pilgrimage for all the people of Western Europe.

The earliest population indeed which has left definite traces is the people which built up the ancient Ægean civilization. We still see their massive constructions at Tarragona and Gerona, as well as in the so-called Talagotes, and similar constructions, in the Balearic Islands, which Antonio Vives believes to be the same type, probably tombs, and dating perhaps from the twentieth to the fifteenth century B.C.[1] The Mediterranean people of the Ægean civilization we may assume to be of a type closely allied to the Iberians. Who the Iberians were is, however, a problem that long perplexed anthropologists. The early investigations of a great anthropologist, Broca, as well as those of Thurnam, followed by the more recent researches of Cartailhac, Siret, and Sergi, have in the main settled this problem. It is fairly clear that the Iberians formed part of a great Mediterranean race which reached Spain from Africa—possibly, as Sergi believes, having their original home in north-east Africa—where they may still be seen in their purest form, by the ancients called Libyans, by the modern Kabyles and Berbers. This race gradually over-spread all the coast of the Mediterranean and in the north-west extended even into Britain in days previous to the arrival of the Celts. Spain as the nearest country to Africa became the special European seat of Eurafrican race and has remained so to the present day, the Basques in their isolated fastnesses, as is

[1] A. Vives, "El Arte Egeo en España" (*Cultura Española*, November 1908. Pierre Paris has pointed out (and Bezzenbuerger agrees) that it is to the Mycenaeans or Ægeans, and not to Greece, that Spain owes the religious and symbolic significance of the bull and cow and the form and style given to these symbols. To an important branch of Ægean culture has been attributed the gourd form of pottery.

now generally recognized, having best preserved, though still with much modification, the primitive Iberian traits. The Celts came at a later date, chiefly to the northern and north-western coast, forming a fringe to the Iberian population, and the Carthaginians, preceded by the Phoenicians, formed a similar fringe along the south and south-western coast. With this southern fringe the Romans mingled their civilization; and then the Visigoths penetrated to the centre of the country and ruled it for many centuries, to be driven to the north of the peninsula by the irresistible Arabs and Berbers who developed in the southern half of the country the most exquisite civilization that Islam has ever attained. Then after five centuries the northern element of the population rolled back with renewed energy to overlay and expel the Mohammedan population. From that time there has been no new immigrations, and so far as the composition of the race has been altered it has been by the more unfortunate methods of banishment, emigration and destruction. An interesting and probably very significant point about the immigrations is that they were largely constituted by similar elements. Cut off on every other side by the Atlantic and the Pyrenees, Spain was chiefly open on the Mediterranean side, and every immigration on this side, probably even to some extent that of the Romans, was mainly composed of some branch, usually African, of the same Mediterranean race. Only the Celts and the Goths brought in new elements, which, however, have failed to modify greatly the general character of the race. The recent researches of anthropologists have shown that the physical characters of the Spanish population reveal a degree of fusion and uniformity which renders them perhaps the purest race in Europe. The absence of fundamental diversity in the racial characteristics of the several provinces, and probably the general lack of pliability in the whole nation, may be explained by this uniformity of constitution. Both by its physical features and also by the race and temper of its population Spain is, far more than any other European country, African in character. I see curious evidence of the affinity between Africa and Spain in the resemblance in literary spirit between the Latin African writers and Spanish writers. Nowhere but in St. Augustine and Tertullian, the most typically African authors, can we find the torrid emotional fervour, the inflexible ethical independence, dominating all other elements of character, which we so often find in the men of Spain.

The resemblance between the Spanish spirit and the African spirit has by none been so well brought out as by the distinguished scholar, Gaston Boissier, and the more impressively since he makes no mention of Spain and is merely concerned to described African characteristics. The African authors who wrote in Latin, he remarks in his attractive work *L'Afrique Romaine* (ch. 6), do not form a compact group with identical character. Yet they reveal common traits and a family air. Thus the greatest of them—Apuleius, St. Cyprian, Arnobius, Lactantius, St. Augustine—have all been rhetoricians. Again, these rhetoricians have all been devout; even Apuleius frequented the temples, was initiated in all the mysteries, and enrolled in the militia of Isis. Again they are all marked by their independence, their diversity, their strong individualism; it has sometimes been said that, born beneath a sky of flame, they are all marked by their violence, a genius of fire, intemperate, incapable of direction or restraint. That was indeed the character of Tertullian, but St. Cyprian was a model of self-restrained moderation, Apuleius a romantic, Lactantius a pure classicist, while Augustine resembles no one, often not even himself. Again the Africans are marked by an originality which is indifferent to elegance, and disdainful of rules, frankly abandoned to its own genius. Thus African literature, according to Boissier, possesses four leading characteristics: a tendency to rhetoric, religious devotion, diverse individuality, indifference to elegance and rules. But these four characteristics are precisely the four characteristics which most clearly mark Spanish literature from Roman days to our own.

This moral element, this peculiar independence, sometimes coarsely fibred, more often finely fibred, seems the predominant element of the Spanish mind. The Spanish are not a great artistic race like the French or the northern Italians, in spite of isolated achievements in painting and architecture; still less are they a race of abstract thinkers and philosophers, like the southern Italians or the Bretons; not one of the pure thinkers of Europe has been a Spaniard; not one of the great discoveries in science has been made in Spain;[1] the Spanish are not even, in the strict sense, an emotional people like the Germans, and the large emancipating emotional personalities, of whom Luther is the supreme type, are not produced by Spain, whose Luther was a Loyola. But to a greater extent even than England Spain is the land of character, of originality, of independence. Character and conduct, alike on the grave and the comic sides, from the subtleties of the theologians to the gusto of the picaresque novelists, have ever occupied the Spaniard in a peculiar degree. In a people more than any other impelled to become the prey of their instincts and passions—by no means always ignoble instincts and passions—conduct and character become matters of more vivid interest than they can ever be to a tamer race. One may note the tendency to sententiousness which characterizes this serious and laconic people; no country is so rich in proverbial wisdom. Nor is it by accident that the greatest and most typical of European moralists is Seneca of Cordova.

Although at the first glance the statement may seem paradoxical, it is probable that in this racial tendency to moral fervour we may really find the ultimate basis of the chief defect in the Spanish character. Sweet-natured, generous, affectionate, faithful as the Spanish man or woman can be in personal relationships, that inflexibility of fibre which is the virtue and quality of the race at its best, easily becomes cruelty. Indifference to the suffering of animals seems natural to Spaniards (except perhaps the Basques), though to a far less extent than to the Moors. The bull-fight, though not originally a Spanish institution but apparently the mediaeval development of Moorish boar-baiting, is certainly a true expression of the people, and though it would be unjust to say that the attraction of the bull-fight is its cruelty, it remains true that a people more sensitive to the infliction of pain could not so long have tolerated a sport in which the infliction of pain is at all events more obvious, if not greater, than in the hunting of foxes or the shooting of pheasants.

[1] At the present time there is not one Spanish man of science, except Ramon y Cajal, the histologist, whose work is followed by the scientific world in general.

But when we talk of Spanish cruelty we must always remember that a Spaniard can be at least as cruel to himself as he is to others. The Spaniard has ever been ready to apply the lash to others, remorselessly, but never more remorselessly than he has applied it to himself. He is only indifferent to the pain of others because he is indifferent to his own pain. Even Strabo noted this aspect of Spanish cruelty; Spanish mothers, he says, slay their children rather than they should fall into the hands of the enemy, and he tells how certain Spaniards when taken prisoners by the Romans, and affixed to the cross, still chanted songs of triumph. One may perhaps say that it is on the side of austerity that Catholicism has appealed so strongly to the Spaniards; Spain was always antagonistic to the domination of Rome, but it was Spain that created the counter-Reformation and saved the Church. It was in Spain that the celibacy of the secular clergy was first declared, a century before it was accepted by the rest of the Christian world. One may recall that the first Christians who were willing to die at the hands of the Church for fidelity to unorthodox opinions, as well as Churchmen who slew them, were alike Spaniards. At a later date the early inquisitors were themselves martyrs; and the violent excesses of a Torquemada and a Lucero were the acts of men who had no brutal thirst of blood, but who naturally and habitually subordinated the infliction of pain to the achievement of their fervid and narrow ideals. The atrocities of the Inquisition, committed on Jew and Moor and heretic, become intelligible when we remember that from the days of Saguntum and Numantia unto our own time the Spaniard has never been surpassed in the capacity for facing calmly and deliberately every form of suffering and death. Nietzsche has preached to a sceptical generation the ennobling virtues that are born of hardness and pain, but that is a lesson that the Spaniard has at no time needed to learn.

  •   •   •   •   •

Not only are the characteristics of the Spanish people, however superficially various, fundamentally the same from Biscay and Asturias to Andalusia and Catalonia, but they have remained the same from the beginning of history. It happens that this opinion is not incapable of verification. When the traveller to-day enters Spain he will, for example, observe that the favourite colour for dresses is black, that the men wear cloaks, while the women are fond of embroidered shawls, their national headdress also being a mantilla coquettishly shading the face, while the hair is done in certain peculiar fashions, especially in an elevated structure. He would also observe that they are fond of the flesh of the goat, that they use oil instead of butter, that they drink water and are extremely frugal and temperate. He might note that the women till the soil and that it is common for two people to ride on one horse. He would be struck by the confidence with which the maimed beggars rely on the passer for charity. He would find the inhabitants sometimes urbane, sometimes with a certain ruggedness of character always brave. And while not avoiding necessary labour he would find that they are very averse to unnecessary labour. Now every one of these observations, literally true to-day, of the manners and morals of the Spanish people was made two thousand years ago by a famous Greek traveller who wrote before the Christian era. If Strabo returned to life to revise his *Geography*, there is probably no part of it which would need so little change as the book on Spain.[1] What ancient writers have told us about Britain is almost wholly meaningless as regards the British to-day; in what they have told us of France and Germany we discern a resemblance to the general character and temper of the people still inhabiting those countries. But in what has come down to us concerning Spain we recognize the very accent and gesture of the modern Spaniard, just as the statue of the Gaditanian dancing girl in the Museum at Naples presents the precise pose of the modern Spanish dancer. The bull-ring and the Church have indeed been added to Spanish institutions, but they have only been grafted on to more ancient habits of the people.

We realize the singular persistence of the Spanish genius if we

[1] Even when the facts have changed their form we may still trace a continuity of tradition. It was customary in Strabo's time for men to be put to death by stoning; it is still common to see dogs so put to death. Strabo tells us that the Iberians thought the Romans mad because they walked for mere pleasure; the same observation to-day is made by many southern peoples, beside the Spanish, concerning the English.

trace the history of a single district. We could not take a better example than Cordova. Even the names of cities seem to have changed less in Spain than elsewhere, and Cordova still remains the name by which it has always been known. Before the Christian era the civilization of which Cordova is the centre was so ancient that Strabo tells us it was thought to possess laws and poems not less than six thousand years old. In any case the inhabitants of the fertile valley of the Guadalquivir, always famed for its olives, were even then regarded as the most polished and urbane people of Spain, and such qualities are the surest index of an ancient civilization. The first important Roman settlement was at Cordova, and from the time that we first begin to trace its history definitely it has never ceased to produce great men. The first of these—as also the first great Latin author of non-Italian origin—was the elder Seneca, as man and as writer a representative of the mixture of sternness and humour which marked alike the early Roman and the Spaniard, as also, it may be added, in later times the English and the Lowland Scotch. The traditions of Cordova were carried on by the younger Seneca and by Lucan, who with much foreign rhetoric exhibits in full development the arrogant and perfervid independence of the Spanish temper; the sentiment of the well-known line:

Victrix causa diis placuit, sed victa Catoni,

represents an attitude which has always been peculiarly Spanish. The establishment of Christianity in no way affected the intellectual position of Cordova, and in the days of Athanasius and Constantine, the greatest of Western ecclesiastics was no Italian, but Hosius, Bishop of Cordova. The Moslems came, but Cordova only flourished the more, and in the fourth century was the most civilized and the most magnificent city in Europe. Almanzor, the greatest statesman and general of Mohammedan Spain, began life as poor a student of Cordova; Ziriab, the most accomplished dilettante and Epicurean of the mediæval world, also belonged to a city equally pre-eminent in the arts of war and of peace. In its famous mosque Cordova possessed a temple which even now is only exceeded in size, though scarcely in interest, by St. Peter's. Before the institution of universities Cordova was the chief centre of European learning, and Albucasis, Albenzoar, Al Hazen were the chief scientific luminaries of their time, while it was a Cordovan of distinguished Cordovan family, Averroës, who by introducing Aristotle to the modern world led to the revival of learning in Europe. When Cordova again became Christian it played a smaller part in the world but never ceased to be a great city. Gonsalvo, *the great Captain*, one of the glories of Spain and Europe in the fifteenth century, was of old Cordovan family. Even to the present Cordova has maintained its reputation as a city to be born in, and Valera, the best novelist and the finest prose-writer of modern Spain, is a son of Cordova. To-day, as we wander through the ever-delightful streets of the ancient city, we are far from conscious of the gloom that broods over the dead cities of Europe; the grass may grow on the streets that were first in Europe to be paved, but we everywhere feel the presence of a race of unconquerable fibre. It is a climate of extremes, like that of Florence, and the men of Cordova and the men of Florence alike possess a peculiar intellectual energy, separating them, as an elect people, from their fellows. But while the energy of Florence has been mainly compressed into a few centuries, that of Cordova has been spread over a period that cannot be measured.

The civilization of Spain thus lies at the most ancient roots of European culture. Spain, we must always remember, was the first-born of Rome among the countries of Europe, the immediate inheritor of Rome's traditions. That is one of the keys to the right understanding of the Spanish genius. Unlike the Gauls who yielded almost immediately to the Roman legions, the Iberians resisted long and savagely; but the fervid tenacity of their resistance was equalled by the ardour with which they afterwards clung to the language and civilization of their conquerors. There was real affinity between the two races; both alike possessed a moral gravity and independence which facilitated assimilation when once the barriers were broken down. Thus it was that, from the first, Spaniards played so large a part at Rome, alike in letters and statecraft. Not only was Balbus of Cadiz the first provincial who ever became consul, but he was the only one ever accorded a triumph, and beside Trajan and Hadrian, Theodosius the Great also belonged to Spain. Quintilian was a typical Spaniard. Columella, the earliest horticultural classic, belonged to Cadiz. Pomponius Mela, who wrote the first account we possess of the ancient world, came from near Gibraltar, while at a later date Orosius, the first Christian historian of the world, came probably from Tarragona. We find Spain playing a prominent part in every century, not less in the Christian world than in the pagan world. Juvencus, the first writer of Latin Christian verse, was a Spaniard, while Prudentius, coming from the same Aragonese district as Martial, was the greatest of early Christian poets before Dante, and while his fame remained at its height for a thousand years, his work is still full of charm for the few who read him. In Prudentius, indeed, we find already in full development all the Spanish qualities: fervid intensity, religious exaltation, ascetic extravagance—without that narrow intolerance which the Spaniards showed in later ages—as well as that vivid picturesque quality, even the humour, which mark the Spanish character from first to last. Nor was Spanish intellectual supremacy confined to the fields of literature. At the end of the fourth century, as the historians of Spain proudly point out, the Pope, the two emperors of the world (Theodosius and his rival Maximus), the great heretic of the day, Priscillian—the first heretic ever put to death by the Church—as well as his persecutors, Idatius and Ithacus, were all Spaniards. At a very early period Spain gained its position as a great theological centre, and in the seventh century it was Spain—with, to some extent, Ireland—which chiefly maintained the intellectual life of Europe. The most prominent intellectual figure of the seventh century is St. Isidorus, the Bishop of Seville, the last philosopher and man of science of the Roman Empire and one of the most influential teachers of the Middle Ages. Then the Moslem invasion came to sweep away the last traditions of the Christianized ancient world, substituting indeed what was in many respects a more exquisite civilization. This in its turn was at last swept away by a reinvigorated Christian Spain, which in the full flowering time of its genius in the seventeenth century produced in Velasquez and in Cervantes the greatest painter and the greatest novelist of Europe, and then relapsed into mediocrity from which it has never since emerged.

.   .   .   .   .

What is the cause of the sudden extinction of all the finest intellectual elements of a civilization that flourished during so vast a period? Before we attempt to answer that question we have to go beyond the characteristics of the Spanish people and to consider the special conditions under which the nation has evolved.

A fact which seems of the most fateful significance in the history of Spain is the ultimate dominion of Castile. When at the end of the fifteenth century the masterful, fervent, bigoted Isabella united Aragon to Castile and drove the Moslems of Granada out of the country, she at once laid the foundation of Spain as a great power in the world and ensured its speedy overthrow. A country that is dominated by its most central region is sure to be badly dominated. The centre may probably contain the strongest race, but it will certainly be unprogressive and conservative to a dangerous extent. In the centre the race will be most homogeneous, with least of that pliability tending to civilization which comes from a fine blending of races, and the centre is necessarily more impregnable to external influences. If we could imagine France dominated by the pure and unprogressive Celts of Auvergne we should have a picture of a wholly different France. Peter the Great knew well what he was about when he transferred the capital of Russia from Moscow to St. Petersburg; and it may be doubted whether the domination of the German Empire by its most remote and least civilized region will eventually prove an unmixed advantage. There can be little doubt that the pre-eminence of Castile has exerted an unhappy influence on Spain. The special inflexibility and fervour of the Spanish people is more unmixed in Castile than elsewhere; in Castile also there was a conflict between the ruling classes and the people, who, while marked by more excellent qualities than their rulers have usually possessed, have seldom shown any desire or aptitude to take the reins into their own hands. Their activities have chiefly run into religious and literary channels, and how great a race they were in temper and capacity we may be content to find witness in the tongue they fashioned, a speech which for the special qualities of strength and beauty can only be equalled by English among the living tongues of Europe. As a people they deserved the highest admiration; as rulers they were entirely unfit to govern an empire. That intense racial fervour, which in the spiritual sphere produced results we may sometimes admire and sometimes deplore, when turned into a practical direction produced only the gloomiest and most suicidal results.

As a typical example on a colossal scale of the Castilian man of the people as ruler we may take the great Cardinal Ximenez. Of humble birth, he spent the first fifty-six years of his life in obscurity, then, turning friar, he became confessor to Queen Isabella and finally Archbishop of Toledo, the greatest ecclesiastic in Europe after the Pope. Simple, austere and humble in his personal life, he was yet arrogant and inflexible in public life, of undaunted will and courage, able to withstand pope and queen and king, to reform completely the unwilling Spanish clergy. Yet so indifferent was he to practical obstacles that he would undoubtedly have met defeat and death on some occasions had it not been for the prudence of others. Founder of a great university, Ximenez nevertheless by the destruction of the priceless libraries of Granada accomplished the greatest holocaust of learning which has ever been in the power of one man, and it was he who, brushing aside wiser counsels, swept away to Africa or to destruction all those Moors whom he could not baptize with his mop, thus creating the piratical Barbary States which were for centuries the scourge of Spain and indeed of Europe. This sober, humble, haughty friar cannot be called a great statesman—for without far-sighted wisdom and moderation no statecraft can benefit any nation—yet it is impossible not to feel some admiration for so supreme an incarnation of those qualities which—sometimes effectively and more often ineffectively—for four hundred years dominated Spain.

Until the days of Ferdinand and Isabella, the history of Spain, though sanguinary and confusing, is on the whole cheerful and certainly picturesque, full of freedom and fine energy, of variegated activities in every field. From the sixteenth century onward it is a record of intense and unrelieved gloom. It was no doubt the influence of Isabella, perhaps the most masterful and powerful woman who ever sat on a throne—in harmony with her wily and rapacious husband, Ferdinand—that finally moulded the temper of Spain, such as it existed when the first great world-power of the modern world, such as we now know it in its decay. Without Isabella there would have been no Ximenez and no Torquemada; without the protection afforded by her great personal character and wifely devotion Ferdinand could not have corrupted the Spanish spirit so safely and so thoroughly. Up to the end of the fifteenth century Spain had for 2,000 years been a land of great men, it had never been a great nation. Even under the rule of wiser kings and better laws that were elsewhere to be found in Europe, the people had preserved a sturdy distrust both of kings and laws. The task that was too great even for Alfonso the Wise was accomplished by the quiet, beautiful, inflexible, remorseless girl who once and for all dominated the firm and stubborn men of Spain; henceforth they were chained to the car of a great state, obedient to the crack of the whip. But that result was attained not only at terrible ultimate cost, but with an effort that would have been impossible to monarchs less bigoted than Isabella, less greedy and unscrupulous than Ferdinand. These qualities were required not only to build up the financial prosperity of United Spain, but to wield the fearful instrument of the Inquisition, by which, above all, Spain was moulded into a homogeneous whole, a great state without great men. Hitherto Spaniards had been tolerant, natively opposed to any interference with individual freedom; intercourse with the cultured Moors had made bigotry difficult; and Spain had taken no part in the Crusades.

The Inquisition met at first with opposition from clergy and laity alike, and not a few inquisitors were slain or grievously injured. Torquemada only became possible in Spain because the religious Isabella and the greedy Ferdinand saw in the Inquisition a marvellous device for the double purpose of exterminating the heretic and appropriating his gold. So, in spite of all pledges, in spite of the pope himself, it was set up throughout the kingdom. A great inquisitor cannot, however, be manufactured by royal mandate, and just as there is something in the Spanish character which makes the bull-fight, though not originally Spanish, the most characteristic of Spanish institutions, so we can see how, when once his humanity and independence had been crushed, the terrible fervour and inflexibility of the Castilian, that power of ferocious concentration on a single aim, lent itself peculiarly to the skilful and thorough manipulation of this awful instrument. It has often been pointed out, and it is needless here to repeat, how the Spanish character was modified by the Inquisition, not merely by the direct elimination of the most independent elements of the population, such as at a later date the revocation of the Edict of Nantes effected the spiritual impoverishment of France, but by the modification of traditions. On the one hand bigotry, greed, bribery, indolence became habits of the governing class, parasitism and servility habits of the governed classes;[1] on the other hand, the reserve and gloom, of which the germs lay in the Spanish character from the first, were intensified in days when the only sure way to be a free man—and that open to but few—was to become oneself a familiar of the Holy Office. Thus was formed the typical Spanish don of the seventeenth century, well known throughout Europe. The free-thinking, free-speaking, free-acting Cid had always been the national hero of Spain; hence-forth the Cid had no more relation to Spanish life than Robin Hood to English life.[2] The last great Spaniard in practical affairs belonging to old Spain was Gonsalvo, the "Gran Capitan", a great soldier, a great diplomatist, a great gentleman; and even he was not wholly untouched at the last by the methods of his master, Ferdinand. From that time it was not in life but in art, in novels, in drama, in

[1] Salillas, the Spanish criminal sociologist, in his instructive book, *Hampa*, has shown how radically parasitism is rooted in the national character, and how truly and significantly this is illustrated in picaresque literature. But it can scarcely be said that we find much of this characteristic until the sixteenth century.

[2] J. Fitzmaurice-Kelly (*Chapters on Spanish Literature*, pp., I et esq.) deals interest-ingly with the Cid—whom he regards with the more idealistic Don Quixote as the two national heroes of Spain—and the literature that grew up around him. The *Poema del Cid* dates from about the middle of the twelfth century, some fifty years after the hero's time, and was probably inspired by the *Chanson de Roland*.

poetry, in painting—and sometimes in religion—that Spain could claim any unmixed reverence. Cervantes, Calderon, Lope de Vega, and Velasquez nobly filled the seventeenth century, together with a group of great religious mystics, above all, St. Teresa, the chief of European woman saints. Since they died Spain has not given the world one manifestation of supreme original genius in any field.

The final seal of Ferdinand and Isabella was stamped upon Spain when their achievements in unifying the country, establishing the Inquisition and extinguishing the Moslem civilization of Grenada culminated in the expedition of Columbus. It was only with reluctance that Isabella could be persuaded to consent to this expedition; she might have divined that she was signing the ultimate fate of Spain. Possibly if the new world could have been left in the capable hands of Columbus the result might have been different. But the newly inaugurated order of things, by which the world was regarded as the prey of rulers, parasites, and friars, was in the first flush of its success. Those colonial methods were inaugurated which only ended yesterday in the Philippines. The new world was pillaged of its wealth, and its population was left to the tender mercies of friars and cut-throats. The home country, already undergoing a slow progress of depopulation through the sanguinary violence of its history from the time of the Romans onward, was drained of its men and its energy. Three centuries later, as we know, the rule of Spain was as extinct in the new world as its genius was in the old world.

. . . .

It is usually the women of the country who present most clearly its fundamental racial character. Certainly it is so in Spain; and whatever the reputation of Spain in other respects Spanish women at all events have never lacked fervent admirers. Even here, however, the admiration of the foreigner has more often been remarkable for its enthusiasm than for its insight. Far from being the gaily dressed beauty who raises her skirts and ostentatiously flirts behind her fan, the typical daughter of Spain is grave, quiet,

unfailingly dignified, simple and home-loving, singularly affectionate in her domestic relationships.[1] Passionate she can doubtless
be, but passion to a Spanish woman is a matter of life and death, far
too serious a matter to be played with, and flirting is unknown to
her. This is the secret of that simple, direct bearing and speech of
the Spanish woman, so free from the embarrassing consciousness
of sex, which renders a Spanish woman so charming, with a charm
in this and in many other respects so unlike that of a Frenchwoman;
and the poorest of Spanish women, however gracious she may be,
has no difficulty in conveying an assurance of the fact that she belongs to herself. The saying of Pope that "most women have no
character at all" would at all events not have suggested itself in
Spain, where the sense of almost self-sufficing self-possession seems
to be the rule among the women of the ordinary population, who
often retain both vitality and charm of manner into old age. There
is no class of the population of whom this is not true, perhaps least
of all that class (on the verge of gipsydom) which still keeps up the
dances of old Spain for the joy of an ever smaller circle. Abroad,
the dances of Spain are transformed by the original skill of an Otero
or a Carmencita (Guerrero being the splendid exception); at home
they are attenuated in polite society, rendered common-place in
cafés chantants, suppressed in their favourite haunts by the unregarding
Spaniard. In Seville nearly every home of real native dancing is now
closed; in Malaga you may think you know everything, and yet
never see or hear of the Chinitas, with its malodorous approach,
with the strange old-world picture it presents within, such as one
sees in seventeenth-century Dutch paintings. Here one may sometimes witness the best performances in Spain. The dancers sit in a
row at the back of the stage, the guitarrist sits in front, and one by
one, or two by two, the dancers come forward, in their exquisite
dresses, the beautiful Manila shawl and the skirt that reaches the
ankles, like great beautiful butterflies, as they sway and bend and

[1] It is common outside Spain to hear the Spaniard, and especially the Spanish
woman, spoken of as lacking the virtues both of sincerity and cleanliness. This is for
the most part the reverse of the truth. It may perhaps be accounted for by the general
belief of the northerner that the southerner is false, and, as regards cleanliness, by
national differences in sanitary and other habits.

curve in those slow solemn movements which mark the most characteristic Spanish dances. In the Near East a dance is a rhythm of the body alone, in the Far East dancing is all done with the arms, in the North with the legs. The most ancient and famous art of dancing in the Western world is a rhythmic and harmonious motion of the whole person, a motion in which the body and limbs, even head and eyes, all play their measured part. It is that above all that marks the dances of Spain as attaining the highest point at which the poetry of movement has ever reached. Even when the dance becomes, as in its essence it often really is, the conventional physical expression of the most profound emotion of human passion, it never loses its reserve or dignity in its added intensity of meaning, nor passes beyond the bounds of art. It is Spain alone which justifies the saying of Nietzsche, that dancing is the highest symbol of perfected human activity.

Every dance-tune in Spain may be a song-tune, and when the dance passes into a song, and we hear that soul-stirring extraordinary chant that is partly Moorish, partly gipsy, wholly Spanish, we begin to understand why its dancing is so peculiarly attractive to all those who are held by the fascination of Spain. In this dying and neglected art we reach the last stronghold in which the spirit of the race has entrenched itself. Dancing is the final embodiment of the genius of Spain, the epitome of its great and sorrowful history.

·   ·   ·   ·   ·

Although it may seem an extravagant assertion that the genius of Spain was extinguished in the seventeenth century, we may fairly claim to measure Spain by the standard she has herself set. From the days of Seneca and Martial to the days of Cervantes and Velasquez, a period of two thousand years, the great men of Spain were the great men of the civilized world. That has never been so since. Spain has produced noble and admirable figures, but they have seldom or never possessed fundamental originality or executive effectiveness. If we look around at the most conspicuous representatives of Spain to-day in literature and art we find none who will stand examination by international standards.

We too often forget, however, that the genius of a nation is not always concentrated in great personalities of unique intellectual pre-eminence. It often happens, and perhaps especially so in the oldest civilizations, that the tree dies at the head, that a general population exhibits personal qualities that have ceased to become conspicuous either in its social or in its intellectual aristocracy. In its disintegration the diffused spirit of a people may still be noble and beautiful. Even on the physical side this is often manifest. I may recall the contrast which strikes the traveller in Russia and in Poland. Russia, a young country with an immense future, is a land of strong personalities dominating a vast population of patient, ugly, unkempt peasants, who are still mainly barbarians. In Poland a country of ancient civilization, where the political and intellectual aristocracy are crushed or decayed, an instinctive culture is the inheritance of the whole people; even your waiter at Warsaw has an air of nobility, and the market girls in the Brama Zelaj have the gracious beauty and bearing of court ladies. In the same way, if you wish to learn to know Spain to-day, it is useless to read the cable messages of newspaper correspondents at Madrid, or even to study modern Spanish literature; it is necessary to live among the people themselves, who are alone to-day the more or less inarticulate exponents of the genius of Spain.

I have already pointed out how, even in some minute peculiarities as those of costume, usually so fleeting, the Spaniards of to-day resemble the Spaniards who lived before the Christian era. It is one of the results of this racial conservatism, that of all European countries except Russia—which has not yet emerged from those ages—Spain alone presents to us something of the aspect of the Middle Ages. The piety of Spain is mediaeval; in the cathedral of Saragossa the unaffected dramatic attitudes of the ecstatic worshippers belong to a time when the religious attitude was natural to all men. Not less mediaeval it seemed when, within the walls of the Troitsa monastery of Central Russia, I noted the peasants on a great feast day crowding into the church as into their own home, to rest and talk and eat. In the modern world men and women have learnt to fear both God and their neighbours, and march into their sacred temples with such decent, self-conscious uniformity, that a church nowadays is the last place in which a lover of human nature would seek to observe his fellows. It is such points as these that indicate the profound difference of atmosphere to which in Spain, as in Russia, we are brought back. As in sacred, so in secular things, Spain clings to the old ways. Everywhere one may see the signs of British and, more especially of late years, Belgian enterprise and industry in Spain, but of Spanish rarely indeed. The Italians have become showmen and restaurant keepers and waiters, to exploit their country as a comfortable and well-kept museum of antiquities. The Spaniard, neither anxious to attract nor to repel the foreigner, calmly maintains his ancient traditions, and in his manners and customs we may still read those generous and chivalric traits which delights us in mediaeval Spain.

In the modern world as we know it to-day, and above all in the English-speaking world, there is nothing that seems to the great mass of the population so worthy of pursuit and so satisfactory as a standard of progress, as the cultivation of commerce, education and politics. Among the common people of Spain these things are dead or have never existed. Commerce, except in Catalonia, is treated with indifference and contempt; education is so neglected that in no European country is there so large a proportion of individuals who can neither read nor write; while the experience of many centuries has shown the people the futility of politics, and there is no motive power to renovate political life as some other countries have been renovated in the past century; Greece and Italy had political independence and unity to fight for; Germany was stirred by a great crisis and the genius of a few strong men; there are none of these things in Spain, and a modern Spanish revolution is but a fresh shuffle of the same worn out cards; the only political activity which really arouses any enthusiasm among the masses is, not socialism, but in accordance with the fundamentally free and independent temper of the people, a kind of moderate anarchism. The splendid energy of the Spaniards of old in war and in religion has passed away without giving place to any enthusiasm for the aims which impassion the modern world. Thus, for instance, Malaga might be one of the greatest ports of the Mediterranean and one of the chief health-resorts of Europe. But although it is as old as the Phoenicians and still bear the same ancient name, its harbour works were only completed yesterday, when trade was already falling into other channels, and even to-day it has scarcely taken a single step to attract the health-seeker to its perpetual warmth and sunshine. The Spaniard is content to live leisurely on the traditions of a great past, on the hope of an infinite *mañana*.

When we live with the Spaniard, however, we learn to recognize that the modern method of compressing the maximum of feverish haste into the day's work—"and for life's sake losing the reasons for living"—is perhaps less wholly desirable than we have sometimes imagined. There is no need to haste after wealth in a land where men are agreed that poverty is not contemptible, and that the best things cannot be bought for money. The only worthy social end that can be reached by money is democratic equality, and that has already been attained more perfectly in Spain than in any newer civilization is even conceivable. There is no new country where equality of social intercourse, courtesy, and sympathy are more general among all classes of the population, and where the habits of an instinctive fine breeding may be found even among the poorest. The sense of personal dignity and consideration for others have already bought all that the *mirage* of wealth only promises. Again, while the absence of education is doubtless a real loss—and certainly to those who measure the civilization of a country by the magnitude of its newspaper press Spain must indeed be contemptible—is it a vast mistake to suppose that there is no education in Spain? The traditions of the old civilization diffused throughout the country constitute an atmosphere in which every boy and girl grow up naturally and which cannot by any effort be produced in the most vigorous and progressive of newer and cruder civilizations. The woman who can with difficulty write her name shows an unfailing instinct where the essentials of good breeding are concerned; the fine-fibred *toreador*, brutal as his occupation may seem to us, need fear no comparison either in physical and mental qualities with the athlete of the English-speaking world. That hideous laugh which rings out in the night air of London—as pathetic in its reckless vacuity as any cry of sorrow—is never heard in the lowest quarter of any Spanish city, not because there is no mirth there, or any forced restraint, but because the gracious traditions of an old civilization are part of the lives of the commonest people. Thus it is that in Spain, unlike those centres in which civilization has ripened too quickly, vulgarity and prudery are alike absent. We have indeed left behind our own civilization and the virtues that belong to it; but we have entered another civilization in which virtues that we vainly and ineffectively strive after are the common possession of the common people.

IF WE consider the nature and distribution of the genius which has flowered on the German racial soil we are at the outset struck by several traits which we may also encounter along other avenues of approach to Germany.

We see, for instance, a certain vagueness of outline in the groups of German genius, with a lack of pronounced character alike in the total body of that genius and in its local sub-divisions. In these respects German genius presents a contrast to French genius which is definitely characterized, whether we consider it as a whole or whether we have regard to its separate local groups. German genius, on the other hand, has often seemed, even to Germans, to be intellectually rather characterless, although, morally, the exponents of German genius have often been marked by strength of character to a high degree.

In association with the comparative characterlessness of German genius, we find also, and no doubt inevitably, a lack of originality and initiative. New ideas, the germs of invention, the intuitions of discovery, have not come from Germany nearly so often as from Italy and France and England. Originality of idea, it is true, is not the only or indeed the chief quality of genius, not even in art where it yet counts for so much. The Germans are supreme in music; most of the supremely beautiful things in music have come from Germany in the broad sense; yet the great musical movements, though nearly all matured by Germans, have scarcely ever originated in Germany, but mostly in the Netherlands and Italy. The comparative infertility of German genius in ideas is more than compensated by the ardour and sensitiveness of its massive receptivity, by its extraordinary ability to develop and organize new ideas to effective ends.

It has thus come about that the orientation of German genius, beyond that of any other great people, is international. This is by no means to say the actual products of German genius are always fitted for international use and enjoyment. That is conspicuously not the case. But the receptiveness of the German mind to international influences renders an international outlook, even when it has been combined with a narrowly Germanic national spirit, singularly easy. No other land has produced, as its supreme representative in literature, so genuinely international a spirit as Goethe. Yet Goethe is only the representative, though in a supreme degree, of an attitude which has never been altogether uncommon in Germany, not even during the Great War, when in the midst of a fever of Pan-Germanism a large number of distinguished Germans publicly maintained, at serious cost to themselves, a vigorously international attitude. In the sphere of genius, the German—however peculiarly national his more popular activities may be, and however unskilful in measuring international reactions—is internationally-minded and even in the lowest regions of industry it is easy for him to adapt himself to the international market.

This internationality of German genius is associated with a remarkably large infusion of foreign blood in its chief representatives. In the genius of no other great European country can we so frequently find a foreign racial admixture. In determining it, we must put aside the presence of the "Alpine" or "Celtic" element as well as of the Slav element. These elements are not "Germanic" in the narrow anthropological sense, but they are so anciently rooted in Germany that we cannot count them foreign, and so wide-spread that if we ruled them out there would be little German genius to deal with. We must only take into account recent and definitely determinable foreign elements in the man of genius's ancestry. In France such elements are remarkably rare. The same may be said (with a few exceptions) of Italy. In England, of which I can speak with assurance on the basis of my own investigations[1] the foreign element is also not common among the most prominent men of genius. But in Germany we find four or five men of the first order of eminence who were of partly foreign origin. The father of Leibnitz, in some ways the finest and most accomplished representative of the noblest German spirit, was of Polish origin. Kant's paternal grandfather was Scotch, Schopenhauer's father was Dutch,

[1] Havelock Ellis, *A Study of British Genius*, p. 26.

Dürer's father was Hungarian, Beethoven's paternal grandfather was Flemish, the mother of the Humboldts was of French Huguenot descent, as was Dubois-Reymond's father, Helmholtz's mother was English, and though it is incorrect to regard Moltke, as is sometimes done, as a Dane, his grandfather was of remote Danish ancestry and his grandmother a French Huguenot. We note here especially the prevalence of French Huguenot blood, also found in a much larger number of German men of genius of the second order. Everywhere that it penetrated this blood has been precious, but it is only in Germany, and more especially Prussia, that the national genius has been so considerably dependent upon it. This immigration of French Protestants, extending back to the Reformation, lasted till the middle of the eighteenth century. They were often the most enlightened and vigorous people of their own nation, and many countries benefited by their invasion, but none so greatly as Germany. The vigour and quality of these stocks were out of all proportion to their size. They furnished precisely what was needed especially in Prussia, and German thinkers have been the first to acknowledge the inestimable benefits thus conferred on the German character and the German genius. When the French Ambassador asked Frederick the Great if he had any message to send to Louis XIV, "I only wish," the king replied, "he would again revoke the Edict of Nantes." Some indeed regarded this element as at one time almost too powerful, for at a time when Berlin numbered only ten thousand inhabitants, half of them were refugees, chiefly French. They established anew the industries destroyed by the Thirty Years' War. They transformed Berlin from a dirty provincial town into a great city. They brought over a number of manufacturers of wool and silk and cloth. It is stated that formerly 10 per cent of the officers in the German Army were of French origin. They were physicians and architects and painters as well. A number of distinguished German scholars, men of science, artists and poets have been of French origin.

Reibmayr has divided German genius into three geographical zones: (1) west of the Ems and of the Rhine from the point where the Rhine turns southwards as far as Mainz, then south of the Main

and of the Danube to Vienna; (2) east of the Ems, the Rhine and
the Neckar up to Lübeck, the Elbe, the Saale, and Regensburg;
(3) the region from the east of the second zone to the Russian,
Polish, and Hungarian frontiers.[1] This more or less longitudinal
division from east to west is not altogether satisfactory, for it not only
includes (in a manner far from uncommon among German scholars)
regions which are in no sense Germanic, but it disregards anthropological distinctions, and, for instance, assimilates peoples who are
so remote racially from each other as those of Schleswig-Holstein
and Bavaria. Racially, and with regard to types of genius, a lati-
tudinal delimitation of zones, from north to south, would be better.
We should thus have a small northern Germanic zone, of more or
less long-headed people, from the Baltic coast through Pomerania,
and Mechlenburg, and Schleswig-Holstein, to Friesland. Then we
should have a much larger racially mixed but largely Slav zone
from a broad Eastern basis in East Prussia, Posen, and Silesia, narrow-
ing down through Saxony, to be diffused and lost towards the
north-west; finally we should have a very broad-headed and dark
"Alpine" zone, yet larger if we include Austria to the south, firmly
entrenched among the hills of Higher Germany and mingling to the
north with the Slav zone. The first zone would comprise many of
the most vigorous, dominating, and tenacious representatives of
German genius; the second would be the great centre of intellectual
and administrative genius; the third, emphasizing elements already
clearly traceable in the second zone, would be the central home
of the peaceable, industrious, poetic, and musical activities of
Germany.

From the historical and developmental point of view, however,
Reibmayr's zones really help us to realize the three stages of the
evolution of the German spirit, and present to us three distinct
and to some extent successive pictures of German genius.

The first zone, that of the west and south, is the least Germanic
of all. It is largely "Celtic", that is to say, more precisely, of Alpine
stock in the west and almost entirely so in the south. The Franks and
the Alemanni who occupied the region between the Rhine, the

[1] A. Reibmayr, *Die Entwicklungsgeschichte des Talentes und Genies.*

Danube, and the Main, absorbed the Latin culture they were in contact with and became civilized when the Germanic hordes to the east were still savages. Thus this region was the source from which all Germany was civilized, and all the sacred shrines of German culture are to be found here. A certain Latin vivacity and a Gallic spirit, a tendency to cosmopolitanism, had always marked the people of this region, even until to-day. There is a graciousness, an international breadth and harmony in the genius of this zone which we find nowhere else in Germany to the same extent. Nicholas of Cusa, who, it has been claimed, opened the modern period of thought, was a man of the Moselle, though his culture was largely Italian, and in the fifteenth century was the chief exponent of progress and reform in religion, science, letters, and philosophy. Charlemagne and Goethe represent the supreme manifestation of the Frankish spirit and both alike reveal its orderly, harmonious, receptive, and genuinely international impulses, while we may add that the Jew Karl Marx, the most important international figure provided by Germany since Goethe, belonged on both sides of his family to the German and Dutch Rhineland.

This Romanized and more or less "Celtic" zone has been from the earliest days the radiating focus of civilization in Germany; Strassburg, especially, was the laboratory in which the arts of the Latin world, and especially of France, were adapted or transmuted for German use. A very large proportion of the poets, artists, and scholars of mediaeval Germany came from Strassburg, just as earlier they came from England and later from Basel. Latin influences flowed down the Rhine and Norse influences worked up it. Thus the Rhine became the sacred source of the Nibelung legend and the homeland of Germanic myth. It is natural that the German should cling to the shrines of Germanic culture which this western zone holds. But it must still be remembered that they are shrines of Germanic culture precisely because they were not purely German. Even in the fifteenth century Thomas Murner, the satirist of Strassburg, one of the leading figures in early German literature, strongly opposed the idea that Alsace is Germanic, even though he himself wrote in German. That is a dispute which, in the nature of things,

THE GENIUS OF GERMANY

can never be really settled by any squabble over the political possession of this region. We have to regard Alsace simply as the natural
mediator between France and Germany.

In this first zone Reibmayr includes to the south the different and
more easterly region of Swabia (largely coinciding with modern
Würtemberg and Baden). Anthropologically this region is in the
highlands and mainly a land of Alpine population, while the river
valleys, lower down, are occupied by a more Germanic people.
Swabia, the land of Schiller and so many other poets and dreamers,
is the great Germanic focus of poetic idealism. The home of
romance, even in philosophy, for Schelling is romantic and Hegel
has been termed "the greatest of romantic philosophers", even in
music, for Mozart's father was from Augsburg. By its large and
harmonious spirit, its freedom from a narrow conception of
patriotism, Swabia resembles the other parts of this first zone. But
it differs from it by yielding an altogether indisputable element of
the pure German spirit and genius, as well as by its historically late
evolution. The ancient Duchy of Swabia played a highly important
part in mediaeval German poetry. In the earliest period the whole
poetic and scholarly activity of Germany may be said to lie between
the two poles of the Monastery of Fulda and the monastery of St.
Gall, and the one was immediately to the north and the other
immediately to the south of the Swabian region understood in the
larger sense. Later, Hartman von Aue was a Swabian, and so, unless
he was a Frank, was Wolfram von Eschenbach. Swabia has a more
important place in the production of poetry than any other German
region. Like the other regions of Germany it has long lost local
character and isolation. But the Swabians were once regarded as
the purest of Germanic races and noted for their quaint and genial
character. They were hostile to novelty, perhaps lacking in initia-
tion, but emotional, idealistic, sensitive to the beauty of Nature,
easily moved by large and sometimes vague ideas. Schiller is the
great and typical poet of this region as Goethe is of the Rhine. But
there are a great number of tender and charming poets to be found
here, among these Hölderlin (revered by young Germany of
to-day), Uhland, Mörike, Kerner, Schubart, Hauff. The last of the

Swabian school, though his reputation was mainly local, was Fischer, while the most distinguished writer of Swabian stock in recent times has been Victor von Scheffel, who wrote *Ekkehard*, the best of German historical novels. In thought and philosophy, Albertus Magnus the Universal Doctor, Sebastian Franck, a pioneer in science and mystical theology, Schelling and Hegel are the great and typical figures.

Swabia leads us into the second or central zone, which was predominant in the evolution of German genius from the fifteenth to the early eighteenth centuries, and has probably contributed its fair share to the total ever since. Here, taking the main stream of history, we are undoubtedly at the core of German genius. Foreign elements are reduced to a minimum. Here was the most obstinate resistance to the acceptance of Christianity and here was the first vigorous and successful effort to throw off Catholicism; here also were produced the tough Germanic pioneers of social democracy. If we believe that the German genius is marked rather by character than by grace, by depth of emotion rather than by clarity of intellect, by industry rather than by artistry—a genius that is rugged, independent, rebellious, and exuberant—it is here, in the land between Hamburg and Nuremburg, that we shall find the great representatives of Germany. Here is the home of Luther, here the home of Lessing, the Father of Protestantism and the Father of Rationalism. We can find no more central and typical German figures than these—the cowled peasant, coarse and sensual and devout and superstitious, who fled from the cloister to mould the spiritual and to some extent even the national fate of Germany, and the Kamenz pastor's son, as many-sided as Luther, and as impulsive a fighter, yet not the child of Luther, but, rather, an Erasmus grown militant, wearing himself out in a perpetual struggle for clarity in intellect, for toleration in morals, for love in religion, so laying spiritual foundations, as yet unbuilt on, not only for Germany but for all humanity.

This region teems with men who have had in them something of the rough vigour and independence of Luther, something of the keen penetration and wide outlook of Lessing, or sometimes men who are at the same time related to both types, like Wilhelm Liebknecht of Upper Hesse (while Bebel's mother was born only a few miles away)—a district where the tough democratic spirit has been peculiarly vigorous. Hence have come philosophers, theologians, scholars, conversationalists, scientists, travellers, merchants, men like Eckhard the mystic, one of the greatest and most typical of Germans, Leibnitz, not less conspicuous, Nietzsche and Schleiermacher and Lotze and Herbart and Reimarus and the brothers Schlegel, Lamprecht; from here also Hans Sachs and Klopstock and Bürger and Rückert. J. P. Richter and Novalis, perhaps the two most peculiarly Germanic of German prose writers, Jacob Grimm and Müllenhoff, the two chief pioneers in Germanic origins; the painters Dürer and Wohlgemüth and Altdorfer and Aldegrever and Kranach; while, as a supreme distinction, here is the home of the great and most purely Germanic makers of music, Bach and Händel (whose father, however, came from Silesia) and Gluck and Weber and Brahms and Wagner. It is in this region, we see, that the most genuine and unmixed products of German genius have been elaborated, often obscure and fantastic and unfitted for exportation, yet, on the other hand, often among the best and finest that has been contributed by any land to human civilization. Here, above all, is the home of the German spirit.[1] It must at the same time be remembered that this central zone is, anthropologically, by no means purely Germanic throughout, and perhaps even less so when we consider its genius than when we take into account the ordinary population.

At the north this zone of genius covers all that part of Germany, from Schleswig-Holstein to Friesland, which the Germans themselves regard as peculiarly "Germanic", the region, that is to say, inhabited by a population approximating to the tall, fair, long-headed people of Scandinavia. This notion of what is "Germanic" is, however, as we know, a superstition; it may have been true two thousand years ago; it has never been true of Germany since

[1] It may be noted that this zone contains the whole of the region which on the basis of house structure and village settlement appears on Meitzen's map as "pure German", a region extending from Schleswig-Holstein along the left banks of the Elbe and the Saale to the Thuringian border of northern Bavaria.

Germany began to be civilized and organized. It is not, therefore, surprising that this northern section of the second zone of genius, while it has produced a number of fine, vigorous, independent, and original men, and some of the best scholars of Germanic origin, cannot show one who ranks among the great Germans of the first order, and not many typical Germans of lesser degree. The men of this northern region have, indeed, on the contrary, often distinguished themselves by their fierce opposition to the more dominant tendencies of Germany as represented by Prussia. This district is the cradle of the Anglo-Saxons and its genius may still be regarded as more nearly Anglo-Saxon than Germanic; though it would be idle to expect it to show that vivacity and complexity which, through the infusion of other elements, have long since modified the Anglo-Saxon genius in England. In modern imaginative literature Frenssen is the most notable representative of this region.

More centrally in this zone we reach Westphalia, a typically Germanic region. "The Westphalians have no genius," said Frederick the Great. But there has here always been a high cultivation of the national root-character. "No people in the world," remarked Erasmus, "deserve more praise for their endurance of labour, their faith, their morals, their simple wisdom and their wise simplicity."

At the south, the second zone is modified, as all these zones are in the south, by becoming softer, more poetic, more harmonious in the manifestation of its genius. As we include Halle in the second zone we must also include Leipzig which lies but a few miles away, not only a great natural centre of exchange, but a typical focus of the central German spirit. Leipzig is Slav in name and origin, and the numerous men of genius it has produced have often revealed a strain of Slav genius down even to the most representative of German plastic artists in recent times, Klinger, who unites mysticism with the clear hard emphasis by which German art in design, revolting violently from the tendencies more harmoniously expressed in music, tends to assert itself, and so has become a kind of modern Dürer. Treitschke has remarked on the "extraordinary confusion of the two and thirty large and innumerable small domains which now pass by the name of the province of Saxony". But this diversity is largely, though by no means altogether, superficial. Saxony, alike the province and the kingdom, appears to be fairly uniform anthropologically, even right into Hanover, and while more Germanic than the region to the south, it is less Germanic than the north and distinctly infiltrated by Slav racial element proceeding from a broad basis in Poland to an apex in Hanover. This Slav influence is pronounced in the origin, the physical appearance, and the name of some of the most typical men of German genius in this zone. Copernicus, born at Thorn was the son of a Pole from Cracow, Leibnitz was of Polish origin, Nietzsche believed the same of himself, Böhme, the most influential of German mystics, belonged to a specially Slavonic region of Eastern Saxony while it is possible that his parents, though German, came from Bohemia; Treitschke was physically a Slav;[1] Händel belonged by birth and maternal ancestry to Halle, a centre of Slav influence; and the prevalence of great composers in this zone itself indicates the presence of the Slav element which in all central Europe is closely associated with musical genius. Putting aside the early masters who come from the Netherlands, only one great German composer, Brahms, came from the north.

It must also be pointed out that not only a great part of Saxony but northern Bavaria and the district still further south are included in the second zone. Here we have a region which, while it is rightly associated with mediaeval and Renaissance German genius, is by race and spirit still more remote than even Saxony from the Germanic north. We are here among the short dark round-heads, a hardy and cheerful people quite unlike the Saxons. They are not melancholic and suicidal like the Saxons, but more inclined to exert violence on others. Näcke, who pointed out these differences, observed that in his experience they were well seen among the insane. They are also found in the army, and Treitschke frequently refers to the unanimous complaints concerning the indiscipline,

---

[1] Broad-shouldered, tall, dark-haired, dark-eyed, dark-complexioned, remarks his biographer Hausrath, Treitschke was unmistakably Slav; Nietzsche was more Polish than German in appearance and when abroad was sometimes mistaken for a Pole.

violence, and love of plunder of the Bavarians, in the campaigns of the early nineteenth century.[1] The same violence and destructiveness to property has been noted of Bavarian troops, alike in the war of 1870 and in the Great War of more recent times, although violence against the person is noted more especially among the Prussians. It seems to be in accordance with these traits that the genius of Bavaria is of a vigorous and enterprising temper rather than, as that of the softer but gifted people to the north of them, mystical and humanitarian and philosophical.

When we reach the third zone we are in the heart of Prussia at the creative focus of modern Germany. We observe at once a different impress on the men of genius here produced. They are less obscure,—less profound, if we so please,—than the men of the central zone often are, and also less intimate; in the fundamental sense they are less Germanic. But while they speak more clearly and in tones more generally intelligible to the world, it cannot be said that on the whole they possess that international spirit of which Goethe is the supreme and unapproached representative. The men of the first zone reached out their arms in a cosmopolitan spirit from the foundation of a soil in which they had themselves become rooted. In the third zone the racial elements of genius are often so recent and so mixed that they have not become rooted, and it is on the basis of an artificial and forced nationalism that their internationalism often arises.

The foreign, and especially the French Huguenot, element in Prussia is, as we have seen, remarkably large and potent. Yet even this precious element, powerful as it has been, and operative even to-day, has not changed the heavy and tough native character. Rohrbach has in recent years lamented the inability of the Germans to come into friendly relations with other peoples, a defect having its root, he believes, and we may well agree, in a note of personal gruffness in intercourse, which proceeded from the originally narrow and militaristic spirit of Prussia.

This third zone has only expressed itself in genius during recent times, and to no pronounced degree (except, as ever, in the south)

[1] See, e.g., Treitschke, *History*, Eng. trans., vol. ii, pp. 697, 701.

until the end of the eighteenth century. But its essential characters appear from the first. Christian Wolf, who was born in 1679, is already the typical representative of Prussian genius, so definitely that the qualities that he represents—orderliness, dogmatism, receptivity, and industry—have sometimes seemed to be the hall-mark of the German mind everywhere. He is typical, also, in this, that, like so many of the most unmistakable representatives of the Prussian spirit, he was not himself a Prussian, but came from Breslau in the days before Silesia was Prussian. It is noteworthy that even the men of scientific military genius produced by this pre-eminently military state—Scharnhorst, Clausewitz, Gneisenau, Moltke—were all outsiders; Arndt, the fiercely patriotic soldier-poet of Prussia, was largely a Swede, as perhaps was Dahlmann, "the master-builder of the German Idea", certainly half Danish, while Fichte, the prophet of Prussianism, and Treitschke, its historical bard, were both Saxons. Even Bismarck, says Lamprecht who knew him, bore unmistakable traces of the Lower Saxon and had a *Platt deutsch* accent.

Christian Wolf was influential in moulding Prussian culture but he has long ceased to make any living appeal. Less than a century later we find in the Humboldt brothers representatives of the Prussian spirit whose genius was of finer and more vital order, Alexander a conquistador in the realms of physical science, and Wilhelm, active alike in science and morals and practical life, an even finer and rarer spirit. By his later activities Wilhelm von Humboldt leads us into the sphere of statesmanship in which the Prussian forceful and organizing temper has, above all, sought expression. Here Bismarck is the supreme representative figure. Bismarck, the man who proclaimed blood and iron as his ideal, the great realist to his own people, and to outsiders (in the words of an Italian) "a barbarian of genius", was far from resembling the conventional image which has often been set up to represent him. A colossus whose appearance reminded the historian Lamprecht of Charlemagne, yet, as Lamprecht himself points out, there was something other than this in Bismarck. A lion-like figure, certainly, but when Bebel met him for the first time he was astonished to hear a high treble voice; this colossus was a bundle of nerves, so full of apprehension that before any great crisis he fell ill, the victim of all sorts of neuralgias, with a feminine sensibility that in his love letters appear like masochism, a creature of moods that were sometimes a torment to himself and to others. Such a man who lived in the moment, and remade his picture of the world every morning, naturally attached importance to what he called "imponderabilia" and the "psychological moment". We cannot estimate the Prussian unless we realize in his character this element of complexity, even morbidity, the marks of a creature too rapidly civilized. Just as Goethe is the supreme figure of the first zone and Luther of the second, so Bismarck is the supreme figure of the third and latest German zone. These three figures include all Germany.

It cannot be said that the third zone in its genuinely Prussian region has proved a favourable soil for any of the forms of art. The rare artists found in this uncongenial atmosphere have mostly led a distracted and tortured existence. The only composer of high eminence in this zone, Schumann (and he was really a Saxon from the peculiarly Slav region of Lusatia), died insane. Heinrich von Kleist, who was probably the finest poet of this land, was a highly morbid creature who spent his short life in restlessly wandering about the world and then committed suicide. Meinhold, the finest imaginative artist in prose of this zone, was the eccentric and unattractive pastor of a remote Baltic village.

The finer spirited and more sensitive children of Prussia have, ever since the days of Frederick William I, looked at their own land and its brutal officialdom with a loathing which has failed to recognize the elements it held of useful and needed discipline. "I think with loathing," said the Prussian Winckelmann, "of this country which groans under the greatest despotism the world has ever known. It is better to be a circumcized Turk than a Prussian. In a country like Sparta the arts cannot thrive." It is Treitschke who quotes that passage, with the remark that to describe the land of the corporal's stick as a "Sparta" was "extremely ideal". Hegel later (in 1801) expressed the keenest antipathy to Prussia, "a state whose dreary emptiness strikes everyone in the first of its villages he enters." If even some of the finest of Germans have thus failed to appreciate German virtues, it must not be a matter of surprise to us if less distinguished foreigners have still oftener exhibited the like failure.

We must go to the extreme east and south, to Polish Prussia and Silesia, among a Slavonized people having much in common with the neighbouring Saxons, to reach a softer and more sympathetic atmosphere. Here we find Angelus Silesïus (his father was a Pole) and Zinzendorf and Eichendorff, all typical Silesians. Händel, of all German composers most akin to the great Russians, was the most Slav, a Silesian of Breslau on his father's side, and from the most Slav region of Central Germany on his mother's. Herder, who was largely an inspirer of the extravagantly cosmopolitan though finely humanitarian universalism by which in the eighteenth century this third zone sometimes went beyond the first zone, was a Silesian through his father, an East Prussian through his mother, and perhaps the finest representative of the Silesian spirit on the spiritual side.[1] On the more practical side we have Bebel, who, while through his mother he belonged to the individualistic, anti-authoritarian people of the Rhineland, derived his sensitive, emotional, humanitarian temper from his Silesian father. The Silesian temperament brings us to the Slav. It must be noted, indeed, that the whole of this eastern zone, even by virtue of its situation against Russia, is necessarily permeated throughout by the Slav element. It expresses itself spiritually in the gift for religion and for music. The majority of the men of genius born in this zone are of partly Slav blood.

When we survey generally the intellectual manifestations of the German spirit—in literature, scholarship, science, philosophy—we seem to be impressed, above all, by the presence of a tendency to a vast and encyclopædic universalism. All the qualities of the German and his defects—his ferocious industry, his insatiable and impartial intellectual appetite, his uncritical formlessness, his often character-less receptivity—combine to aid in the creation of many-sided achievements of stupendous magnitude. Germany produced the

[1] Schleiermacher, who harmoniously united mystical devotion with free critical inquiry, was only a Silesian by birth, not by race.

first great representative of this type, the thirteenth century Dominican monk of Swabia, Albertus Magnus, the Universal Doctor. It also produced the last, one of the most inspiring figures ever produced in any land, Leibnitz, a man of genuine cosmopolitan spirit, at least as much at home in Paris as in his own Leipzig, and writing his chief work in French or Latin, inventor and discoverer, thinker and philosopher, statesman and jurist, a penetrating pioneer into the future, always occupied in the task of uniting seeming antagonisms in some higher synthesis. Leibnitz remains the greatest representative of Germany's most fruitful spiritual activity.

There has been no great encyclopædic philosopher since Leibnitz. The immense importance of synthetic and unifying vision is, however, still well recognized, and is nowhere so widely attempted as in Germany. No modern man of science has been so various as Helmholtz, no modern psychologist so systematically comprehensive as Wundt, no anthropologist so universal as Virchow. And if we turn to less conspicuous men, it is only in Germany that we can find a writer like Eduard Reich, who patiently sets forth his own personal impressions of the universe in twenty octavo volumes of six hundred to eight hundred pages each.

No figure has appeared in Germany since 1870 of any significance to the world in general; for Nietzsche began writing before that date and Wagner had been composing for half a century. The prominence in Germany during the past half century of a peculiarly intense and aggressive form of nationalism, with its accompanying ideals of State supremacy, has been equally disastrous to German genius and German internationalism. The Germans began to misunderstand their own international affinities. Then appeared an idea—like so many other German ideas, having its origin outside Germany—which turned the real fact inside out. Instead of recognizing the fact that German genius is to a remarkable extent non-German in origin, it was argued that non-German genius was really German. This doctrine, of which Woltmann was a chief propagandist, was more especially applied to Italy, and most of the great Italian figures—Dante, Boccaccio, Giotto, Leonardo da Vinci, Raphael, Buonarroti, Titian, and many others—were regarded as really of Germanic origin. A few years ago Otto Hauser in his *Weltgeschichte der Literatur*, seeing in all the most significant manifestations of the cultures of other countries the features of a Germanic mixture (*Einschlag*), assumed that the Etruscans were Germans and found that the humour of Italian literature is *echt Germanisch*. If, however, we put aside such speculations and seek a genuine Germanic element in conspicuous modern European men of genius, where its presence could easily be demonstrated, we seldom find it, and it would be hazardous to suppose that it was ever more conspicuous than it is to-day. The influence of Germans during recent times in other countries than their own has been shown, not by the production of high genius but by more humble though valuable qualities of citizenship, so that, as Ferrero has pointed out, they have often formed a valuable cement in non-German communities. The vagaries of anthropological pan-Germanism are really, however, a reaction against a premature and too extreme cosmopolitanism in a world not yet ready for so humane an idea. That reaction must not conceal from us those more characteristic traits of genuine internationalism which have peculiarly distinguished the greatest men of Germany—Leibnitz and Kant and Goethe and Wilhelm von Humboldt and Nietzsche and so many others—during the most brilliant flowering period of the German genius. It is not possible to doubt that the future will witness a renaissance of that spirit.

AFTERWORD

NATIONALISM AND PEACE[1]

ALL WHO have thought deeply about the advent of a future world of peace have recognized the immense importance of the problem of nationalism. But that problem is far from being faced as widely or as vigorously as it needs to be.

The reason largely is that there are two very different kinds of nationalism, one good, the other bad. We fear to attack one lest we should be suspected of attacking the other. Tolstoy's ferocious denunciation of patriotism hardly allowed for the existence of a good patriotism.

In its ideals and its earlier stages nationalism may be altogether admirable. It is not an ancient ideal, it belongs to recent centuries, the offspring of Renaissance Sovereignty and Revolutionary Rights, as Delisle Burns pointed out in a, for the most part, admirable little book on *Political Ideals* published more than twenty years ago and even more actual to-day than when it was written.

The most famous exponent of the aims of nationalism was Mazzini, preceded in Germany by the philosopher Fichte, and the aims of these eminent pioneers were worthy of unqualified approval. It is significant that they spoke for Italy and Germany, Italy especially being the early home of such ideals. There were special reasons in the sufferings and struggles of Italy and Germany why, in early times, if not indeed much later, their best political minds should be set in this direction. It was not, however, until 1848 that nationalism became a dogma. In the first place it was the right of a people to democratic self-control free from internal disunion and external oppression. Far from any aggressive or hostile attitude, nationalist states, Mazzini declared, freed from the rule of kings and privileged classes, would live in harmony and fraternity with other countries. And he considered of immense importance the existence not merely of rights but of duties in co-operation with other countries, since every

---

[1] This essay is probably the last composition Havelock Ellis wrote. It was completed in the spring of 1939; he died on July 8th, 1939. F. D.

country, with its own special qualities, has a mission to fulfil towards humanity.

As we know only too well, the development of nationalism has seldom, if ever, followed these lines. The ideal has indeed been exactly reversed. The nationalism which was to mean co-operation with other nations in a common service to the highest aims of human civilization, has come to mean an aggressive attitude deliberately nourished by propaganda, a jealous envy of the possessions, spiritual and material, of other nations, a latent hostility prepared to break out into open warfare against neighbouring countries which seemed to lack the ability to defend themselves. This is the tragically distorted shape of nationalism which now prevails, most vigorously and conspicuously no doubt in the totalitarian countries, but quite definitely, even if less obtrusively, in so called democratic lands. This nationalism, spurred on by pride and a lust for conquest, has, under the impetus of trade rivalries, expanded into modern Imperialism. Its influence is shown by the fact that every country claims "sovereignty". This simply means that every country's self-interest ranks above the interests and rights of all other nations and admits no duties towards them. It has become a dogma, with all the force of a sacred religious myth, so that the assertion of it may never be questioned. There can never be a good and peaceful world so long as each nation claims "sovereignty".

But there is hope. This pernicious nationalism is being undermined. On the surface the nationalist political myth still rules, but when we penetrate to the economic realities developing beneath, the myth is seen to be meaningless. This is clearly set forth by Francis Delaisi in his notable book: *Political Myths and Economic Realities*. The dignified and romantic myth is still loudly proclaimed because it is not easy to propagandize the more realistic aims of war and to induce the masses to die for rubber, potash, fertilizers, and so forth.

In peacetime the economic realities of life are more subtly penetrative every day in the lives of the citizens who are constantly fed on the beautiful myth of a national sovereignty superior to the rest of the world and independent of it. Yet in most civilized countries, even outside Europe, from the moment when on getting out of bed the citizen washes himself with soap having its source on the Congo, he is all day in contact with articles from all over the world until he goes to bed under an eiderdown quilt from Norway to dream that his country is completely self-supporting and able to snap its fingers at all other countries. He is really a citizen of the world without knowing it. That is the tragedy of our time. "The world," as Delaisi concluded, "will only acquire equilibrium when interdependence has gained the same value as salvation for the Christian, equality for the democrat, and the fatherland for the patriot."

When we contemplate the earth to-day from a scientific view-point the most significant fact is its decreased size. During millions of years it was not easy for any living creature to move more than a short distance over its surface without perishing. To-day the human animal (though even he only after hundreds of thousands of years) can traverse it in a few days which are rapidly becoming a few hours. This facility of movement, in a less degree but for an ever increasing number of people, is altering the spiritual atmosphere for the whole human species. We can no longer afford to be indifferent to people at a distance, because they are in reality no longer at a distance. It has become fatally easy for them to be our enemies as well as our friends. The immense extent and range of commerce, the recently increased powers of agricultural productivity, have enabled nations to exercise trade rights of freedom or restriction which may be in the highest degree baneful or helpful to themselves or to other nations. There is no longer any possibility of isolation in the world and the isolationist nation does not belong to our time.

Island nations no longer exist, certainly not in civilization. Great Britain realized a very long time ago, in spite of geography, that it is not an island, and has developed that realization on a rather large scale. The United States have taken longer to realize that the days of isolationist nationality are over. This indeed was natural. Not only by its size and fairly compact character, as well as its position surrounded by oceans and other countries which, at all events now and in the future, are as harmless as the ocean, there was every excuse for regarding the United States as an island. Until lately the isolationist attitude has seemed reasonable. It seems so no longer.

But any such change of national attitude is in the long run fruitless unless it marks the individual attitude. What is the individual attitude towards the individuals of other nations? In most cases, without doubt, unsatisfactory. It is usually made up of prejudices, largely based on political or supposed "patriotic" notions and fed by the mischievous provender of an unwholesome press altogether reckless of facts. The attitude towards the concrete individual is indeed almost or quite indistinguishable from the attitude towards the abstract nation.

But there is always a healthy reaction to this absurd and unsociable attitude. It is always possible for many to realize that, whatever the minor differences, the people even of hostile nations must be in the main very like ourselves. At the present time one of our main tasks in the cause of the world's progress is to spread this really very common-sense view.

One way in which we can carry it out is by learning to know personally—or to enable other people to know personally—individuals of other nations. Many interesting friendships are formed in this way and lead the friend to form friendly feelings towards the whole nation to which the other friend belongs. Contacts of this kind are nowadays more or less automatically formed owing to the shrinkage of the world and increased individual intercourse, even putting aside the immensely increased contacts of recent years due to the floods of immigrant refugees. But deliberate efforts are being made on a considerable scale to increase such contacts.

But this movement does not by any means always work so smoothly as the optimist assumes. Even at the most youthful age the youngster of one nation is not naturally apt to fall on the neck of the youngster of another nation. He is quite as likely to devise unpleasant nicknames for him and to exercise the popular gesture of contempt. At a slightly older age the schoolboy or schoolgirl is highly critical, and easily finds objection in unfamiliar ways of speech or of conduct which are simply the outcome of foreign habits or a different national tradition. So that an antagonistic attitude may be encouraged rather than dispelled. Or the influence may act reversely and after a considerable stay in, for instance, a totalitarian land and subjected to its terrific propaganda, it is possible to become antagonistic to the traditions and ideals of one's own land.

So that we must always remember how susceptible is the youthful mind and how easily apt to acquire new prejudices. It thus happens that many who were ready and eager to aid the visits of students and others to foreign countries have been worried to find that the result has been the opposite of that desired.

What we need is evidently something more than contact with strangers in a strange land. There must be preparation for that visit to a strange land. What is especially needed, and hardly ever received, is a certain amount of early education in the elements of history. I do not of course mean a training in those eighty volumes of the Cambridge Histories recently completed, however desirable it may be for the teachers themselves to have access to that great and splendid work to which the first scholars of many lands have contributed. I have much more in mind a small volume, also only now published (at far too high a price) though not recently written, Pirenne's *History of Europe to the Sixteenth Century*. Pirenne was a Belgian professor at Ghent University, carried away by the Germans during the Great War and shut up in camps in various German towns and villages in the course of which he lectured to huge audiences on history, until he was found to be "very dangerous". Then it occurred to him to write a history of Europe. He had but few books to consult and only small school exercise books to write on. But he had behind him thirty-five years of study, and, of far more importance, he was a man of genius with an original and stimulating mind such as is seldom given to history. So that he was able to write a book which the best judges consider far superior to any other on the same scale, and really making clear the main movements and great forces in European history.

Though Pirenne's *History* has only now been published he had elsewhere expressed his opinion that Germany's discipline and spirit of obedience, her militarism and lack of political ability were largely explained by the rebirth of serfdom in the sixteenth century. If that had been made clear to the youthful visitors they would have acquired a more sympathetic outlook on the differences between Germany and the nations of the west.

But it is quite possible to acquire a sympathetic vision even in the recognition of opposed traits. In a book, *Reaching for the Stars*, by Miss Norah Waln, who is of Quaker origin and possesses its serene traits, this is illustrated. After living in Germany she finds the Germans an honest and good race, fond of beauty and order, and subject to sometimes rather befogging bursts of mysticism. She cannot understand how so lovable a people can at present condone persecution and crude heroics, and even debase the arts for which they are specially gifted. But she sees both sides, and refuses to allow one side to blind her to the other.

We need to approach the people of another nation with open minds, clear vision, and intelligent understanding of what to expect. Then on that abstract foundation a concrete and emotional relationship may wholesomely develop.

I have been speaking of Germany but the same is true of other nations.

The charge sometimes brought against the pioneers of a future world of peace is that they have no constructive ideas and are doing nothing but talk to bring to birth the new world they foresee. If such a charge were well-founded there is certainly no excuse for it. Even if we confine ourselves to the highly important point I am here discussing, every individual can co-operate. Anyone may forge a little link of brotherhood or at least of understanding. Some day, perhaps, every boy and girl will have become at home in a foreign country, and there could be no more useful step towards the abolition of war. Something may be done in this direction even by those who stay at home. The radio, for instance, could be most useful.

No one can be at home with the peoples and the speech of many lands. There is no more urgent need to-day than an auxiliary common language. No reasonable person desires to abolish any native language. But we need in addition a method of expression intelligible to the educated person of any land. This realization has long existed among a minority; it is time it became common to the majority; and it is a question that might relevantly and profitably be taken up by the League of Nations, however doubtful we may be of the aims that League was instituted to carry out. Some people hold that everyone should be acquainted with English and French; that is not an altogether satisfactory solution. The best is probably a simple artificial language fairly apt for the people of any country, whether or not the choice of Esperanto is made, and it would be possible to make a better one. If ever our national governments set up the proposed Ministry of International Friendship—I see little sign of this at present—it is with such activities as these that it will be largely concerned.

They are certainly becoming urgent. Only some three centuries ago the earth was a vast and mostly unknown place inhabited by completely strange human creatures and no human being had ever circumvented it. Now, under totally different conditions, never was the need for economic unity in business and spiritual unity in aim so acute. Let everybody take some part. Then at last the universal brotherhood of all peoples, which in the eighteenth century was the pious aspiration of the philosophic Condorcet, may become an established fact.

INDEX

INDEX

A

Ægeans, the, 198
Akbar, Emperor, 166
Aksakov, Sergei, 145, 154–5
Alans, the, 107
Albenzoar, 205
Albucasis, 205
Aldegrever, 225
Alexinsky, 85–6
Alemanni, the, 221
Alexander I, 162
Alfonso the Wise, 187, 209
Al Hazen, 205
Almanzor, 204
Altdorfer, 225
Anacharsis, 108
Andreyev, Leonid, 88, 156–7
Angles, the, 39, 41
Anglo-Saxons, the, 39–41
Antoine, 132
Anutchin, 103, 104
Apulcius, 200
A quoi tient la Supériorité des Anglo-Saxons, 32
A quoi tient l'Infériorité Française, 32
Arabazhin, 119
Arabian Nights, 135
Arabs, the, 199
Arbo, 105
Aristotle, 196, 205
Arndt, 229
Arnobius, 200
Arnold, Matthew, 18, 179
Arroz Y Tartana, 190
Askold, 111
Athanasius, St., 33
At the Russian Front, 170
Aue, Hartman von, 223
Augustine, St., 200
Austen, Jane, 144
Auvergnats, the, 198
Averroës, 205

B

Bach, Johann Sebastian, 225
Bacon, Francis, 55, 59, 70
—, Roger, 55, 70
Bakst, Leon, 133
Bakunin, Michail, 89
Balakirev, 129
Balbus, 186, 205
Balzac, Honoré de, 140, 152
Baring, Hon. Maurice, 81, 98, 115, 146, 165
Basques, the, 24, 194–5, 198–9, 201
Bazalgette, Léon, 32
Beauplan, 95, 148
Bebel, 225, 229, 231
Beddoes, Dr. Thomas, 22
Beethoven, Ludwig van, 190, 220
Belgae, the, 38
Beltov, 119
Beowulf, 49
Berbers, the, 198, 199
Berengaria, 187
Bergson, Henri Louis, 84
Berkeley, George, 55
Berlioz, Hector, 130
Bezzenbuerger, 198
Bismarck, Prince Otto von, 229, 230
Blake, Admiral Robert, 57
—, William, 56
Bloch, Adolph, 105
Boccaccio, Giovanni, 232
Bogdanov, 104
Böhme, 227
Boieldieu, 128
Boissier, Gaston, 200
Boniface, St., 54
Boris Gudunov, 130
Borodin, Alexander P., 124, 129, 130
Bossi, Professor, 159
Bouchier, 194, 196
Buonarroti, Michelangelo, 232
Boyhood, 145

INDEX

BRAHMS, JOHANNES, 125, 225, 227
Bretons, the, 24
BRIGHT, JOHN, 70
BROCA, PAUL, 198
BROWNE, SIR THOMAS, 49, 179
BROWNING, ELIZABETH BARRETT, 179
BRÜCKNER, 74, 116, 134
Brythons, the, 37
BUBNOV, J. V., 171
BULGAKOV, 178
Bulgarians, the, 99
Bulletin, Société d'Anthropologie, 107
BUNYAN, JOHN, 9
BÜRGER, 225
BURNE-JONES, SIR E. C., 48
BURNS, DELISLE, 234
BYRON, LORD GEORGE GORDON, 56, 119,
    139, 140
Byzantines, the, 166

C

CAJAL, RAMON Y, 201
CALDERON, PEDRO, 211
CAMPOAMOR, 194
Canas Y Barro, 190
CANUTE, KING, 42
CARACCIOLI, 90
CARDUCCI, GIOSUÈ, 189
CARMENCITA, 212
Carnets de Voyage, 30
CARPENTER, EDWARD, 143
CARTAILHAC, 198
Carthaginians, the, 199
CASANOVA, GIOVANNI JACOPO, 81, 148,
    176
CATHERINE II, 74, 166
Celtiberians, the, 197
Celts, the, 37–8, 197–9
CERVANTES, SHAVEDRA MIGUEL DE, 58,
    186, 188, 207, 211, 213
CHADWICK, SIR JAMES, 161
CHALIAPIN, FEDOR IVANOVICH, 131
CHANCELLOR, RICHARD, 73, 78
Chanson de Roland, 49, 210
CHAPMAN, GEORGE, 56, 189
Chapters on Spanish Literature, 210
CHARLEMAGNE, EMPEROR, 222

CHARLES VII, 30, 31
CHAUCER, GEOFFREY, 56, 57, 137, 189
CHEKHOV, ANTON, 82, 123, 131–4, 141,
    155–8, 177
CHELYSHEV, 76, 95
Cheremisses, the, 104
CHEREPNIN, 130
Childhood, 145
CHKHEIDZE, 86, 91, 168
Chronicles, 79
CHUBB, PERCIVAL, 11
CID, THE, 188, 194, 210
Cimmerians, the, 107
CLAUSEWITZ, 229
CLIVE, LORD ROBERT, 70
Cloak, The, 140
COBBETT, WILLIAM, 40
COLERIDGE, SAMUEL TAYLOR, 49
COLLAS, G. F., 78
COLUMBUS, CHRISTOPHER, 52, 211
COLUMELLA, 206
COMMODUS, LUCIUS, 187
*Comptes-rendus Congrès International de
    Médicine,* 103, 105
CONDORCET, MARIE, MARQUIS DE, 240
CONSTABLE, JOHN, 48
COOK, CAPTAIN JAMES, 70
Co-operativeMovement in Russia, The, 171
COPERNICUS, NICOLAUS, 173, 227
COURNOS, JOHN, 157
CRABBE, REV. GEORGE, 49
Created Legend, The, 157
Croatians, the, 99
CROME, JOHN, 48
CROMER, LORD, 47
CROMWELL, OLIVER, 46, 59
CUI, CAESAR, 129, 130
Cultura España, 198
CURIE, MADAME, 149
CYPRIAN, ST., 200
Czechs, the, 99

D

Dacians, the, 107
DAHLMANN, 229
Daily Chronicle, 86
Dance of Life, The, 14

244

DANILOV, 79
DANTE, ALIGHIERI, 189, 206, 232
DARGOMYJSKY, 128–30
DARWIN, CHARLES ROBERT, 64, 70, 85
DAVIDSON, THOMAS, 11–12
Dead Souls, 140
DE GAULTIER, JULES, 13
DE GOURMONT, REMY, 25
DE GUZMÁN, FERNÁN PÉREZ, 188
DELAISI, FRANCIS, 235, 236
DEL-NEGRO, PROFESSOR, 16
DEMENTYEV, 162
DENIKER, DR., 21, 22
Der Fall Gogol, 140
DE ROBERTY, 175
Description of Ukraine, 148
Dialogues, 106
DIAGHILEV, SERGIE PAVLOVICH, 133
DICKENS, CHARLES, 85, 134, 137, 152
DIDEROT, DENIS, 19
Die Entwicklungsgeschichte des Talentes und
        Genies, 221
DILLON, DR., "E. B. LANIN", 91
DIODORUS, SICULAS, 187
DISRAELI, BENJAMIN, 46
DOMITIAN, TITUS FLAVIUS, 187
Don Quixote, 140, 210
DOSTOYEVSKY, FEODOR MIKHAILOVITCH,
        96, 119, 140–2, 145–6, 153, 156–8,
        178
DRAKE, SIR FRANCIS, 70
Drops of Blood, 157
DRYDEN, JOHN, 25
DUBOIS-REYMOND, 220
Du Développement des Idées Révolution-
        naires en Russie, 147, 167
DÜRER, ALBRECHT, 220, 225, 226
DURNOVO, GENERAL, 177

E

ECKHARD, JOHANNES, 225
EHRLICH, PAUL, 70
EICHENDORFF, JOSEPH, BARON VON, 231
Ekkehard, 224
El Pueblo, 192
Epic Songs of Russia, 135, 148
ERASMUS, DESIDERIUS, 226

ESCHENBACH, WOLFRAM VON, 223
Esthétique de la Langue Française, 25
Eugene Onegin, 118, 134, 135
Europa, 103
Europe Giovane, 91
Europe's Debt to Russia, 83
Euscarians, the, 194–5
EYCK, HUBERT VAN, 63

F

FALKLAND, LUCIUS CARY, 66
FALSTAFF, SIR JOHN, 50, 142
Family Chronicles, 145, 154–5
FERDINAND V, 208–11
FERRERO, GIULELMO, 91, 233
FICHTE, JOHANN GOTTLIEB, 84, 229, 234
FIELDING, HENRY, 144
Finns, the, 102 et sqq.
FISCHER, 224
Fishermen, The, 161
FITZMAURICE-KELLY, J., 210
FLETCHER, GILES, 76
FLORENCE, MAY, 125
FOKIN, MICHAIL, 133
FONVIZIN, DENIS, 138–9
FORD, JOHN, 119
FORTESCUE, SIR JOHN, 68
Forum Philosophicum, 16
FOUILLÉE, 54, 100, 115, 165
FRANCK, SEBASTIAN, 224
FRANKLIN, ALFRED, 161
Franks, the, 221
FREDERICK THE GREAT, 220, 226
FREDERICK WILLIAM I, 66, 230
FREEMAN, PROFESSOR E. A., 42
FRENSSEN, GUSTAV, 226
Frisians, the, 39, 41
FÜRTWANGLER, WILHELM, 108

G

GAINSBOROUGH, THOMAS, 48
Galicians, the, 198
GALILEO, 173
Gallic tribes, the, 23
GARSHIN, 158
Gascons, the, 24

Gauls, the, 23, 205
Generaciones, 188
GEORGE, HENRY, 143
Georgians, the, 167–8
Geography, 203
GERRERO, 40
Geschichte des Flagellantismus, 78
GIBBON, EDWARD, 100, 187
GILDAS, 51, 60
GIOTTO, DI BONDONE, 232
GLADSTONE, HON. WILLIAM EWART, 46
GLAZUNOV, ALEXANDER, 129, 130
GLINKA, MICHAIL IVANOVICH, 115, 120, 128, 130, 135
GLUCK, CHRISTOPHER WILLIBALD, 225
GNEISENAU, 229
GODWIN, WILLIAM, 55, 57
GOETHE, JOHANN WOLFGANG VON, 84, 219, 222, 223, 228, 230, 233
GOGOL, NIKOLAI VASILIEVICH, 82, 131, 139, 140, 141, 154, 155, 156, 158
Goidels, the, 37
Golden Cockerel, The, 73, 130
GONCHAROV, IVAN, 119, 141, 149, 153–4, 167
GONCOURT, EDMOND DE, 141
GONSALVO, 205, 210
GORKY, MAXIM, 87, 88, 131, 146, 155–7
Goths, the, 107, 199
GRAHAM, STEPHEN, 91, 163
Great Russians, the, 100, 165
GRÉTRY, 128
GREY, SIR JOHN, 68
GRIGOROVICH, 156, 161
GRIMM, JACOB, 136, 225
GUERRERO, 212

H

HADDON, A. C., 5
HADRIAN, 187, 206
HAKLUYT, RICHARD, 58, 59, 73
Hamlet, 119, 142, 154
Hamlet of Shtchigry, 119
Hampa, 210
HAMPDEN, JOHN, 46
HÄNDEL, GEORGE FREDERICK, 125, 126, 225, 227, 231
HANSSON, LAURA MARHOLM, 150

HAPGOOD, ISABEL, 135, 148
HARDENBURG, BARON VON, "NOVALIS", 225
HARVEY, WILLIAM, 173
HAUFF, 223
HAUSER, OTTO, 233
HAUSRATH, 227
Havelok, 49
HEGEL, GEORG WILHELM, 223, 224, 230
HEINE, HEINRICH, 139
HELMHOLTZ, HERMAN VON, 220, 232
Henry VI, 19
HENRY, O., 158
HENZEY, 196
HERACLITUS, 15
HERBERSTEIN, BARON, 80, 123, 177
HERDER, JOHANN GOTTFRIED VON, 231
HERODOTUS, 78, 106, 107, 108, 196
Hero of Our Own Time, 140
Hero Tales and Legends of the Serbians, 135
HERRICK, ROBERT, 57
HERZEN, ALEXANDER, 86, 117, 119, 147, 167, 170, 174, 177, 178
HINDENBURG, PAUL VON, 84
HINTON, JAMES, 10, 11, 15
HIRT, 197
Historia de la Guerra Europa, 192
History, 228
History of Europe to the Sixteenth Century, 238–9
History of Materialism, 12–13
History of Penal Methods, 78
History of Russia, 104, 106, 110, 165, 169
History of Russian Literature, 116
HOBBES, THOMAS, 55, 70
HOGARTH, WILLIAM, 70
HOLBEIN, HANS, 63
HÖLDERLIN, 223
HOMER, 108
HOMYAKOV, 86
HOSIUS, 204
House of the Dead, The, 145
HUGO, VICTOR, 34
Huguenots, the, 19, 44, 228
HUMBOLDT, ALEXANDER VON, 220, 229
—, WILHELM VON, 62, 194–5, 220, 233
HUME, DAVID, 55, 70
Hungarians, the, 114

Huns, the, 107
Huss, John, 173
Huxley, Julian, 5
Huysmans, Joris Karl, 30, 153
Hygiène, 161

I

Ibañez, Vincente Blasco, 189–93
Iberians, the, 194–5, 197, 198, 205
Ibsen, Henrik Johan, 42, 132
Idatius, 206
Idiot, 153
Il Travatore, 130
Interpretation of the Russian People, 137, 150
Isabella of Castile, 187, 207–9, 211
Isidorus, St., 206
Ithacus, 206
Ivan Goncharov, 154
Ivan the Terrible, 73, 74, 85
Ives, George, 78

J

Jaime, 188
Jaimes, St., 198
Jenghiz Khan, 166
Jenkinson, Anthony, 73
Jesuits, the, 55
Jesup North Pacific Expedition, The, 121
Joan of Arc, 19, 30, 31–2
Jonson, Ben, 189
Jordaens, Jakob, 62
Jordanus, 103, 104, 106
Jourdain, M., 25
Journal, 141
Jubainville, D'Aubus, 197
Juliana, 54
Jutes, the, 39
Juvencus, 206

K

Kabyles, the, 198
Kafirs, the, 107
Kant, Immanuel, 219, 233
Kantemir, Prince, 138
Karamzin, 87, 138, 179, 185
Kaus, Otto, 140
Keats, John, 49, 57

Kerner, 223
Khilkov, Prince, 88
King Lear, 50, 142
Kipling, Rudyard, 158
Kitchener, Lord, 47
Kleist, Heinrich von, 230
Klinger, 226
Klopstock, Friedrich Gottlieb, 225
Klyuchevsky, 104–6, 110, 111, 165, 169
Knox, John, 54
Koltsov, Alexis Vasilevitch, 165
Korolenko, 177
Kostomarov, 101
Kovalevsky, M., 80, 152, 169, 173
Kranach, Lucas, 225
Kropotkin, Prince Peter, 88, 141, 156, 177, 178
Kryzhanich, Yuri, 167
Kunik, 105
Kuprin, 157–8
Kymri, the, 107

L

La Barraca, 190, 192
Là-Bas, 30
Lactantius, 200
Laforgue, 182
La France ou L'Angleterre?, 86
L'Afrique Romaine, 200
Lamprecht, 225, 229
Landor, Walter Savage, 56, 65
Lange, 12–13
Lanin, E. B. (Dr. Dillon), 91
La Race Slave, 109
L'Art Russe, 120, 122
La Russie Epique, 135
Laufer, Berthold, 120, 121
Lawrence Family, 68
Lebedev, 173
Leibnitz, Gottfried von, 219, 225, 227, 232, 233
L'Empire des Tsars, 115
Leo, Emperor, 169
Le Rire, 180
Lermontov, Mikhail, 133, 134, 138, 140, 154
Leroy-Beaulieu, 102, 111, 115, 173
Les Ibères, 194–6

LESSING, GOTTHOLD EPHRAIM, 84, 224
Letters of a Russian Traveller, 87, 138
LEVITOV, 93
Libyans, the, 198
LIDDELL, R. SCOTLAND, 153, 170
LIE, JONAS, 53
LIEBKNECHT, WILHELM, 225
Life for the Tsar, A, 128, 135
Life in Nature, 10, 15
Life of Jesus, 9
Life of Johannes Brahms, 125
Ligurians, the, 197
LINZELBACH, 109
LIRONDELLE, ANDRÉ, 119
LISZT, FRANZ, 130
Little Russians, the, 100–1, 151, 162, 165
LIVY, 197
LLOYD GEORGE, 46
LOBACHEVSKY, 173
LOCKE, JOHN, 55, 70
Lollards, the, 54
LOMONOSOV, MICHAIL VASILIEVITCH, 76, 137, 139
LOPATIN, 84
Los Muertos Mandan, 190
LOTZE, RUDOLF HERMANN, 225
LOUIS XIV, 220
LOYOLA, ST. IGNATIUS, 201
LUCAN, 204
LUCERO, 202
LUCIAN, 107
LUTHER, MARTIN, 173, 201, 224, 230
LYSKA, ELIZABETH, 174

M

Mabinogion, 48, 49, 50, 135
Macbeth, 142
MAGNUS, ALBERTUS, 224, 232
MAJOR, R. H., 73
MALORY, SIR THOMAS, 49
MALTHUS, THOMAS ROBERT, 151
Marching on Tanga, 182
MARCUS AURELIUS, EMPEROR, 187
MARHOLM, LAURA, 146, 149, 150
MARLOWE, CHRISTOPHER, 56
MARTIAL, MARCUS, 194, 206, 213
MARX, KARL, 222

Massagetes, the, 107
MAUPASSANT, GUY DE, 158
MAXIMUS, 206
Mayflower, the, 52
MAZON, ANDRÉ, 154
MAZZINI, GIUSEPPE, 234
MECHNIKOV, 173
MEINHOLD, 230
MEITZEN, 225
Memoirs of Casanova, 81
Memoirs of Danilov, 79
Memoirs of a Doctor, 145
MENDELEYEV, 173
MERCUTIO, 50
MEREDITH, GEORGE, 149
MEREJKOVSKI, 82, 83
Meri, the, 104
MEROBAUDES, 188
MILL, JOHN STUART, 10, 55
MILTON, JOHN, 25, 56, 57, 189
MILYUKOV, PAVEL, 75, 104, 107, 111, 122, 128, 162, 178
Mind, 11
Modern Customs and Ancient Laws of Russia, 80, 152, 169
MOLTKE, HELMUTH JOHANNES, 220, 229
MONTAIGNE, MICHEL DE, 27, 62
Moors, the, 201
Mordrins, the, 104
MÖRIKE, 223
MORRIS, WILLIAM, 57
Morte d'Arthur, 49, 135
MORYSON, FYNES, 38
MOZART, WOLFGANG AMADEUS, 223
MÜLLENHOFF, 109, 225
MURALT, 69, 179, 182, 184, 185
MURNER, THOMAS, 222
MUSORGSKY, 124, 126, 129, 130
Mycenaeans, the, 198
My Slav Friends, 151

N

NÄCKE, 227
NAPOLEON I, 18, 43, 90
Nationalization of Health, The, 161
Natural History, 106
NEKRASOV, 133, 134

NELSON, LORD HORATIO, 47, 70, 90
NESTOR, 79, 106
Neuri, the, 106
New Europe, The, 159
NEWTON, SIR ISAAC, 64, 70
NICHOLAS OF CUSA, 222
NIEDERLE, L., 105, 109
NIETZSCHE, FRIEDRICH WILHELM, 12, 125, 130, 202, 213, 225, 227, 232, 233
Normans, the, 24, 27, 30, 31, 42–4, 66, 68
Norsemen, the, 110–11, 165
Notes upon Russia, 80, 123
"NOVALIS," BARON VON HARDENBURG, 225
NOVIKOV, 165
NUMANTIA, 202

O

Oblomov, 119, 154
Old House, The, 157
OLEG, 110, 111
Onegin, 154
On the Russian Front, 153
OROSIUS, 206
Ossetes, the, 107
OSTROVSKY, 132
OTERO, 212
Othello, 142

P

PAINE, THOMAS, 55
PANIN, IVAN, 139
PARIS, PIERRE, 198
PARNELL, CHARLES STEWART, 46
PASCAL, BLAISE, 25
PAVLOV, PROF. IVAN, 173
Pechorin, 154
PENN, WILLIAM, 69
PERROT, 196
PETER THE GREAT, 74, 76, 82, 100–1, 137, 138, 148, 162, 167, 169, 207
Petit Jehan de Saintré, 25
PETROVITCH, 135
PHLIPON, 194–7
Phoenicians, the, 195, 199
Picards, the, 24
Pierre Bezukhov, 154
Pilgrim's Progress, 9

PIRENNE, 238–9
PITT, WILLIAM, 46
PLINY THE ELDER, 106, 196, 197
Poema del Cid, 210
Poems (by Pushkin), 139
Poles, the, 99, 113–14
Political Ideals, 234
Political Myths and Economic Realities, 235
POMPONIUS MELA, 206
Popular Science Monthly, 109
POTANIN, 121
POWYS, A. R., 13
Principle of Population, 151
PRISCILLIAN, 206
PROCOPIUS, 169
PROUDHON, PIERRE JOSEPH, 143
PRUDENTIUS, 206
PSEUDO-CAESARIUS, 106
Psychologie des Peuples Européens, 115
PTOLEMY, 106
Punch, 180–1
PURCELL, HENRY, 62
Puritans, the, 54–5
PUSHKIN, ALEXANDER, 115, 118, 119, 120, 124, 133, 134, 135, 138, 139–40, 149, 154, 158
PYESHKOV (MAXIM GORKY), 155–6

Q

Quakers, the, 55, 67
QUINTILIAN, MARCUS, 206

R

Races of Europe, The, 104, 109, 194
RADISCHEV, 138
RALEIGH, SIR WALTER, 59
RAMBAUD, ALFRED NICOLAS, 135
RANSDEN, HERMIONE, 150
RAPHAEL, SANZIO, 232
RASPUTIN, GRIGORY EJIMOVICH, 159
Reaching for the Stars, 239
REIBMAYR, A., 220, 221, 223
REICH, EDUARD, 232
REIMANUS, 225
REINECKE, PAUL, 108, 120
Relation between Ancient Russia and Scandinavia, The, 110

REMBRANDT, HARMENS VAN RIJN, 63
RENAN, ERNEST, 9
Report on Condition of Women and Child Wage-Earners in the U.S.A., 162
Resurrection, 153
REYNOLDS, SIR JOSHUA, 48
—, ROTHAY, 151
RICHARDSON, SAMUEL, 144, 152
RICHTER, J. P., 225
RIMSKY-KORSAKOV, NICHOLAS, 73, 115, 124, 129, 130
RIPLEY, W. Z., 103, 104, 109, 111, 125, 194
ROBERTSON, PROFESSOR CROOM, 11
Robinson Crusoe, 64, 140
RODERIC, BISHOP, 188
ROHRBACH, 228
ROLLAND, ROMAIN, 126
ROLLE, 54
Romans, the, 199, 205
ROSSETTI, DANTE GABRIEL, 28
ROUSSEAU, JEAN-JACQUES, 19, 73, 82, 138, 143
ROWLANDSON, THOMAS, 181
RUBENS, SIR PETER PAUL, 62, 63
RUBINSTEIN, ANTON GRIGOROVICH, 124-5, 129
RÜCKERT, 225
RURIK THE OARSMAN, 110, 165
Rusalka, 128
Ruslan and Lyndmila, 128
RUSSELL, BERTRAND, 12
Russia and Europe, 86
Russian Literature, 156
Russian People, The, 81, 98, 115, 146
Russian Review, 86, 101, 132
Russia's Message, 82, 178

S

SACHER-MASOCH, 79
SACHS, HANS, 225
SALILLAS, 210
SALISBURY, ROBERT ARTHUR, 46
Sangre Y Arena, 190
SANTILLANA, 188
Sarmatians, the, 107
SAROLEA, CHARLES, 83

SAVINA, MADAME, 131
Savoyards, the, 113
Saxons, the, 27, 39, 41, 66
Scandinavians, the, 109-10
SCHARNHORST, GERHARD VON, 229
SCHEFFEL, VICTOR VON, 224
SCHELLING, FRIEDRICH VON, 223, 224
SCHILLER, JOHANN CHRISTOLPH, 223
SCHLEGEL, AUGUST WILHELM VON, 225
SCHLEIERMACHER, FRIEDRICH ERNST, 225, 231
SCHMIDT, DR., 16
SCHOPENHAUER, ARTHUR, 219
SCHUBART, 223
SCHULZE-GÄVERNITZ, PROFESSOR VON, 166
SCHUMANN, ROBERT ALEXANDER, 230
SCOTT, SIR WALTER, 134, 152
SCOTUS ERIGENA, JOHANNES, 55
Scythians, the, 77, 107, 108, 109, 120-1
Semblanzas, 188
SENECA THE ELDER, 204
SENECA THE YOUNGER, 201, 204, 213
Senilia, 141
Serbs, the, 99
SERGI, PROFESSOR, 21, 69, 103, 198
SHAFTESBURY, EARL OF, 62
SHAKESPEARE, WILLIAM, 19, 28, 42, 50-1, 56, 85, 115, 118, 119, 137, 142, 154, 159-60
Shakespeare en Russie, 119
SHELLEY, PERCY BYSSHE, 57, 140
SHIDLOVSKY, 101, 102
SIDNEY, SIR PHILIP, 18, 189
SILESIUS, ANGELUS, 231
SIRET, 198
Sketch of Russian Culture, 104
Skizzen Russischer Kulturgeschichte, 122
Slavs, the, 80, 99, 100, 102 et sqq., 109, 125, 168-9, 173, 226-7, 231
SMETANA, FRIEDRICH, 76
SMIDOVICH, DR., "VERESAYER," 145
SMITH, CAPTAIN JOHN, 69
SMOLLETT, TOBIAS GEORGE, 144
Social Contract, The, 82
"SOLOGUB," TETERNIKOV, 134, 157
SOLOVYEV, VLADIMIR, 84, 175
Sous le Pluie de Fer, 182

SOROLLA, JOAQUIN, 192
Soul of Spain, The, 196
Spain Under the Roman Empire, 194
SPENCER, HERBERT, 55, 70, 85
SPENSER, EDMUND, 56, 189
SPINOZA, BARUCH, 11
Sportsman's Note-Book, 141
STABO, 195, 196
STAHOVITCH, MICHEAL, 178
STANISLAVSKY, CONSTANTIN, 131–2, 133
STASOV, VICTOR, 121, 136
"STENDHAL," MARIE BEYLE, 140
Steppes, The, 123
STERNE, LAURENCE, 25, 85, 134, 152, 179
STOWE, H. B., 137
STRABO, 38, 196, 202–4
STRUTHIUS, 173
STRUVE, 86
Studies in the Psychology of Sex, 80
Study of British Genius, 45, 147, 219
SUMAROKOV, 137
Swabians, the, 223–4
SWIFT, JONATHAN, DEAN, 25
SWINBURNE, ALGERNON CHARLES, 62
Swiss, the, 113
SYUTAYEV, 143

T

TACITUS, CORNELIUS, 103
TAILLEFER, 49
TAINE, HIPPOLYTE ADOLPHE, 30, 147, 183
TALBOT, DR., 163
TAMERLAINE, 56
TARDIEU, CHARLES, 182
TARNOWSKA, COUNTESS MARIA, 159
Tartars, the, 107, 111, 121, 166, 168–9
Tartessians, the, 195–7
TCHAIKOVSKY, PETER ILYICH, 124, 129, 130
Tempest, The, 50
TEMPLE, ARCHBISHOP FREDERICK, 43
TENNYSON, LORD ALFRED, 18
Terres Maudites, 192
TERTULLIAN, QUINTUS, 200
TETERNIKOV, "SOLOGUB," 157
TEXTE, PROFESSOR, 19
THACKERAY, WILLIAM MAKEPEACE, 18
THEODOSIUS THE GREAT, 206

THOMSEN, VILHELM, 109, 110
THURNAM, 198
TIMUR, 166
TITIAN, 232
TOLSTOY, COUNT LEO NIKOLAYEVITCH, 82, 83, 88, 115, 139, 140, 141, 142–5, 146, 149, 153–6, 158, 178, 234
Tolstoy as Man and Artist, 82, 83
TORQUEMADA, TOMÁS DE, 202, 209
Tower of Babel, 125
Tracts Upon Russia, 177
TRAHERNE, 49, 54
TRAJAN, MARCUS, 106, 187, 206
TREITSCHKE, 226–30
Tunguses, the, 120
Turditaneans, the, 195–7
TURGENYEV, IVAN SERGEYVICH, 76, 79, 82, 119, 139, 140, 141, 149, 155
TURNER, JOSEPH MALLORD WILLIAM, 48, 62

U

UHLAND, JOHANN LUDWIG, 223

V

VALERA, JUAN, 189, 205
Varangians, the, 110, 165
VARLAMOV, 76, 131
Vascones, the, 195
VAUGHAN, 54
VEGA, GARCILASSO DE LA, 188
—, LOPE DE, 188, 211
VELASQUEZ, DIEGO RODRIGUEZ, 186, 206, 211, 213
Venedi, the, 106
Venus and Adonis, 50
VERESHCHAGIN, VASILI, 146
"VERESAYEV," DR. SMIDOVICH, 145
VERHAEREN, EMILE, 62
VERLAINE, PAUL, 34
Vie Privée d'Autrefois, 161
Vikings, the, 53
VILLON, FRANÇOIS, 34
VINCI, LEONARDO DA, 232
VIOLLET-LE-DUC, EUGÈNE, 120, 122
VIRCHOW, RUDOLF, 102, 232
Virgin Soil, 149

Visigoths, the, 23, 199
VIVES, ANTONIO, 198
VLADIMIR, ST., 136
Volkswirtschaftliche Studien aus Russland, 166
VOLTAIRE, FRANÇOIS MARIE, 19, 68, 70
Voyages of the English Nation, 59

W

WAGNER, WILHELM RICHARD, 190, 225, 232
WALISZEWSKY, 144, 175
WALLING, W. E., 82, 178
Walloons, the, 38
WALN, NORAH, 239
WASHINGTON, GEORGE, 69
Wealth of Nations, 59
WEBER, CARL MARIA VON, 225
We Europeans, 5
WELLINGTON, DUKE OF, 47
Weltgeschichte der Literatur, 233
Wends, the, 99, 106
Werke, 130
We Women and Our Authors, 150
White Russians, the, 100, 102
Who is to Blame?, 119
WIENER, L., 78, 91, 137, 139, 150, 175
WILLIAM III, 82
WILLIAM THE CONQUEROR, 44

WILLIAMS, DR. HAROLD, 93, 124, 175
WILSON, RICHARD, 48
WINCKELMANN, 230
WOHLGEMÜTH, 225
WOLF, CHRISTIAN, 229
WOLTMANN, 232
WORDSWORTH, WILLIAM, 27, 57
WUNDERER, J. D., 102
WUNDT, WILHELM, 232
WÜRTEMBURG, DUKE OF, 43

X

XIMENEZ, CARDINAL, 208, 209

Y

YOUNG, FRANCIS BRETT, 182

Z

ZABOROWSKI, 107
ZABYELIN, 170
ZAKHAROV, GENERAL, 170
ZAMACOIS, 190
Zeitschrift für Ethnologie, 108
ZINZENDORF, 231
ZIRIAB, 204
ZMIGRODZKI, 106
ZOLA, EMILE EDOUARD, 152, 189-90